A TREASURY OF GREAT THOUGHTS
from Ancient to Modern Times

Other books by Rev. John A. O'Brien:

THE FAITH OF MILLIONS (1938)
TRUTHS MEN LIVE BY (1946)
THE LIFE OF CHRIST (1957)
WHY I BECAME A CATHOLIC (1958)
FIRST MARTYRS OF NORTH AMERICA (1960)
ROADS TO ROME (1960)
GOD AND EVOLUTION (1961)
ETERNAL ANSWERS FOR AN ANXIOUS AGE (1962)
CATCHING UP WITH THE CHURCH (1967)
FAMILY PLANNING IN AN EXPLODING POPULATION (1968)

A Treasury of Great Thoughts
from Ancient to Modern Times

Compiled and Edited by

JOHN A. O'BRIEN, Ph.D.
Author-in-Residence at
The University of Notre Dame

A World of Books That Fill a Need

FREDERICK FELL PUBLISHERS, INC.   NEW YORK

Copyright © 1973 by Rev. John A. O'Brien

All rights reserved. No part of this book may be reproduced in any form or by any means without the prior written permission of the Publisher excepting brief quotes used in connection with reviews.

For information address:
Frederick Fell Publishers, Inc.
386 Park Avenue South
New York, N. Y. 10016

Library of Congress Catalog Card No. 73-80452

Published simultaneously in Canada by
George J. McLeod, Limited, Toronto 2B, Ontario

Manufactured in the United States of America

International Standard Book Number 0-8119-0224-2

A good book is the precious life-blood of a master-spirit, embalmed and treasured up on purpose to a life beyond life. *John Milton*

To
My Dear Friends and Co-Workers
Mr. and Mrs. W. Clement Stone
With the Esteem and Affection of
John A. O'Brien

Table of Contents

Introduction   9
The Torch of Enthusiasm   11
Gratitude: The Heart's Memory   16
Religion Gives Meaning to Life   22
Peace: Man's Urgent Need   30
Contentment: Secret of Happiness   39
True Greatness: How to Achieve It   50
Brotherhood: Goal of Mankind   60
Growing Old Gracefully   68
Getting Along Together   78
Habit Sculptures Character   89
Courtesy Beautifies Human Life   98
Wit and Humor   106
Wisdom: A Precious Jewel   113
The Art of Kindness   122
Christ: Teacher of Mankind   129
Home: Citadel of Happiness   137
Pathways to God   147
Quest for Life's Meaning   155
Faith Gives Meaning to Life   167

Life Beyond the Grave	181
The Art of Courageous Living	196
Self-Control: A Regal Power	212
Laughter: The Best Medicine	220
Hope Must Never Die	229
Friendship Enriches Life	236
How Love Helps You	252
The Companionship of Good Books	263
Prayer: Man's Link with God	271
How to Achieve Success	283
Making Life Worthwhile	293
Religion: Man's Bond with God	309
Humility Becomes Everyone	318
Patience and Perseverance Win the Victory	325
Conquering Fear, Anxiety, Worry	334
Uses of Adversity	345
Conscience: An Inner Voice	355
Dreamers of Dreams	365
The Quest for Happiness	372
Truth Will Make You Free	392

Introduction

For approximately forty years I have had the habit of copying in notebooks thoughts which stirred me with their truth, profundity and insight as well as their charm and felicity of expression. Often I would find myself saying: "That is worth remembering. It merits being integrated into my thinking and becoming a permanent possession of my intellectual life. It will give me light, joy, inspiration and guidance through all the years."

Travelers who encounter spectacularly beautiful scenery will often stop to photograph it to enrich their memory and thus make it part of their permanent possessions. Upon returning home, they delight in sharing with neighbors and friends the breath-taking beauty of scenery which surpassed their ability to describe. In this *Treasury* I seek to share with you thoughts which rival the Grand Canyon in grandeur and the Matterhorn in rugged beauty.

My objective in the presentation of these thoughts is not only to afford you intellectual delight and inspiration but also to help you to deal more effectively with the problems of daily life. Thoughts which guide and inspire have a permanent value and one needs to refer to them frequently and even daily.

For this reason I have chosen certain basic themes which vitally concern all men and women. Then I have selected from the writings of noted thinkers, both ancient and modern, observations which throw light and guidance upon these topics.

Hence the book is both inspirational and of practical helpfulness. To get the most out of this book it is recommended that you confine yourself to one chapter daily until the entire book is read. Thereafter it is recommended that you limit yourself to perusing slowly and reflectively only one or two pages each day and to memorize one quotation.

Thus in the course of a year hundreds of great thoughts will have become your own. No matter what your physical surroundings may be, you will live in the company of the great thinkers and seers of the race. No king on his gilded throne could have such regal, delightful and inspiring company. Furthermore, they will come and go at your pleasure.

To share with my readers the greatest thoughts which I have encountered in more than forty years of daily reading has been for me a labor of love. Not a penny will come to me in remuneration. The royalties will go directly to the University of Notre Dame, where they will help deserving students of all faiths, races and colors to get a good education. The great thoughts in this volume are the lighthouses which will steer us safely through the darkness, bewilderment and complexity of modern civilization.

John A. O'Brien, Ph.D.
University of Notre Dame

The Torch of Enthusiam

Every great and commanding movement in the annals of the world is the triumph of enthusiasm. Nothing great was ever achieved without it.
Ralph Waldo Emerson

I would rather be ashes than dust. I would rather that my spark would burn out in a brilliant blaze than be stifled by dry-rot. I would rather be a superb meteor, every atom of me in magnificent glow, than a sleepy and permanent planet. The proper function of man is to live, not to exist.
Jack London

Nothing is so contagious as enthusiasm. It is the real allegory of the tale of Orpheus; it moves stones and charms brutes. It is the genius of sincerity and truth accomplishes no victories without it.
Edward G. Bulwer-Lytton

None are so old as those who have outlived enthusiasm.
Henry David Thoreau

Enthusiasm is that secret and harmonious spirit which hovers over the production of genius, throwing the reader

of a book, or the spectator of a statue, into the very ideal presence whence these works have really originated. A great work always leaves us in a state of musing.
Isaac D'Israeli

Enthusiasm is grave, inward, self-controlled; mere excitement outward, fantastic, hysterical, and passing in a moment from tears to laughter.
John Sterling

Enthusiasm is a virtue rarely to be met with in seasons of calm and unruffled prosperity. It flourishes in adversity, kindles in the hour of danger, and awakens to deeds of renown. The terrors of persecution only serve to quicken the energy of its purposes. It swells in proud integrity and, in the purity of its cause, it can scatter defiance amid hosts of enemies.
Thomas Chalmers

Enlist the interests of stern morality and religious enthusiasm in the cause of political liberty, as in the time of the old Puritans, and it will be irresistible.
Samuel Taylor Coleridge

Every production of genius must be the production of enthusiasm.
Isaac D'Israeli

Enthusiasm is the leaping lightning, not to be measured by the horse-power of the understanding.
Ralph Waldo Emerson

A little ginger 'neath the tail
Will oft for lack of brains avail.
T. F. MacManus

Enthusiasm moves the world. *A. J. Balfour*

The prudent man may direct a state; but it is the enthusiast who regenerates or ruins it.
Edward G. Bulwer-Lytton

I see you stand like greyhounds in the slips,
Straining upon the start.
Shakespeare

The method of the enterprising is to plan with audacity and execute with vigor; to sketch out a map of possibilities and then to treat them as probabilities.
Christian N. Bovee

I shall grow old, but never lose life's zest, because the road's last turn will be the best.
Henry Van Dyke

A man can succeed at almost anything for which he has unlimited enthusiasm. *Charles M. Schwab*

All noble enthusiasms pass through a feverish stage, and grow wiser and more serene. *William E. Channing*

Enthusiasm is derived from the Greek word signifying "God in us." Its origin throws light upon its deepest meaning and shows its kinship with inspiration, zeal, dedication and determination.
John A. O'Brien

Let us recognize the beauty and power of true enthusiasm; and whatever we may do to enlighten ourselves or others, guard against checking or chilling a single earnest sentiment.
Henry T. Tuckerman

Whatever you attempt, go at it with spirit.
David Starr Jordan

Opposition always inflames the enthusiast, never converts him.
Johann C. von Schiller

Apathy can only be overcome by enthusiasm, and enthusiasm can only be aroused by two things: first, an ideal which takes the imagination by storm; secondly a definite intelligible plan for carrying that ideal into practice.
Arnold Toynbee

All that is necessary for the triumph of evil is for good men to do nothing.
Edmund Burke

Enthusiasm is the state of caring—really caring.
Arthur Gordon

Enthusiasm transforms a lazy person into a tireless worker and changes a coward into a brave man, willing to stake his life for a cause. *John A. O'Brien*

Gratitude:
The Heart's Memory

Gratitude is not only the greatest of virtues, but the parent of all the others. *Marcus Tullius Cicero*

If a man carries his cross beautifully and makes it radiant with glory of a meek and gentle spirit, the time will come when the things that now disturb will be the events for which he will most of all give gratitude to God.
Anonymous

Let but the commons hear this testament,
Which, pardon me, I do not mean to read,
And they would go and kiss dead Caesar's wounds
And dip their napkins in his sacred blood,
Yea, beg a hair of him for memory,
And, dying, mention it in their wills,
Bequeathing it as a rich legacy
Unto their issue.
Shakespeare

I am disposed to say grace upon twenty other occasions in the course of the day besides my dinner. I want

a form for setting out upon a pleasant walk, for a moonlight ramble, for a friendly meeting, or a solved problem. Why have we none for books, those spiritual repasts—a grace before Milton—a devotional exercise proper to be said before reading *The Faerie Queen?*
Charles Lamb

Cicero calls gratitude the mother of virtues, the most capital of all duties, and uses the words grateful and good as synonymous terms, inseparably united in the same character.
Julius Bate

Gratitude is a fruit of great cultivation; you do not find it among gross people.
Samuel Johnson

From David learn to give thanks for everything. Every furrow in the Book of Psalms is sown with the seeds of thanksgiving.
Jeremy Taylor

No man is in true health who cannot stand in the free air of heaven, with his feet on God's free turf, and thank his Creator for the simple luxury of physical existence.
T. W. Higginson

Gratitude to God makes even a temporal blessing of heaven.
William Romaine

Gratitude is the heart's memory.
French proverb

If gratitude is due from children to their earthly parent, how much more is the gratitude of the great family of men due to our Father in heaven.

Hosea Ballou

If one should give me a dish of sand and tell me there were particles of iron in it, I might feel for them with the finger in vain. But let me take a magnet and sweep through it, and how would that draw to itself the most invisible particles by the mere power of attraction! The unthankful heart, like my finger in the sand, discovers no mercies. But let the thankful heart sweep through the day, and as the magnet finds the iron, so it will find, in every hour, some heavenly blessings, only the iron in God's sand is gold. *Oliver Wendell Holmes*

He who receives a benefit should never forget it; he who bestows should never remember it.

Pierre Charron

Give a grateful man more than he asks.

Portuguese proverb

May silent thanks at least to God be given with a full heart;
Our thoughts are heard in heaven.

William Wordsworth

O God, if thou shouldst chain me to a bed for the rest of my life, it would not suffice to thank thee for the days

I have lived. If these words are the last that I shall ever write, let them be a hymn to thy goodness.
Antoine Frédéric Ozanam

Gratitude preserves auld friendships and begets new.
Scottish proverb

Some people complain because God put thorns on roses, while others praise him for not putting roses among thorns. *Anonymous*

John Henry Jowett said: "Gratitude is a vaccine, an antitoxin, and an antiseptic." This is a most searching and true diagnosis. Gratitude can be a vaccine that can prevent the invasion of a disgruntled attitude. As antitoxins prevent the disastrous effects of certain poisons and diseases, thanksgiving destroys the poison of faultfinding and grumbling. When trouble has smitten us, a spirit of thanksgiving is a soothing antiseptic. *Clinton C. Cox*

No metaphysician ever felt the deficiency of language so much as the grateful. *Caleb C. Colton*

> O Lord that lends me life,
> Lend me a heart replete with thankfulness!
> *Shakespeare*

Gratitude takes three forms: a feeling in the heart, an expression in words, and a giving in return.
Anonymous

>Sweet is the breath of vernal shower,
>The bee's collected treasures sweet,
>Sweet music's melting fall, but sweeter yet
>The still small voice of gratitude.
>>*Thomas Gray*

Thou hast given so much to me . . . Give one thing more, a grateful heart. *George Herbert*

There is no lovelier way to thank God for your sight than by giving a helping hand to someone in the dark.
Helen Keller

>The bridegroom may forget the bride,
>>Was made his wedded wife yestreen;
>The monarch may forget the crown
>>That on his head an hour has been;
>The mother may forget the child
>>That smiles sae sweetly on her knee;
>But I'll remember thee, Glencairn,
>>And a' that thou hast done for me.
>>*Robert Burns*

One is tempted to accept life as it is and to forget the men and women of yesterday whose wisdom and sacrifices made it possible for us to have the privileges we now enjoy. Political liberty, universal suffrage, popular education, religious tolerance, trial by jury and the Bible in our own language are some of the blessings which were secured for us by the sacrifice of others. When one loses his sense of gratitude, it is wise to return and study the

history of the centuries and seek to appraise the contribution which others have made to civilization.
Samuel M. Lindsay

Life owes me nothing. One clear morn
Is boon enough for being born;
And be it ninety years or ten,
No need for me to question when.
While Life is mine, I'll find it good,
And greet each hour with gratitude.
Anonymous

Religion Gives Meaning to Life

Religion pure and undefiled before God the Father is this: to give aid to orphans and widows in their tribulation, and to keep oneself unspotted from the world.
St. James the Apostle

Religion is the basis of civil society, and the scourge of all good and of all comfort. *Edmund Burke*

Christians must realize that they have one Church, one Cross, one Gospel. Every church must put its treasures into a safe-deposit box and issue common money, a common money of love, which we need so much.
Athenagoras

The submergence of self in the pursuit of an ideal, the readiness to spend oneself without measure, prodigally, almost ecstatically, for something intuitively apprehended as great and noble, spend oneself one knows not why—some of us like to believe that this is what religion means.
Benjamin N. Cardozo

I could not be interested in any man's religion if his knowledge of God did not bring him more joy, did not brighten his life, did not make him want to carry his joy into every dark corner of the world. I have no understanding of a longfaced Christian. If God is anything, he must be joy. *Joe E. Brown*

Of all the dispositions and habits which lead to political prosperity, religion and morality are indispensable supports. In vain would that man claim the tribute of patriotism who should labor to subvert these great pillars of human happiness, these firmest props of the duties of men and citizens. *George Washington*

A vital religion proves itself both by moral responsibility in creating tolerable forms of community and justice, and by a humble awareness of human imperfectibility. Above all, it preserves a sense of ultimate majesty and meaning, transcending all our little majesties and partial meanings.
Reinhold Niebuhr

Religion is the vision of something which stands beyond, behind, and within, the passing flux of immediate things; something which is real, and yet waiting to be realized; something which is a remote possibility, and yet the greatest of present facts; something that gives meaning to all that passes, and yet eludes apprehension; something whose possession is the final good, and yet is beyond all reach; something which is the ultimate ideal, and the hopeless quest. *Alfred N. Whitehead*

A man who puts aside his religion because he is going into society is like one taking off his shoes because he is about to walk on thorns. *Richard Cecil*

The body of all true religion consists in obedience to the will of the Sovereign of the world, in a confidence in his declarations, and an imitation of his perfections.
Edmund Burke

Above all, I try to avoid the temptation to which anyone who speaks to heathens is subject, to "preach the law." It is difficult not to cite the Ten Commandments and thus prepare for the gospel people to whom lying, stealing and immorality are second nature. I strive to awaken in their hearts the longing for peace with God. When I speak of the difference between the restless and the peaceful heart, the wildest of my savages knows what is meant. And when I portray Jesus as he who brings peace with God to the hearts of men, they comprehend him.
Albert Schweitzer

Nothing that is worth doing can be achieved in a lifetime; therefore we must be saved by hope. Nothing which is true or beautiful or good makes complete sense in any immediate context of history; therefore, we must be saved by faith. Nothing we do, however virtuous, can be accomplished alone; therefore we are saved by love.
Reinhold Niebuhr

The contours of old religions have been changed and their outlines blurred but religion remains and always will remain. I am speaking of religion as belief colored with emotion, an elemental sense of piety or reverence for life summing up man's certanty as to what is right and noble.
Lin Yutang

It is only religion, the great bond of love and duty to God, that makes any existence valuable or even tolerable.
Horace Bushnell

Religion is a candle inside a multicolored lantern. Everyone looks through a particular color, but the candle is always there. *Mohammed Naguib*

If at some period in the course of civilization we seriously find that our science and our religion are antagonistic, then there must be something wrong either with our science or with our religion. *Havelock Ellis*

... In their essence there can be no conflict between science and religion. Science is a reliable method of finding truth. Religion is the search for a satisfying basis for life. ... If our religious leaders are to bring to the present day the vital, living spirit of their faith, they must take science seriously ... a world that has science needs, as never before, the inspiration that religion has to offer. ... Beyond the nature taught by science is the spirit that gives meaning to life. *Arthur H. Compton*

The final test of religious faith ... is whether it will enable men to endure insecurity without complacency or despair, whether it can so interpret the ancient verities that they will not become mere escape hatches from responsibilities but instruments of insights into what civilization means. *Reinhold Niebuhr*

There need not be in religion, or music, or art, or love, or goodness, anything that is against reason; but never while the sun shines will we get great religion, or music, or art, or love, or goodness, without going beyond reason.
Harry Emerson Fosdick

By its enemies religion has been called a drug. It is a drug, and furthermore, the only drug that can counteract the virus of hatred now flowing in the blood of men and nations. *Francis Cardinal Spellman*

    And I have felt
    A presence that disturbs me with a joy
    Of elevated thoughts; a sense sublime
    Of something far more deeply interfused,
    Whose dwelling is the light of setting suns,
    And the round ocean and the living air,
    And the blue sky, and in the mind of man;
    A motion and a spirit, that impels
    All thinking things, all objects of all thought,
    And rolls through all things.
William Wordsworth

Religion is the reaching out of one's whole being—mind, body, spirit, emotions, intuitions, will—for completion, for inner unity, for true relation with those about us, for right relation to the universe in which we live. Religion is *life*, a certain kind of life, life as it could and should be, a life of harmony within and true adjustment without—life, therefore, in harmony with the life of God himself.
Henry P. van Dusen

Those who make religion to consist in the contempt of this world and its enjoyments, are under a very fatal and dangerous mistake. As life is the gift of heaven, it is religion to enjoy it. He, therefore, who can be happy in himself, and who contributes all in his power toward the happiness of others, answers most effectually the ends of his creation, is an honor to his nature, and a pattern to mankind. *Joseph Addison*

Many would like religion as a sort of lightning rod to their houses, to ward off, by and by, the bolts of divine wrath. *Henry Ward Beecher*

Real religion is a way of life, not a white cloak to be wrapped around us on Sunday morning and then tossed aside into the 6-day closet of unconcern.
William A. Ward

Science without religion is lame, religion without science is blind. *Albert Einstein*

There is a signature of wisdom and power impressed on the works of God, which evidently distinguishes them from the feeble imitations of men. Not only the splendor of the sun, but the glimmering light of the glowworm, proclaims his glory. *John Newton*

I do not know how philosophers may ultimately define religion; but from Micah to James it has been defined as service to one's fellow men rendered by following the great rule of justice and mercy, of wisdom and righteousness. *Theodore Roosevelt*

True religion shows its influence in every part of our conduct; it is like the sap of a living tree, which penetrates the most distant boughs. *William Penn*

My altars are the mountains and the ocean,
Earth, air, stars—all that springs from the great Whole,
Who hath produced and will receive the soul.
Lord Byron

I would not give much for your religion unless it can be seen. Lamps do not talk, but they do shine.
Charles H. Spurgeon

Religion—that voice of the deepest human experience.
Matthew Arnold

Religion is a soul with its allegiance fixed, moving about the common streets with the stamp and seal of *forever* on it. It is bolted down to eternity as an engine is bolted down to a cement floor, lest it shake itself to pieces in ten minutes. *Paul E. Scherer*

Some people want a religion that will make them feel respectable, but not require that they be.
Banking

Religion is the fear and love of God; its demonstration is good works; and faith is the root of both, for without faith we cannot please God; nor can we fear and love what we do not believe.
William Penn

> Whoever sees 'neath winter's field of snow
> The silent harvest of the future grow
> God's power must know.
>
> The heart that looks on when the eyelids close,
> And dares to live his life in spite of woes,
> God's comfort knows.
> *John Tyndall*

Peace:
Man's Urgent Need

Blessed are the peacemakers for they shall be called the children of God. *St. Matthew 5:9*

Where there is peace, God is. *George Herbert*

If it is possible, as much as lieth in you, live peaceably with all men. *St. Paul*

How beautiful upon the mountains are the feet of him that bringeth good tidings, and that preachest peace; of him that sheweth forth good, that preachest salvation, that saith to Sion: Thy God shall reign. *Isaiah*

Glory to God in the highest, and on earth peace, good will toward men. *St. Luke*

Let there be no strife, I pray thee, between thee and me. *Genesis 13:8*

I could not live in peace if I put the shadow of a wilful sin between myself and God. *George Eliot*

A fact does not become a truth until people are willing to act upon it; the fact that war is now a losing proposition for everybody will not flower into an effective truth until we are prepared to make as many sacrifices for our children's future peace as for their present comforts.
Sydney J. Harris

Ah! when shall all men's good
Be each man's rule, and universal peace
Lie like a shaft of light across the land,
And like a lane of beams athwart the sea?
Alfred, Lord Tennyson

Agree with thine adversary quickly, whilst thou art in the way with him. *St. Matthew 5:25*

A peace is of the nature of a conquest:
For then both parties nobly are subdued,
And neither party loses.
Shakespeare

From the cradle to his grave a man never does a single thing which has any first and foremost object save one, to secure peace of mind, spiritual comfort, for himself.
Mark Twain

A Chinese sage was asked by a farmer when will the

world truly know peace. The sage said, follow me. And he brought the man to the side of a brook and the Chinese sage put his hand on the head of the farmer and pressed it into the water until finally the farmer came up gasping for air, for life itself. And the sage said: there is your answer. When man wants peace, when he wants peace as much as you have just wanted air, when he comes up gasping for peace, when he wants to give everything in himself to have peace, as you have given everything to have air, he will have peace. *Anonymous*

>Joy is like restless day; but peace divine
>   Like quiet night;
>Lead me, O Lord, till perfect day shall shine.
>   Through Peace to Light.
>
>*Adelaide A. Procter*

Since reason condemns war and makes peace an absolute duty; and since peace cannot be effected or guaranteed without a compact among nations, they must form an alliance of a peculiar kind, which may be called a pacific alliance, different from a treaty of peace inasmuch as it would forever terminate all wars, whereas the latter ends only one. *Immanuel Kant*

May the peace of God which surpasses all understanding guard your hearts and your minds in Christ Jesus.
St. Paul

>Drop thy still dews of quietness till all our striving cease;
>   Take from our souls the strain and stress,

And let our ordered lives confess
The beauty of thy peace.

John Greenleaf Whittier

Dr. Robert Oppenheimer, who supervised the creation of the first atomic bomb, appeared before a Congressional committee. They inquired of him if there was any defense against the weapon.

"Certainly," the great physicist replied. "And that is"—Dr. Oppenheimer looked over the hushed, expectant audience and said softly—"peace."

Anonymous

Her ways are ways of pleasantness, and all her paths are peace.

Proverbs 3:17

No more shall the war cry sever,
   Or the winding rivers be red;
They banish our anger forever
   When they laurel the graves of our dead.
Under the sod and the dew,
   Waiting the judgment day;
Love and tears for the blue,
   Tears and love for the gray.

Francis M. Finch

The world will never have lasting peace so long as men reserve for war the finest human qualities. Peace, no less than war, requires idealism and self-sacrifice and a righteous and dynamic faith. *John Foster Dulles*

It is when we all play safe that we create a world of utmost insecurity. *Dag Hammarskjold*

> Not thus doth peace return!
> A blessed visitant she comes;
> Honour in his right hand
> Doth lead her like a bride.
> *Robert Southey*

The Bible teaches us that there is no foundation for enduring peace on earth, except in righteousness; that it is our duty to suffer for that cause if need be; that we are bound to fight for it if we have the power; and that if God gives us the victory we must use it for the perpetuation of righteous peace. *Henry van Dyke*

Peace will never be entirely secure until men everywhere have learned to conquer poverty without sacrificing liberty to security. *Norman Thomas*

The first and fundamental law of nature, which is, *to seek peace and follow it.* *Thomas Hobbes*

With peace in his soul a man can face the most terrifying experiences. But without peace in his soul he cannot manage even as simple a task as writing a letter. *An English psychiatrist*

The grim fact is that we prepare for war like precocious giants and for peace like retarded pygmies.
Lester B. Pearson

Let the bugles sound the *Truce of God* to the whole world forever.
Charles Sumner

> In peace there's nothing so becomes a man
> As modest stillness and humility.
Shakespeare

The "price of peace" can never reach such dimensions as to equal the smallest fraction of war's deadly cost.
Abba Eban

To be glad of life because it gives you the chance to love and to work and to play and to look up at the stars, to be satisfied with your possessions but not contented with yourself until you have made the best of them, to despise nothing in the world except falsehood and meanness and to fear nothing except cowardice, to be governed by your admirations rather than by your disgusts, to covet nothing that is your neighbor's except his kindness of heart and gentleness of manners, to think seldom of your enemies, often of your friends, and every day of Christ, and to spend as much time as you can, with body and with spirit, in God's out-of-doors, these are little guideposts on the footpath to peace.
Henry van Dyke

The real problem is in the hearts and minds of men. It is

not a problem of physics but of ethics. It is easier to denature plutonium than to denature the evil spirit of man.
Albert Einstein

To plunder, to slaughter, to steal, these things they misname empire; and where they make a desert, they call it peace. *Calgacus*

What we now need to discover in the social realm is the moral equivalent of war: something heroic that will speak to men as universally as war does, and yet will be as compatible with their spiritual selves as war has proved itself to be incompatible. *William James*

Peace cannot be kept by force. It can only be achieved by understanding. *Albert Einstein*

What mankind wants is not merely the absence of war but real peace. The mere possibility of another world war is a haunting nightmare. You cannot stand indefinitely on the brink of a precipice and pray that the sense of balance will never forsake you or that you may never be pushed into the chasm. It is an ordeal which may of itself produce the fatal loss of equilibrium. *Moshe Sharett*

Though not a "peace-at-any-price" man, I am not ashamed to say that I am a peace-at-almost-any-price man.
Sir John Lubbock

Peace! and no longer from its brazen portals
The blast of war's great organs shakes the skies!

But beautiful as songs of the immortals,
　The holy melodies of love arise.
　　　　　　　　　　Henry Wadsworth Longfellow

They shall beat their swords into ploughshares, and their spears into pruninghooks: nation shall not lift up sword against nation, neither shall they learn war any more.
　　　　　　　　　　　　　　　　　　Isaiah 2:4

Yet there we follow but the bent assign'd
By fatal nature to man's warring kind:
Mark! where his carnage and his conquests cease!
He makes a solitude, and calls it peace!
　　　　　　　　　　　　　Lord Byron

To discover a system for the avoidance of war is a vital need of our civilization; but no such system has a chance while men are so unhappy that mutual extermination seems to them less dreadful than continued endurance of the light of day.　　　　　　　　*Bertrand Russell*

Till the war-drum throbb'd no longer, and the battle-flags
　were furl'd
In the parliament of man, the federation of the world.
　　　　　　　　　　　　Alfred, Lord Tennyson

The High Contracting Parties solemnly declare in the names of their respective peoples that they condemn recourse to war for the solution of international controversies, and renounce it as an instrument of national policy

in their relations with one another. The High Contracting Parties agree that the settlement or solution of all disputes or conflicts of whatever nature or of whatever origin they may be, which may arise among them, shall never be sought except by pacific means.
Articles I and II of the Pact of Paris

Were half the power that fills the world with terror,
   Were half bestowed on camps and courts,
Given to redeem the human mind from error,
   There were no need of arsenals and forts.
Henry Wadsworth Longfellow

Contentment:
Secret of Happiness

I have learned, in whatsoever state I am, therewith to be content. *Philippians 4:11*

> And Freedom, leaning on her spear,
>   Laughs louder than the laughing giant;
> Some good bank-stock, some note of hand,
>   Or trifling railroad share,
> I only ask that fortune send
> A little more than I shall spend.
> *Oliver Wendell Holmes*

A contented mind is the greatest blessing a man can enjoy in this world; and if, in the present life, his happiness arises from the subduing of his desires, it will arise in the next from the gratification of them.
Joseph Addison

> I was too ambitious in my deed,
> And thought to distance all men in success,
> Till God came to me, marked the place, and said,
> "Ill doer, henceforth keep within this line,

Attempting less than others," and I stand
And work among Christ's little ones, content.
Elizabeth Barrett Browning

The secret of contentment is knowing how to enjoy what you have, and to be able to lose all desire for things beyond your reach. Lin Yutang

God, grant me the serenity to accept the things I cannot change, courage to change the things I can, and wisdom to know the difference.
Motto of Alcoholics Anonymous

A harvest of peace is produced from a seed of contentment. Anonymous

Content is the philosopher's stone, which turns all it touches into gold. Thomas Fuller

A man who finds no satisfaction in himself, seeks for it in vain elsewhere. François Duc de la Rochefoucauld

Resign every forbidden joy; restrain every wish that is not referred to God's will; banish all eager desires, all anxiety; desire only the will of God; seek him alone and supremely, and you will find peace.
François de Salignac de La Mothe-Fénelon

Dig a hole in the garden of your thoughts. Into it put all your disillusions, disappointments, regrets, worries, troubles, doubts and fears, and forget. Cover well with the earth of fruitfulness. Water it from the well of content. Sow on top the seeds of hope, courage, strength, patience and love. Then, when the time of gathering comes, may your harvest be a rich and fruitful one.
Anonymous

Content makes poor men rich; discontent makes rich men poor. *Benjamin Franklin*

It is right to be contented with what we have, never with what we are. *Sir James Mackintosh*

> We'll therefore relish with content,
> Whate'er kind Providence has sent,
>   Nor aim beyond our pow'r;
> For, if our stock be very small,
> 'Tis prudent to enjoy it all,
>   Nor lose the present hour.
> *Nathaniel Cotton*

A man whose heart is not content is like a snake which tries to swallow an elephant. *Chinese proverb*

Fit thyself into the environment that thou findest on earth, and love the men with whom thy lot is cast.
Marcus Aurelius

An ounce of contentment is worth a pound of sadness to serve God with.
Thomas Fuller

Dear little head, that lies in calm content
  Within the gracious hollow that God made
On every human shoulder, where he meant
  Some tired head for comfort should be laid.
Celia L. Thaxter

Great tranquillity of heart is his who cares for neither praise nor blame.
Thomas à Kempis

Happy the man, of mortals happiest he,
Whose quiet mind from vain desires is free;
Whom neither hopes deceive, nor fears torment,
But lies at peace, within himself content.
George Granville

Submission is the only reasoning between a creature and its maker and contentment in his will is the best remedy we can apply to misfortunes.
Sir William Temple

Then be content, poor heart!
God's plans, like lilies pure and white, unfold:
We must not tear the close-shut leaves apart.
Time will reveal the calyxes of gold!
May Louise R. Smith

Do not despise your situation; in it you must act, suffer, and conquer. From every point on earth we are equally near to heaven and to the infinite.
Henri F. Amiel

>Happy the man whose wish and care
> A few paternal acres bound,
>Content to breathe his native air
> In his own ground.
>Whose herds with milk, whose fields with bread,
> Whose flocks supply him with attire,
>Whose trees in Summer yield him shade;
> In Winter, fire.
>*Alexander Pope*

Contentment is a pearl of great price, and whoever procures it at the expense of ten thousand desires makes a wise and a happy choice. *John Balguy*

>There is a jewel which no Indian mines can buy,
> No chymic art can counterfeit;
>It makes men rich in greatest poverty,
> Makes water wine; turns wooden cups to gold;
> The homely whistle to sweet music's strain,
>Seldom it comes; to few from Heaven sent,
>That much in little, all in naught, *Content*.
>*John Wilbye*

He will easily be content and at peace, whose conscience is pure. *Thomas à Kempis*

43

My crown is in my heart, not on my head;
Not deck'd with diamonds and Indian stones,
Nor to be seen: my crown is called content;
A crown it is that seldom kings enjoy.
Shakespeare

Contentment with the divine will is the best remedy we can apply to misfortunes. *Sir William Temple*

Envy deserves pity more than anger, for it hurts nobody so much as itself. It is a distemper rather than a vice: for nobody would feel envy if he could help it. Whoever envies another, secretly allows that person's superiority.
Horace Walpole

With only plain rice to eat, with only water to drink, and with only an arm for a pillow, I am still content.
Confucius

Contentment produces, in some measure, all those effects which the alchymist ascribes to what he calls the philosopher's stone; and if it does not bring riches, it does the same thing by banishing the desire of them. If it cannot remove the disquietudes arising from a man's mind, body, or fortune, it makes him easy under them.
Joseph Addison

It is our duty to compose our character, not to compose books, and to win, not battles and provinces, but order and tranquillity for our conquest of life.
Michel de Montaigne

'Tis better to be lowly born,
And range with humble livers in content,
Than to be perk'd up in a glistening grief,
And wear a golden sorrow.
Shakespeare

Content has a kindly influence on the soul of man, in respect of every being to whom he stands related. It extinguishes all murmuring, repining, and ingratitude toward that Being who has allotted us our part to act in the world. It destroys all inordinate ambition; gives sweetness to the conversation, and serenity to all the thoughts; and if it does not bring riches, it does the same thing by banishing the desire of them. *Joseph Addison*

It is not miserable to be blind; it is miserable to be incapable of enduring blindness. *John Milton*

When the world trembles I'm unmoved,
When cloudy, I'm serene;
When darkness covers all without
I'm always bright within.
Daniel Defoe

If two angels were sent down from heaven, one to conduct an empire, and the other to sweep a street, they would feel no inclination to change employments.
John Newton

Nor hell nor heaven shall that soul surprise,
Who loves the rain,

And loves his home,
And looks on life with quiet eyes.
Frances Shaw

My God, give me neither poverty nor riches, but whatsoever it may be thy will to give, give me, with it, a heart that knows humbly to acquiesce in what is thy will.
Gotthold, pseud. for Christian Scriver

Nothing can bring you peace but yourself. Nothing can bring you peace but the triumph of principle.
Ralph Waldo Emerson

Resign every forbidden joy; restrain every wish that is not referred to God's will; banish all eager desires, all anxiety; desire only the will of God; seek him alone and supremely, and you will find peace.
François de Salignac de La Mothe Fénelon

Joy is indeed a precious quality which very few experience in their lives. The person who knows how to enjoy life will never grow old no matter how many years he can call his own. It is easy to be happy at specific times, but there is a certain art in being happy and contented every day. *Ora Capelli*

There is a sense in which a man looking at the present in the light of the future, and taking his whole being into account, may be contented with his lot: that is Christian contentment. But if a man has come to that

point where he is so content that he says, "I do not want to know any more, or do any more," he ought to be changed into a mummy! Of all hideous things a mummy is the most hideous; and of mummies, the most hideous are those that are running about the streets and talking.
Henry Ward Beecher

Serenity comes to the man who lives with an unfaltering faith in an unfailing God. The person who lives with eternity in his heart will find a strange calm in his spirit.
Joseph R. Sizoo

The fountain of content must spring up in the mind; and he who has so little knowledge of human nature as to see happiness by changing anything but his own disposition, will waste his life in fruitless efforts, and multiply the griefs which he proposes to remove.
Samuel Johnson

Peace of mind may transform a cottage into a spacious manor hall; the want of it can make a regal park an imprisoning nutshell. *Joshua L. Liebman*

True contentment depends not upon what we have; a tub was large enough for Diogenes, but a world was too little for Alexander. *Caleb C. Colton*

The truest kinship with humanity would lie in doing as humanity has always done, accepting with sportsmanlike

relish the estate to which we are called, the star of our happiness, and the fortunes of the land of our birth.
G. K. Chesterton

The noblest mind the best contentment has.
Edmund Spenser

When Pyrrhus was about to sail for Italy, Cineas, a wise and good man, asked him what were his intentions and expectations. "To conquer Rome," said Pyrrhus. "And after that?"

"We will subdue Carthage, Macedonia, all Africa and all Greece." "And when we have conquered all we can, what shall we do?"

"Do? Why, then we will sit down and spend our time in peace and comfort." "Ah, my Lord," said the wise Cineas, "what prevents our being in peace and comfort now?"
George L .Walton

Quiet minds cannot be perplexed or frightened, but go on in fortune or misfortune at their own private pace, like a clock during a thunderstorm.
Robert Louis Stevenson

The mind is a river; upon its water thoughts float through in a constant procession every conscious moment. It is a narrow river, however, and you stand on a bridge over it and can stop and turn back any thought that comes along, and they can come only in single file, one at a time. The art of contentment is to let no thought pass that is going to disturb you.
Frank Crane

There is but one way to tranquillity of mind and happiness, and that is to account no external things thine own, but to commit all to God. *Epictetus*

When God sorts out the weather and sends rain,
Why rain's my choice.
James Whitcomb Riley

O what a glory doth this world put on
For him who, with a fervent heart, goes forth
Under the bright and glorious sky, and looks
On duties well performed, and days well spent!
Henry Wadsworth Longfellow

True Greatness: How to Achieve It

All things that we see standing accomplished in the world are properly the outer material result, the practical realization and embodiment of thoughts that dwell in the great men sent into the world.
Thomas Carlyle

And I smiled to think God's greatness
   flowed around our incompleteness,
Round our restlessness, his rest.
Elizabeth Barrett Browning

Difficulty is a nurse of greatness, a harsh nurse, who rocks her foster children roughly, but rocks them into strength and athletic proportions. The mind, grappling with great aims and wrestling with mighty impediments, grows by a certain necessity to the stature of greatness.
William Cullen Bryant

Genius is one percent inspiration and ninety-nine percent perspiration.
Thomas A. Edison

But be not afraid of greatness: some are born great, some achieve greatness, and some have greatness thrust upon them. *Shakespeare*

Great men stand like solitary towers in the city of God.
Henry Wadsworth Longfellow

> Why, man, he doth bestride the narrow world
> Like a Colossus, and we petty men
> Walk under his huge legs and peep about
> To find ourselves dishonorable graves.
> *Skakespeare*

If any man seeks for greatness, let him forget greatness and ask for truth, and he will find both.
Horace Mann

A great man is one who has conquered himself. He has brought order, discipline and meaning into his life and prevented it from becoming the aimless, self-centered, repulsive existence to which he is drawn by his inherited weaknesses. The process begins when a man brings a center of interest into his life. This interest must be something inspiring and elevating. If you push these requirements far enough, the center of his life can only be God.
Harold Oxley

> Dear Lord, but once before I pass away
> Out of this hell into the starry night
> Where still my hopes are set in Death's despite,
> Let one great man be good, let one pure ray

Shine through the gloom on this my earthly day
From one tall candle set upon a height.
Alfred B. Douglas

Great men are they who see that spiritual is stronger than any material force; that thoughts rule the world.
Ralph Waldo Emerson

The greatest man is he who chooses the right with invincible resolution; who resists the sorest temptations from within and without; who bears the heaviest burdens cheerfully; who is calmest in storms, and most fearless under menace and frowns; and whose reliance on truth, on virtue, and on God, is most unfaltering.
William E. Channing

No saint, no hero, no discoverer, no prophet, no leader ever did his work cheaply and easily, comfortably and painlessly, and no people was ever great which did not pass through the valley of the shadow of death on its way to greatness.   *Walter Lippmann*

A great man is made up of qualities that meet or make great occasions.   *James Russell Lowell*

Greatness is not mortal. The qualities which the great have to give, they give perpetually. Their gifts are taken into the pattern of life, and they appear thereafter in the fabric of lives of nations, renewing themselves as the leaves of the trees are renewed by the seasons.
Robert Trout

Genius is the capacity for taking infinite pains.
Thomas Carlyle

He fought a thousand glorious wars,
    And more than half the world was his,
And somewhere, now, in yonder stars,
    Can tell, mayhap, what greatness is.
William M. Thackeray

No man has come to true greatness who has not felt in some degree that his life belongs to his race, and that what God gives him he gives him for mankind.
Phillips Brooks

Truly great persons are more interested in controlling themselves than in controlling others. If monuments are put up to honor persons less worthy than themselves, they do not mind, for humility is one of their traits. It is probable that Einstein, acclaimed as the greatest scientist of his time, was more humble than most of the students at the university where he taught. Greatness is modest; it avoids publicity. *Clinton E. Bernard*

Greatness and goodness are not means, but ends!
Hath he not always treasures, always friends,
The good great man? three treasures, Love, and Light,
And Calm Thoughts, regular as infant's breath;
And three firm friends, more sure than day and night,
Himself, his Maker, and the Angel Death!
Samuel Taylor Coleridge

Thine, O Lord, is the greatness and the power, and the glory, and the victory, and the majesty: for all that is in heaven and in the earth is thine; thine is the kingdom, O Lord, and thou art exalted as head above all.
I Chronicles 29:11

The hero is one who kindles a great light in the world, who sets up blazing torches in the dark streets of life for men to see by. The saint is the man who walks through the dark paths of the world, himself a "light."
Felix Adler

Greatness is a spiritual condition worthy to excite love, interest, and admiration; and the outward proof of possessing greatness is, that we excite love, interest, and admiration. *Matthew Arnold*

As the marsh-hen secretly builds on the watery sod,
Behold I will build me a nest on the greatness of God;
I will fly in the greatness of God as the marsh-hen flies
In the freedom that fills all the space 'twixt the marsh
   and the skies. *Sidney Lanier*

There are stars whose light reaches the earth only after they themselves have disintegrated and are no more. And there are men whose scintillating memory lights the world after they have passed from it. These lights which shine in the darkest night are those which illumine for us the path. *Hannah Senesh*

No great man lives in vain. The History of the world is but the Biography of great men.
Thomas Carlyle

The wisest man could ask no more of Fate
Than to be simple, modest, manly, true,
Safe from the Many, honored by the Few;
To count as naught in the World, or Church or State,
But inwardly in secret to be great.
James Russell Lowell

This is the final test of a gentleman: His respect for those who can be of no possible service to him.
William Lyon Phelps

Great men are the gifts of kind Heaven to our poor world; instruments by which the Highest One works out his designs; light-radiators to give guidance and blessing to the travelers of time. *Moses Harvey*

No horse gets anywhere until he is harnessed. No steam or gas ever drives anything until it is confined. No Niagara is ever turned into light and power until it is tunneled. No life ever grows great until it is focused, dedicated, disciplined. *Harry Emerson Fosdick*

The superior man is the providence of the inferior. He is eyes for the blind, strength for the weak, and a shield for the defenseless. He stands erect by bending above the fallen. He rises by lifting others.
Robert G. Ingersoll

The names and memories of great men are the dowry of a nation. *Pasquale Villari*

Whosoever will be chief among you, let him be your servant. *Matthew 20:27*

To bear up under loss; to fight the bitterness of defeat and the weakness of grief; to be victor over anger, to smile when tears are close; to resist disease and evil men and base instincts; to hate hate, and to love love; to go on when it would seem good to die; to look up with unquenchable faith in something ever more about to be—that is what any man can do, and be great.
Zane Grey

He alone is worthy of the appellation who either does great things, or teaches how they may be done, or describes them with a suitable majesty when they have been done; but those only are great things which tend to render life more happy, which increase the innocent enjoyments and comforts of existence, or which pave the way to a state of future bliss more permanent and more pure. *John Milton*

Man's unhappiness, as I construe, comes of his Greatness; it is because there is an infinite in him, which with all his cunning he cannot quite bury under the Finite.
Thomas Carlyle

The truly great consider first, how they may gain the approbation of God; and secondly, that of their own con-

science; having done this, they would then willingly conciliate the good opinion of their fellowmen.
Caleb C. Colton

  The heart ran o'er
With silent worship of the great of old!
The dead but sceptred sovereigns, who still rule
Our spirits from their urns.
Lord Byron

He is truly great that is little in himself, and that maketh no account of any height of honors.
Thomas à Kempis

I count him a great man who inhabits a higher sphere of thought, into which other men rise with labor and difficulty.
Ralph Waldo Emerson

  Rightly to be great
Is not to stir without great argument,
But greatly to find quarrel in a straw,
When honour's at the stake.
Shakespeare

Nothing great comes into being all at once; not even the grape or the fig. If you say to me now, "I want a fig," I shall answer, "That requires time." Let the tree blossom first, then put forth its fruit, and finally let the fruit ripen.
Epictetus

None of those who have been raised to a loftier height by riches and honors is really great. Why then does he seem great to you? It is because you are measuring the pedestal along with the man.
Lucius Annaeus Seneca

The measure of a master is his success in bringing all men round to his opinion twenty years later.
Ralph Waldo Emerson

> The heights by great men reached and kept
>   Were not attained by sudden flight,
> But they, while their companions slept,
>   Were toiling upward in the night.
Henry Wadsworth Longfellow

What is a great life? It is the dream of youth realized in old age. *Alfred De Vigny*

> That man is great, and he alone,
> Who serves a greatness not his own
>   For neither praise nor pelf:
> Content to know and be unknown:
>   Whole in himself.
Owen Meredith

Not a day passes over the earth but men and women of no note do great deeds, speak great words, and suffer noble sorrows. Of these obscure heroes, philosophers, and martyrs the greater part will never be known till that hour when many that were great shall be small, and the small great. *Charles Reade*

To dwell in the wise house of the world,
To stand in true attitude therein,
To walk in the wide path of men,
In success to share one's principles with the people,
In failure to live them out alone,
To be incorruptible by riches or honors,
Unchangeable by poverty,
Unmoved by perils or power:
These I call the qualities of a great man.
Mencius

Brotherhood:
Goal of Mankind

Love one another with fraternal charity.   *St. Paul*

The belief in the brotherhood of man stems from the conviction that God is the father of us all, regardless of race, color or creed.   *John A. O'Brien*

> Blow wind of God and set us free
> from hate and want of charity;
> Strip off the trappings of our pride,
> and give us to our brother's side.
> *William S. Braithwaite*

However serious may be that which divides us, that which unites us is greater still, for we are brothers and we have the certitude of being united in Christ.
Cardinal Paul-Emile Leger

After so many years of separation, after such painful polemics, what else can we do but again love one another, listen to one another and pray for one another?
Pope Paul VI

Where'er I roam, whatever realms to see,
My heart untravell'd fondly turns to thee;
Still to my brother turns with ceaseless pain,
And drags at each remove a lengthening chain.
Oliver Goldsmith

A new commandment I give you, that you love one another: that as I have loved you, you also love one another. By this will all men know that you are my disciples, if you have love for one another.
John 13:34, 35

However degraded or wretched a fellow mortal may be, he is still a member of our common species.
Lucius Annaeus Seneca

Brotherhood must have a religious basis if it is to have any real significance. Without faith in the fatherhood of God, as Jesus and the prophets preached it, people have a pretty hard time being brotherly. They drift off into hated societies, or more often, into the society of the indifferent.
Edwin T. Dahlberg

Jesus throws down the dividing prejudices of nationality, and teaches universal love, without distinction of race, merit, or rank. A man's neighbor is every one that needs help.
J. C. Geikie

A peaceful world depends upon better understanding and respect for each other in a spirit of brotherhood and adherence to ethical principles. If these are lost, civilization gradually disappears. *Herman W. Steinkraus*

The universe is but one great city, full of beloved ones, divine and human, by nature endeared to each other.
Epictetus

Dostoevski causes one of his characters to [say]: "I am X in an indeterminate equation. I am a sort of phantom in life who has lost all beginning and end, who has forgotten his own name." The affirmation that we find in the Gospel causes us to confront every man with the words, "I know your real name. You are not an X in an indeterminate equation or a phantom in life, you are a child of God, you are a brother of mine in Christ."
Harold A. Bosley

The crest and crowning of all good, life's final star, is Brotherhood. *Edwin Markham*

Brotherhood doesn't come in a package. It is not a commodity to be taken down from the shelf with one hand. It is an accomplishment of soul-searching prayer and perseverance. *Oveta C. Hobby*

Whoever in prayer can say, "Our Father," acknowledges and should feel the brotherhood of the whole race of mankind. *Tryon Edwards*

And when with grief you see your brother stray,
Or in a night of error lose his way,

Direct his wandering and restore the day . . .
Leave to avenging Heaven his stubborn will.
Fear, O, remember, he's your brother still.
Jonathan Swift

We are members of one great body, planted by nature in a mutual love, and fitted for a social life. We must consider that we were born for the good of the whole.
Lucius Annaeus Seneca

If any lift of mine may ease
  The burden of another,
God give me love and care and strength
  To help my ailing brother.
Anonymous

Brotherhood, once a dream and a vision, has now become a dire necessity. *Louis L. Mann*

Behold, how good and how pleasant it is for brethren to dwell together in unity! *Psalms 133:1*

Let us no more be true to boasted race or clan,
But to our highest dream, the brotherhood of man.
Thomas C. Clark

Help thy brother's boat across, and lo! thine own has reached the shore. *Old Hindu proverb*

God, what a world if man in street and mart,
Felt that same kinship of the human heart
Which makes them, in the face of fire and flood,
Rise to the true meaning of Brotherhood.
Ella Wheeler Wilcox

Of a truth men are mystically united; a mysterious bond of brotherhood makes all men one. *Thomas Carlyle*

If a man says, I love God, and hateth his brother, he is a liar. *I John 4:20*

Just the thought of brotherhood has a sobering effect on me, for it reminds me that I am only a transitory member of a very large family called Humanity.
Bellamy Partridge

I sought my soul, but my soul I could not see; I sought my God, but my God eluded me; I sought my brother, and found all three. *Anonymous*

Our doctrine of equality and liberty and humanity comes from our belief in the brotherhood of man, through the fatherhood of God. *Calvin Coolidge*

Slav, Teuton, Kelt, I count them all
  My friends and brother souls,
With all the peoples, great and small,
  That wheel between the poles.
Alfred, Lord Tennyson

When people universally realize that all are united by the common bond of mortality and by the basic needs . . . the need to worship and to love, to be housed and fed, to work and play, perhaps we will have learned to understand, which is to love spiritually, and there will be peace and brotherhood on earth. Without brotherhood, peace is not possible.
Faith Baldwin

Science can make a neighborhood of the nations, but only Christ can make the nations into a Brotherhood.
John Holland

The race of mankind would perish from the earth did they cease to aid each other.
Sir Walter Scott

>I met a little maid
>   A rosy burden bearing;
>"Is he not heavy?" I said
>   As past me she was hurrying.
>She looked at me with grave, sweet eyes,
>   This fragile little mother,
>And answered in swift surprise:
>   "Oh, no Sir, he's my brother."

Anonymous

The universe is but one great city, full of beloved ones, divine and human by nature, endeared to each other.
Epictetus

The world is now too dangerous for anything but the truth, too small for anything but brotherhood.
Adlai Stevenson

The answer to the question, "Am I my brother's keeper?" must always be "No! I am my brother's brother."
Dr. Paul Klapper

The opportunity to practice brotherhood presents itself every time you meet a human being.
Jane Wyman

The best way to prove to yourself that you're not superior to a brother man of different color or creed is to get acquainted with him.   Globe Gazette (Mason City, Iowa)

Whoever degrades another degrades me,
And whatever is done or said returns at last to me.
Walt Whitman

We yearn for world brotherhood so passionately we can't wait to spend $300 on a television set to see some brother get beaten up good in a fast ten rounds.
Fine Paper Salesman

You can't hold a man down without staying down with him.
Booker T. Washington

Whosoever is angry with his brother without a cause shall be in danger of the judgment. *Matthew 5:22*

> Yes, you'd know him for a heathen
> If you judged him by the hide,
> But bless you, he's my brother,
> For he's just like me inside.
> *Robert Freeman*

Growing Old Gracefully

A graceful and honorable old age is the childhood of immortality.
Pindar

For just as I approve of a young man in whom there is a touch of age, so I approve of the old man in whom there is some of the flavor of youth. He who strives thus to mingle youthfulness and age may grow old in body, but old in spirit he will never be.
Marcus Tullius Cicero

Maturity, we now know, need be no dull routine of a defeated and resigned adulthood. It can rather be the triumphant use of powers that all through our childhood and youth have been in preparation.
Harry A. Overstreet

As winter strips the leaves from around us, so that we may see the distant regions they formerly concealed, so old age takes away our enjoyments only to enlarge the prospect of the coming eternity.
Jean Paul Richter

>Since more than half my hopes came true
>   And more than half my fears
>Are but the pleasant laughing-stock
>   Of these my middle years: . . .
>Shall I not bless the middle years?
>   Not I for youth repine
>While warmly round me cluster lives
>   More dear to me than mine.
>   *Sarah N. Cleghorn*

A diplomat is a man who remembers a lady's birthday but forgets her age.   *Anonymous*

Childhood itself is scarcely more lovely than a cheerful, kindly, sunshiny old age.   *Lydia Maria Child*

>Be wise with speed;
>A fool at forty is a fool indeed.
>   *Edward Young*

Each part of life has its own pleasures. Each has its own abundant harvest, to be garnered in season. We may grow old in body, but we need never grow old in mind and spirit. We must make a stand against old age. We must atone for its faults by activity. We must exercise the mind as we exercise the body, to keep it supple and buoyant. Life may be short, but it is long enough to live honorably and well. Old age is the consummation of life, rich in blessings.   *Marcus Tullius Cicero*

I venerate old age; and I love not the man who can look without emotion upon the sunset of life, when the dusk of evening begins to gather over the watery eye, and the shadows of twilight grow broader and deeper upon the understanding. *Henry Wadsworth Longfellow*

> Abide with me, fast falls the eventide;
> The darkness deepens; Lord, with me abide.
> *Henry F. Lyte*

When I was young I was amazed at Plutarch's statement that the elder Cato began at the age of eighty to learn Greek. I am amazed no longer. Old age is ready to undertake tasks that youth shirked because they would take too long. *W. Somerset Maugham*

How beautiful can time with goodness make an old man look. *Douglas Jerrold*

> And not by eastern windows only,
> When daylight comes, comes in the light;
> In front, the sun climbs slow, how slowly,
> But westward, look, the land is bright.
> *Arthur H. Clough*

A man's age is as unimportant as the size of his shoes if his interest in life is not impaired, if he is compassionate and if time has mellowed his prejudices.
Douglas Meador

Like a morning dream, life becomes more and more bright the longer we live, and the reason of everything appears more clear. What has puzzled us before seems less mysterious, and the crooked paths look straighter as we approach the end. *Jean Paul Richter*

> I shall grow old, but never lose life's zest,
> Because the road's last turn will be the best.
> *Henry van Dyke*

If wrinkles must be written upon our brows, let them not be written upon the heart. The spirit should not grow old.
James A. Garfield

Old men's eyes are like old men's memories; they are strongest for things a long way off. *George Eliot*

> Spring still makes spring in the mind
>   When sixty years are told;
> Love makes anew this throbbing heart,
>   And we are never old.
> Over the winter glaciers
>   I see the summer glow,
> And through the wild-piled snowdrift,
>   The warm rosebuds below.
> *Ralph Waldo Emerson*

When one finds company in himself and his pursuits, he cannot feel old, no matter what his years may be.
Amos Bronson Alcott

One's age should be tranquil, as childhood should be playful. Hard work at either extremity of life seems out of place. At mid-day the sun may burn, and men labor under it; but the morning and evening should be alike calm and cheerful. *Matthew Arnold*

> So life's year begins and closes;
> Day, though short'ning, still can shine;
> What though youth gave love and roses,
> Age still leaves us friends and wine.
> *Thomas Moore*

As for old age, embrace and love it. It abounds with pleasure if you know how to use it. The gradually declining years are among the sweetest in a man's life; and I maintain that even when they have reached the extreme limit, they have their pleasure still.
Lucius Annaeus Seneca

The vices of old age have the stiffness of it too; and as it is the unfittest time to learn in, so the unfitness of it to unlearn will be found much greater.
Robert South

Rashness is a quality of the budding-time of youth, prudence of the harvest-time of old age.
Marcus Tullius Cicero

The thing to do is neither to fear old age nor to fight it, but to accept it without tension and use it. When I say "use it," I do not mean bear it, accommodate yourself to it, but take hold of it and make something out of it. That's what nature does. She does not die drably; she puts on her most gorgeous robes in autumn, her yellows and her flaming reds, and dies gloriously. *E. Stanley Jones*

That man never grows old who keeps a child in his heart. A healthy old fellow, who is not a fool, is the happiest creature living. *Sir Richard Steele*

Your young men shall see visions, and your old men shall dream dreams. *Acts 2:17*

> Let me grow lovely, growing old
> So many fine things to do;
> Laces, and ivory, and gold,
> And silks need not be new.
> And there is healing in old trees,
> Old streets a glamour hold;
> Why may not I, as well as these,
> Grow lovely, growing old?
> *Karle W. Baker*

When one becomes indifferent to women, to children, and to young people, he may know that he is superannuated, and has withdrawn from what is sweetest and purest in human existence. *Amos Bronson Alcott*

> And if I should live to be
> The last leaf upon the tree
> In the spring,

> Let them smile, as I do now,
> At the old forsaken bough
> Where I cling.
>
> *Oliver Wendell Holmes*

Youth is happy because it has the ability to see beauty. Anyone who keeps the ability to see beauty never grows old. *Franz Kafka*

There are three classes into which all the women past seventy years of age I have ever known, were divided: that dear old soul; that old woman; that old witch.
Samuel Taylor Coleridge

> A little more tired at close of day,
> A little less anxious to have our way;
> A little less ready to scold and blame;
> A little more care of a brother's name;
> And so we are nearing the journey's end,
> Where time and eternity meet and blend.
>
> *Rollin J. Wells*

To keep young, every day read a poem, hear a choice piece of music, view a fine painting, and if possible, do a good action. *Johann Wolfgang von Goethe*

There cannot live a more unhappy creature than an ill-natured old man, who is neither capable of receiving pleasures, nor sensible of conferring them on others.
Sir William Temple

Age is not all decay; it is the ripening, the swelling, of the fresh life within, that withers and bursts the husk.
George Macdonald

Nearly two-thirds of all the greatest deeds ever performed by human beings—the victories in battle, the greatest books, the greatest pictures and statues—have been accomplished after the age of sixty.
Albert E. Wiggam

Of earthly blessing age is not the least,
   Serene its twilight sky, the journey past;
Like that rare draught at Cana's marriage feast,
   Life's best wine is the last.
Frances E. Pope

To know how to grow old is the masterwork of wisdom, and one of the most difficult chapters in the great art of living.
Henri F. Amiel

When we are out of sympathy with the young, then I think our work in this world is over.
George Macdonald

The more we live, more brief appear
   Our life's succeeding stages;
A day to childhood seems a year,
   And years like passing ages.
Thomas Campbell

The only way any woman may remain forever young is to grow old gracefully. *W. Beran Wolfe*

> So take the hint, the hands of Time
> Are pointing, not unkindly,
> Back to the hills we used to climb
> While prospects beckoned blindly.
> *Laurence Housman*

Think of what the world would have missed had a retirement age, even at 70, been universally enforced. Gladstone was Prime Minister of England at 83; Benjamin Franklin helped frame the Constitution of the U.S. at 80; Oliver Wendell Holmes retired from the Supreme Court bench at 91; Henry Ford, when past 80, took up the presidency of the Ford Motor Co. for the second time; and Alonzo Stagg was named the "Football Man of the Year" at 81. Dr. Lillian J. Martin learned to drive an automobile when she was 76 years old, and at the same age founded the Old Age Center in San Francisco, where she received aged people as students. She continued to direct it until her death at 91.

Wingate M. Johnson

> For we are old, and on our quick'st decrees
> The inaudible and noiseless foot of Time
> Steals ere we can effect them.
> *Shakespeare*

Drawing near her death, she sent most pious thoughts as harbingers to heaven; and her soul saw a glimpse of happiness through the chinks of her sickness-broken body. *Thomas Fuller*

Certainly old age has a great sense of calm and freedom; when the passions relax their hold, then, as Sophocles says, you have escaped from the control not of one master, but of many. *Plato*

>Youth with swift feet walks onward in the way;
>　The land of joy fills all before his eyes;
>Age, stumbling, lingers slowly day by day,
>　Still looking back, for it behind him lies.
>Fail not for sorrow, falter not for sin,
>But onward, upward, till the goal ye win!
>*Frances A. Kemble*

Getting Along Together

So whatever you wish that men do to you, do so to them; for this is the law and the prophets.
St. Matthew 7:9

Thou shalt love thy neighbor as thyself.
St. Matthew 19:19

The secret of loving others is to see in the face of every other person the lineaments of the countenance of Christ and to remember the Saviour's words, recorded in the Gospel according to St. Matthew: "Amen, I say to you, as long as you did it for one of these, the least of my brethren, you did it for me." *John A. O'Brien*

I do not want to know the man who lives a few doors from me, for if I knew him I would be robbed of the luxury of hating him. *Charles Lamb*

How much suffering must humanity endure before it finally learns to put the whole before the part, to understand that only in the safety of a community of nations can any nation find its own safety?
Sumner Wells

Always respect the dignity of those who are with you and, above all, the freedom of every human being.
Pope John XXIII

All happy families are alike, but every unhappy one is unhappy in its own way. *Count Leo N. Tolstoy*

As are families, so is society. If well ordered, well instructed, and well governed, they are the springs from which go forth the streams of national greatness and prosperity, of civil order and public happiness.
William M. Thayer

A holy family, that make
Each meal a supper of the Lord.
Henry Wadsworth Longfellow

When men are animated by the charity of Christ, they feel united, and the needs, sufferings and joys of others are felt as their own. *Pope John XXIII*

Hast thou heard a word against thy neighbor? Let it die within thee, trusting that it will not burst thee.
Ecclesiastes 19:10

It is a terrible, an inexorable, law that one cannot deny the humanity of another without diminishing one's own; in the face of the victim one sees oneself.
James Baldwin

The happiest moments of my life have been the few which I have passed at home in the bosom of my family.
Thomas Jefferson

A happy family is but an earlier heaven.
Sir John Bowring

> W'en you see a man in woe,
> Walk right up and say "hullo."
> Say "hullo" and "how d'ye do,"
> "How's the world a-usin' you?" . . .
> W'en you travel through the strange
> Country t'other side the range,
> Then the souls you've cheered will know
> Who you be, an' say "hullo."
> *Sam Walter Foss*

If you want your neighbor to know what Christ will do for him, let the neighbor see what Christ has done for you.   Times, All-Church Press (Houston, Texas)

> Anything, God, but hate;
> I have known it in my day,
> And the best it does is scar your soul
> And eat your heart away.
> Man must know more than hate.
> As the years go rolling on;
> For the stars survive and the spring survives,
> Only man denies the dawn.
> God, if I have but one prayer
> Before the cloud-wrapped end,

I'm sick of hate and the waste it makes.
Let me be my brother's friend.

Anonymous

The family is a society limited in numbers, but nevertheless a true society, anterior to every state or nation, with rights and duties of its own, wholly independent of the commonwealth. *Pope Leo XIII*

A house without a roof would scarcely be a more different home than a family unsheltered by God's friendship, and the sense of being always rested in his providential care and guidance. *Horace Bushnell*

He who joins in sport with his own family will never be dull to strangers. *Titus M. Plautus*

Looking through the wrong end of a telescope is an injustice to the astronomer, to the telescope, and to the stars; likewise, looking at our neighbor's faults instead of the attributes gives us an incorrect conception of ourselves, our neighbor, and our God.

William A. Ward

I will do more than live and let live. I will live and help live. *Walter W. Van Kirk*

Civilization varies with the family, and the family with civilization. Its highest and most complete realization is

found where enlightened Christianity prevails; where woman is exalted to her true and lofty peak as equal with the man; where husband and wife are one in honor, influence, and affection, and where children are a common bond of care and love. This is the idea of a perfect family.
William Aikman

He that loves not his wife and children, feeds a lioness at home, and broods a nest of sorrow.
Jeremy Taylor

To God be humble, to thy friend be kind,
And with thy neighbors gladly lend and borrow.
His chance to-night, it may be thine to-morrow.
William Dunbar

A split atom and a split mankind cannot co-exist indefinitely on the same planet. *Liston Pope*

If God has taught us all truth in teaching us to love, then he has given us an interpretation of our whole duty to our households. We are not born as the partridge in the wood, or the ostrich of the desert, to be scattered everywhere; but we are to be grouped together, and brooded by love, and reared day by day in that first of churches, the family.
Henry Ward Beecher

The security and elevation of the family and of family life are the prime objects of civilization, and the ultimate ends of all industry. *Charles W. Eliot*

We can never be the better for our religion if our neighbor is the worse for it.
Anonymous

A man is like a letter of the alphabet; to produce a word, it must combine with another.
Benjamin Mandelstamm

"The last word" is the most dangerous of infernal machines, and the husband and wife should no more fight to get it than they would struggle for the possession of a lighted bombshell.
Douglas Jerrold

The family is one of nature's masterpieces.
George Santayana

You've got to save your own soul first, and then the souls of your neighbors if they will let you; and for that reason you must cultivate, not a spirit of criticism, but the talents that attract people to the hearing of the word.
George Macdonald

I don't set up to be no judge of right and wrong in men,
I've lost the trail sometimes myself an' may get lost again;
An' when I see a chap who looks as though he'd gone astray,
I want to shove my hand in his an' help him find the way.
J. A. Foley

Woman is the salvation or the destruction of the family. She carries its destiny in the folds of her mantle.
Henri F. Amiel

When the black-lettered list to the gods was presented
(The list of what Fate for each mortal intends),
At the long string of ills a kind goddess relented,
And slipped in three blessings—wife, children, and friends.
William R. Spencer

Man is a special being, and if left to himself, in an isolated condition, would be one of the weakest creatures; but associated with his kind, he works wonders.
Daniel Webster

Hell is where no one has anything in common with anybody else except the fact that they all hate one another and cannot get away from one another and from themselves.
Thomas Merton

Kindness is the golden chain by which society is bound together.
Johann Wolfgang von Goethe

One day when famine had wrought great misery in Russia, a beggar, weak, emaciated, all but starved to death, asked for alms. Tolstoy searched his pockets for a coin but discovered that he was without as much as a copper piece. Taking the beggar's worn hands between his own, he said: "Do not be angry with me, my brother; I have nothing with me." The thin, lined face of the beggar became illumined as from some inner light, and he whispered in reply: "But you called me brother. That was a great gift."
Wesley Boyd

No man is an island entire; every man is part of the main. If a clod be washed away by the sea, Europe is the less, as well as if a promontory were, as well as if a manor of thy friends or thine own were. Any man's death diminishes me because I am involved in mankind, and therefore never send to know for whom the bell tolls; it tolls for thee. *John Donne*

Twenty thousand years ago the family was the social unit. Now the social unit has become the world in which it may truly be said that each person's welfare affects that of every other. *Arthur H. Compton*

The brotherhood of man is not a dream; it is a fact. And if mankind is to survive as a species, this fact must be recognized. This curious point where biology and religion meet must be our new point of departure, the only basis for a brave new world, its alternative being war and chaos. *Stuart Cloete*

There is a destiny that makes us brothers;
None goes his way alone:
All that we send into the lives of others
Comes back into our own.
Edwin Markham

The best way to uncolor the negro is to give the white man a white heart. *Ivan N. Panin*

'Tis the human touch in this world that counts,
The touch of your hand and mine,

Which means far more to the fainting heart
Than shelter and bread and wine;
For shelter is gone when the night is o'er,
And bread lasts only a day,
But the touch of the hand and the sound of the voice
Sing on in the soul alway.
Spencer M. Free

The days of the rugged individualist are over and the days of the cooperative individual are here. The pioneer on his homestead was independent and could go it alone. His descendants, whether at the plow, or loom or desk, whether in village or city, are interdependent. The pioneer forged a free world on his own; his children's children must find their way with all other peoples to a free world. *Paul G. Hoffman*

There is more power in the open hand than in the clenched fist. *Herbert N. Casson*

We must learn to live together as brothers or we will perish together like fools. *Martin Luther King, Jr.*

Thomas Carlyle tells of an Irish widow who, for the support of her three children, appealed to charitable establishments in Edinburgh, where her husband died. Continually rebuffed, she fell exhausted, contracted typhus fever, died, and infected her street. Seventeen others perished as a consequence. Am I my brother's keeper? Carlyle concludes, "Had human creature ever to go lower for proof?" *Eldon L. Johnson*

When we understand each other, we find it difficult to cut one another's throats. *Van Wyck Brooks*

We ask the leaf, "Are you complete in yourself?" And the leaf answers, "No, my life is in the branches." We ask the branch, and the branch answers, "No my life is in the root." We ask the root, and it answers, "No my life is in the trunk and the branches and the leaves. Keep the branches stripped of leaves, and I shall die." So it is with the great tree of being. Nothing is completely and merely individual. *Henry Emerson Fosdick*

We make our friends; we make our enemies, but God makes our next-door neighbor. That is why the old religions and the old scriptural language showed so sharp a wisdom when they spoke, not of one's duty toward humanity, but of one's duty toward one's neighbor. Duty toward humanity may take the form of some choice which is personal or even pleasurable. But we have to love our neighbor because he is there. He is the sample of humanity that is actually given us.

G. K. Chesterton

We do not want the men of another color for our brothers-in-law, but we do want them for our brothers.
Booker T. Washington

> There are hermit souls that live withdrawn
>   In the peace of their self-content;
> There are souls like stars that dwell apart,
>   In a fellowless firmament;

There are pioneer souls that blaze their paths
   Where highways never ran,
But let me live by the side of the road,
   And be a friend to man.

Sam Walter Foss

Habit Sculptures Character

Character is that which reveals moral purpose, exposing the class of things a man chooses or avoids.
Aristotle

Every man's character is the arbiter of his fortune.
Publilius Syrus

In contrast with the man who acts on motives of expediency, the man of character acts on principle. The former is changeable like the weather vane; the latter is constant and dependable. Character is not to be confused with reputation, intellectual ability, personality or social attractiveness.
　　Character is an inner quality by means of which a man steadfastly obeys the moral law and follows the dictates of his own conscience, "come hell or high water."
John A. O'Brien

A man never reveals his own character more vividly than when portraying the character of another.
Jean Paul Richter

A good character is, in all cases, the fruit of personal exertion. It is not inherited from parents; it is not created by external advantages; it is no necessary appendage of birth, wealth, talents or station; but it is the result of one's own endeavors, the fruit and reward of good principles manifested in a course of virtuous and honorable action. *J. Hawes*

Before we realize it, most of us have become mere walking bundles of habits, which we will carry with us to our dying day. So the destiny which each one carves out for himself, both in this world and in the world to come, may be said in truth to be the result of the habits which he forms. *John A. O'Brien*

> Sow a thought and reap an act.
> Sow an act and reap a habit.
> Sow a habit and reap a character.
> Sow a character and reap a destiny.
> *Anonymous*

The qualities of character, hidden or buried, are revealed eventually even as the quality of a building is revealed under the stress of time and storm. When we do less than our best we cheat ourselves. We are the architects and builders of our own characters and must of necessity dwell within them. *George E. Mayo*

> We all are blind until we see
> That in the human plan,
> Nothing is worth the making

If it does not make the man.
Why build these cities glorious
If man unbuilded goes?
In vain we build the world unless
The builder also grows.
Edwin H. Markham

A good character carries with it the highest power of causing a thing to be believed. *Aristotle*

One ship drives east and another drives west
   With the selfsame winds that blow.
  'Tis the set of the sails
  And not the gales
    Which tells us the way to go.
Like the winds of the sea are the ways of fate,
   As we voyage along through life:
  'Tis the set of a soul
  That decides its goal,
    And not the calm or the strife.
Ella Wheeler Wilcox

Character is the result of two things: mental attitude and the way we spend our time. *Elbert Hubbard*

An honest man is the noblest work of God.
Alexander Pope

It is in trifles, and when he is off his guard, that a man best shows his character. *Arthur Schopenhauer*

As there is much beast and some devil in man, so is there some angel and some God in him. The beast and the devil may be conquered, but in this life never destroyed.
Samuel Taylor Coleridge

Character is like a tree, and reputation like its shadow. The shadow is what we think of it; the tree is the real thing. *Abraham Lincoln*

Mankind is made up of inconsistencies, and no man acts invariably up to his predominant character. The wisest man sometimes acts weakly, and the weakest sometimes wisely. *Lord Chesterfield*

Character must stand behind and back up everything— the sermon, the poem, the picture, the play. None of them is worth a straw without it.
J. G. Holland

The crown and glory of life is character. It is the noblest possession of a man, constituting a rank in itself, and estate in the general good will; dignifying every station, and exalting every position in society. It exercises a greater power than wealth and secures all the honor without the jealousies of fame. It carries with it an influence which always tells; for it is the result of proved honor, rectitude, and consistency—qualities which, perhaps more than any others, command the general confidence and respect of mankind. *Samuel Smiles*

More knowledge may be gained of a man's real character by a short conversation with one of his servants than from a formal and studied narrative, begun with his pedigree and ended with his funeral.   *Samuel Johnson*

Character is perfectly educated will.
Novalis (Baron Friedrich von Hardenberg)

In the end, we are all the sum total of our actions. Character cannot be counterfeited, nor can it be put on and cast off as if it were a garment to meet the whim of the moment. Like the markings on wood which are ingrained in the very heart of the tree, character requires time and nurture for growth and development.

Thus also, day by day, we write our own destiny; for inexorably we become what we do. This I believe, is the supreme logic and the law of life.
Madame Chiang Kai-shek

One man is made of agate, another of oak; one of slate, another of clay. The education of the first is polishing; of the second, seasoning; of the third, rending; of the fourth moulding.   *John Ruskin*

If you can talk with crowds and keep your virtue, or walk with kings—nor lose the common touch, if neither foes nor loving friends can hurt you, if all men count with you, but none too much; if you can fill the unforgiving minute with sixty seconds' worth of distance run, yours is the earth and everything that's in it, and—which is more—you'll be a man, my son.   *Rudyard Kipling*

A man is what he is, not what men say he is. His character no man can touch. His character is what he is before God. His reputation is what men say he is. That can be damaged. For reputation is for time. Character is for eternity. *John B. Gough*

> When wealth is lost, nothing is lost;
> When health is lost, something is lost
> When character is lost, all is lost!
> *Anonymous*

Character and personal force are the only investments that are worth anything. *Walt Whitman*

Every temptation that is resisted, every noble aspiration that is encouraged, every sinful thought that is repressed, every bitter word that is withheld, adds its little item to the impetus of that great movement which is bearing humanity onward toward a richer life and higher character. *John Fiske*

If I take care of my character, my reputation will take care of itself. *Dwight L. Moody*

In the destiny of every moral being there is an object more worthy of God than happiness. It is character. And the great aim of man's creation is the development of a grand character and grand character is, by its very nature, the product of probationary discipline.
Austin Phelps

Let us not say, Every man is the architect of his own fortune; but let us say, Every man is the architect of his own character. *G. D. Boardman*

Fame is a vapor, popularity an accident, riches take wings. Only one thing endures, and that is character.
Horace Greeley

If we work upon marble, it will perish; if we work upon bronze, time will efface it; if we build temples, they will crumble into dust; but if we work upon immortal souls, if we imbue them with just principles of action, with fear of wrong and love of right, we engrave on those tables something which no time can obliterate, and which will brighten and brighten through all eternity.
Daniel Webster

Only what we have wrought into our character during life can we take away with us. *Alexander Humboldt*

I pray thee O God, that I may be beautiful within.
Socrates

The miracle, or the power, that elevates the few is to be found in their industry, application, and perseverance under the promptings of a brave, determined spirit.
Mark Twain

Parents can't change the color of their child's eyes, but

they can help give the eyes the light of understanding and warmth of sympathy. They can't much alter the child's features, but they can in many ways help endow it with the glow of humaneness, kindness, friendliness . . . which may in the long run bring a lot more happiness than the perfection that wins beauty contests.
Amram Scheinfeld

The noblest contribution which any man can make for the benefit of posterity, is that of a good character. The richest bequest which any man can leave to the youth of his native land, is that of a shining, spotless example.
Robert C. Winthrop

The harder you throw down a football and a good character, the higher they rebound; but a thrown reputation is like an egg. *Austin O'Malley*

Talents are best nurtured in solitude; character is best formed in the stormy billows of the world.
Johann Wolfgang von Goethe

There is nothing so fatal to character as half-finished tasks. *David Lloyd George*

There is not a man or woman, however poor they may be, but have it in their power, by the grace of God, to leave behind them the grandest thing on earth, character; and their children might rise up after them and thank God that their mother was a pious woman, or their father a pious man. *Norman Macleod*

The best characters are made by vigorous and persistent resistance to evil tendencies; whose amiability has been built upon the ruins of ill-temper, and whose generosity springs from an over-mastered and transformed selfishness. Such a character, built up in the presence of enemies, has far more attraction than one which is natively pleasing.
Henry M. Dexter

Since character is the sum of our habits, the laws which form our habits form also our characters. Hence the ten laws of character formation may be summarized as follows:

1. Make your nervous system your ally instead of your enemy.
2. Launch yourself upon the new practice with as vigorous and determined an initiative as possible.
3. Continue this initiative and don't allow failures to discourage you because effort despite an occasional defeat is accumulative and will eventually triumph.
4. Never allow any exception in regard to your resolution.
5. Grasp the first opportunity to translate your resolve into action and utilize every emotional prompting along the line of the habit you wish to form.
6. Careful, whole-hearted effort must be put into the work of forming a habit.
7. Tell your friends about your resolution.
8. Start with little things rather than with big ones.
9. Make the practice of the habit as pleasant as possible and the failure to practice it as unpleasant as you can.
10. Keep the faculty of effort alive in you by a little gratuitous exercise every day.

John A. O'Brien

Courtesy Beautifies Human Life

Courtesy is a smile in action.   *John A. O'Brien*

A gentleman never heard a story before.
Austin O'Malley

He may freely receive courtesies who knows how to requite them.   *John Ray*

> How sweet and gracious, even in common speech,
> Is that fine sense which men call courtesy!
> Wholesome as air and genial as the light,
> Welcome in every clime as breath of flowers,
> It transmutes aliens into trusting friends,
> And gives its owner passport round the globe.
> *James T. Fields*

Hail! ye small sweet courtesies of life; for smooth do ye make the road of it, like grace and beauty, which beget inclinations to love at first sight; it is ye who open the door and let the stranger in.   *Laurence Sterne*

Americans can never be called ill-mannered people. It has been estimated that we pay more than ten million dollars every year in toll charges in order to add the polite word "please" to our telegrams. *Anonymous*

A man's hat in his hand never did him any harm.
Italian proverb

High erected thoughts seated in a heart of courtesy.
Sir Philip Sidney

As charity covers a multitude of sins before God, so does politeness before men.
Lord Greville

A man's own good-breeding is his best security against other people's ill manners. *Lord Chesterfield*

Courtesy on one side only lasts not long.
George Herbert

Life is not so short but that there is always time enough for courtesy. *Ralph Waldo Emerson*

Politeness is to goodness what words are to thought. It tells not only on the manners, but on the mind and the heart; it renders the feelings, the opinions, the words, moderate and gentle. *Joseph Joubert*

Nothing is ever lost by courtesy. It is the cheapest of the pleasures; costs nothing and conveys much. It pleases him who gives and him who receives, and thus, like mercy, is twice blessed. *Erastus Wiman*

Fair words brake never bone.
Anonymous

> Shepherd, I take thy word,
> And trust thy honest offer'd courtesy,
> Which oft is sooner found in lowly sheds
> With smoky rafters, than in tap'stry halls,
> And courts of princes.
> *John Milton*

Small kindnesses, small courtesies, small considerations, habitually practised in our social intercourse, give a greater charm to the character than the display of great talents and accomplishments. *M. A. Kelty*

A polite man is one who listens with interest to things he knows about, when they are told to him by a person who knows nothing about them.
Philippe de Mornay

If a man be gracious and courteous to strangers it shows he is a citizen of the world. *Francis Bacon*

Discourtesy does not spring merely from one bad quality, but from several—from foolish vanity, from ignorance of what is due to others, from indolence, from stupidity, from distraction of thought, from contempt of others, from jealousy. *Jean de la Bruyere*

Manners are the happy ways of doing things. If they are superficial, so are the dewdrops which give such a depth to the morning meadows. *Ralph Waldo Emerson*

Politeness is a desire to so contrive it, by word and manner, that others will be pleased with us and with themselves. *[Charles de Secondat, Baron de la Brède et de Montesquieu]*

There is no outward sign of politeness which has not a deep, moral reason. Behavior is a mirror in which every one shows his own image. There is a politeness of the heart akin to love, from which springs the easiest politeness of outward behavior. Politeness is not always the sign of wisdom, but the want of it always leaves room for suspicion of folly. *Walter Savage Landor*

If we treat people too long with that pretended liking called politeness, we shall find it hard not to like them in the end. *Logan Pearsall Smith*

Truth, uttered with courtesy, is heaping coals of fire on the head; or, rather, throwing roses in the face.
St. Francis de Sales

There is a courtesy of the heart; it is allied to love. From it springs the purest courtesy in the outward behavior.
Johann Wolfgang von Goethe

In our disturbed and uncertain age, not knowing where we are going, how and if we shall get there, the least we can do in our common predicament is to treat one another with a certain amount of respect. It is more important and more urgent today to teach our children this humble form of tolerance—courtesy and good manners are nothing else but that—than to try to convince them that capitalism is better than communism, or vice versa. If history has proved something, it is that means and ways are more important than the distant ends.
Romain Gary

Politeness has been defined as artificial good nature; with much greater propriety it may be said that good nature is natural politeness. *Stanislas Leszczynski*

Politeness is like an air-cushion; there may be nothing in it, but it eases our jolts wonderfully. Politeness is fictitious benevolence. It supplies the place of it among those who see each other only in public, or but little. The want of it never fails to produce something disagreeable to one or other. *Samuel Johnson*

It takes no personal development nor stature to be tactless or inconsiderate. Such behavior is nothing more than immaturity seeking expression. It is an unconscious effort to conceal or cover up our sense of inferiority and of inadequacy. The mature person, on the other hand, lives on the level of human equation. He need not belittle in order to make himself an equal. He has the sense of adequacy within himself. He needs no false props to bolster his sense of importance.

Tom D. Eilers

To speak kindly does not hurt the tongue.

French proverb

There is no outward sign of true courtesy that does not rest on a deep moral foundation.

Johann Wolfgang von Goethe

In all the affairs of life, social as well as political, courtesies of a small and trivial character are the ones which strike deepest to the grateful and appreciating heart.

Henry Clay

Politeness has been well defined as benevolence in small things. *Thomas Babington Macaulay*

The whole of heraldry and chivalry is in courtesy. A man of fine manners shall pronounce your name with all the ornament that titles of nobility could add.

Ralph Waldo Emerson

Manners are of more importance than laws. Upon them, in a great measure, the laws depend. The law touches us

but here and there, and now and then. Manners are what vex or soothe, corrupt or purify, exalt or debase, barbarize or refine us, by a constant, steady, uniform, insensible operation, like that of the air we breathe in.
Edmund Burke

When saluted with a salutation, salute the person with a better salutation, or at least return the same, for God taketh account of all things. *Koran*

> Of courtesy, it is much less
> Than courage of heart or holiness,
> Yet in my walks it seems to me
> That the grace of God is in courtesy.
> *Hilaire Belloc*

We should be as courteous to a man as we are to a picture, which we are willing to give the advantage of the best light. *Ralph Waldo Emerson*

Politeness is to human nature what warmth is to wax.
Arthur Schopenhauer

Rudeness is the weak man's imitation of strength.
Eric Hoffer

Self-respect is at the bottom of all good manners. They are the expression of discipline, of good-will, of respect for other people's rights and comfort and feelings.
Edward S. Martin

The test of good manners: to bear patiently with bad ones.
Solomon I. Gabirol

Tact is the knack of making a point without making an enemy.
Howard W. Newton

Wit and Humor

For health and the constant enjoyment of life, give me a keen and ever present sense of humor; it is the next best thing to an abiding faith in providence.
G. B. Cheever

Humor is consistent with pathos, whilst wit is not.
Samuel Taylor Coleridge

Humor is falling downstairs if you do it while in the act of warning your wife not to. *Kenneth Bird*

Everything is funny as long as it is happening to somebody else. *Will Rogers*

Although he had much wit,
He was very shy of using it.
Samuel Butler

The world is a perpetual caricature of itself; at every moment it is the mockery and the contradiction of what it is pretending to be. But as it nevertheless intends all the time to be something different and highly dignified, at the next moment it corrects and checks and tries to cover up the absurd thing it was; so that a conventional world, a world of masks, is superimposed on the reality, and passes in every sphere of human interest for the reality itself. Humor is the perception of this illusion, whilst the convention continues to be maintained, as if we had not observed its absurdity.

George Santayana

True humour springs not more from the head than from the heart; it is not contempt, its essence is love; it issues not in laughter, but in still smiles, which lie far deeper. It is a sort of inverse sublimity, exalting as it were, into our affections what is below us, while sublimity draws down into our affections what is above us.

Thomas Carlyle

An ounce of mother-wit is worth a pound of school-wit.

German proverb

I live in a constant endeavor to fence against the infirmities of ill-health and other evils of life by mirth. I am persuaded that every time a man smiles—but much more so when he laughs—it adds something to this fragment of life.

Laurence Sterne

It is not humor to be malignant.

Latin proverb

With the fearful strain that is on me night and day, if I did not laugh I should die.   *Abraham Lincoln*

A wit is a very unpopular denomination, as it carries terror along with it; and people in general are as much afraid of a live wit, in company, as a woman is of a gun.
Lord Chesterfield

There is certainly no defence against adverse fortune which is, on the whole, so effectual as an habitual sense of humor.   *T. W. Higginson*

Humor is the electric atmosphere; wit is the flash.
H. R. Haweis

We love a joke that hands us a pat on the back while it kicks the other fellow down stairs.
C. L. Edson

A grain of wit is more penetrating than the lightning of the night-storm, which no curtains or shutters will keep out.   *Ralph Waldo Emerson*

These poor gentlemen endeavor to gain themselves the reputation of wits and humorists by such monstrous conceits as almost qualify them for bedlam; not considering that humor should always lie under the check of reason, and that it requires the direction of the nicest judgment, by so much the more as it indulges itself in the most boundless freedoms.   *Joseph Addison*

There must be more malice than love in the heart of all wits.   *R. B. Haydon*

Wit may be a thing of pure imagination, but humor involves sentiment and character. Humor is of a genial quality; dwells in the same character with pathos, and is always mingled with sensibility.
Henry Giles

Fools are only laugh'd at; wits are hated.
Alexander Pope

Wit makes its own welcome, and levels all distinctions. No dignity, no learning, no force of character, can make any stand against good wit.   *Ralph Waldo Emerson*

> Great wits are sure to madness near allied,
> And thin partitions do their bounds divide.
> *John Dryden*

Wit is the sudden marriage of ideas which before their union were not perceived to have any relation.
Mark Twain

He's winding up the watch of his wit; by and by it will strike.   *Shakespeare*

It is with wits as with razors, which are never so apt

to cut those they are employed on as when they have lost their edges. *Jonathan Swift*

I shall ne'er be ware of mine own wit till I break my shins against it. *Shakespeare*

Nothing more smooth than glass, yet nothing more brittle; nothing more fine than wit, yet nothing more fickle.
H. C. Bohn

Professed wits, though they are generally courted for the amusement they afford, are seldom respected for the qualities they possess. *Sydney Smith*

Those who jest with good taste are called witty.
Aristotle

The distinction between a witticism and a low, rude joke is that the former may be indulged in, if it be seasonable, and in hours of relaxation, by a virtuous man; the latter is unworthy of any human being.
Marcus Tullius Cicero

The true touchstone of wit is the impromptu.
Molière [Jean Baptiste Poquelin]

True wit is nature to advantage dress'd,
What oft was thought, but ne'er so well expressed.
Alexander Pope

There is not, perhaps, any harder task than to tame the natural wildness of wit. *Thomas Ticknell*

Thy wit is a very bitter sweeting: it is most sharp sauce.
Shakespeare

Those who cannot miss an opportunity of saying a good thing . . . are not to be trusted with the management of any great question. *William Hazlitt*

Wit's an unruly engine, wildly striking
Sometimes a friend, sometimes the engineer.
George Herbert

Wit is folly unless a wise man hath the keeping of it.
John Ray

Wit may be defined as a justness of thought and a facility of expression, or (in the midwives' phrase) a perfect conception with an easy delivery.
Alexander Pope

Wit raises human nature above its level; humor acts a contrary part, and equally depresses it.
Oliver Goldsmith

Wit is that which is at once natural and new; that which, though not obvious, is, upon its first production, acknowledged to be just; that which he that never found it wonders how he missed. *Samuel Johnson*

Wit consists in discerning the resemblance between things that differ, and the difference between things that are alike. *Anna Louise de Stael*

Wit is the clash and reconcilement of incongruities, the meeting of extremes round a corner.
Leigh Hunt

Wisdom:
A Precious Jewel

Happy is the man that findeth wisdom, and the man that getteth understanding. . . . Her ways are ways of pleasantness, and all her paths are peace. . . . Wisdom is the principal thing; therefore get wisdom; and with all thy getting get understanding. *Proverbs 4:5*

Common-sense in an uncommon degree is what the world calls wisdom. *Samuel Taylor Coleridge*

Fortunately or otherwise, we live at a time when the average individual has to know several times as much in order to keep informed as he did only thirty or forty years ago. Being "educated" today, requires not only more than a superficial knowledge of the arts and sciences, but a sense of interrelationship such as is taught in few schools. Finally, being "educated" today, in terms of the larger needs, means preparation for world citizenship; in short, education for survival. *Norman Cousins*

He who provides for this life, but takes no care for eternity, is wise for a moment, but a fool forever.
John Tillotson

Great is wisdom; infinite is the value of wisdom. It cannot be exaggerated; it is the highest achievement of man.
Thomas Carlyle

God gives man wisdom as he gives them gold; his treasure house is not the mint, but the mine. A wise man's day is worth a fool's life. *Arabic saying*

He is a wise man who does not grieve for the things which he has not, but rejoices for those which he has.
Epictetus

There are but two classes of the wise; the men who serve God because they have found him, and the men who seek him because they have found him not.
Richard Cecil

After the event even a fool is wise. *Homer*

In an active life is sown the seed of wisdom; but he who reflects not, never reaps; has no harvest from it, but carries the burden of age without the wages of experience; nor knows himself old, but from his infirmities, the parish register, and the contempt of mankind. And age, if it has not esteem, has nothing.
Edward Young

It takes a clever man to turn cynic and a wise man clever enough not to. *Fannie Hurst*

The children of this world are in their generation wiser than the children of light. *St. Luke 16:8*

He is happy in his wisdom who learned at another's expense. *Plautus*

Among mortals second thoughts are wisest.
Euripides

It is better to sit with a wise man in prison, than with a fool in paradise. *Anonymous*

The divine essence itself is love and wisdom.
Emanuel Swedenborg

A wise man will not communicate his differing thoughts to unprepared minds, or in a disorderly manner.
Benjamin Whichcote

The Delphic oracle said I was the wisest of all the Greeks. It is because that I alone, of all the Greeks, know that I know nothing. *Socrates*

Men who know themselves are no longer fools; they stand on the threshold of the Door of Wisdom.
Havelock Ellis

To have a low opinion of our own merits and to think highly of others is an evidence of wisdom.
Thomas à Kempis

He who thinks wisdom is greater than virtue will lose his wisdom.
Hebrew proverb

He who learns the rules of wisdom without conforming to them in his life is like a man who ploughs in his field but does not sow.
Saadi

The doorstep to the temple of wisdom is the knowledge of our own ignorance.
Charles H. Spurgeon

The wise man is also the just, the pious, the upright, the man who walks in the way of truth. The fear of the Lord, which is the beginning of wisdom, consists in a complete devotion to God.
Otto Zockler

God hath chosen the foolish things of the world to confound the wise.
I Corinthians 1:27

Wisdom is to the mind what health is to the body.
François Duc de La Rochefoucauld

Our grandfathers could wait for a twice-a-week stagecoach without running a temperature; modern man gets mad if

he misses one section of a revolving door. Life is gulped down, not savored. The only new vice of the past three hundred years is the breathless blasphemy of speed. Pascal's profound word is considered mere gibberish: "The unhappiness of mankind is due to one thing, we have not the wisdom to remain in tranquility at home."
James W. Clarke

No man can be wise on an empty stomach.
George Eliot

The mintage of wisdom is to know that rest is rust, and that real life is in love, laughter, and work.
Elbert Hubbard

Such is the nature of men that however they may acknowledge many others to be more witty, or more eloquent, or more learned, yet they will hardly believe there be many so wise as themselves.
Thomas Hobbes

The wise man has his foibles, as well as the fool. But the difference between them is, that the foibles of the one are known to himself and concealed from the world; and the foibles of the other are known to the world and concealed from himself.
J. Mason

The art of being wise, is the art of knowing what to overlook.
William James

The fear of the Lord is the beginning of wisdom.
Psalms 111:10

The first consideration a wise man fixeth upon is the great end of his creation; what it is, and wherein it consists; the next is of the most proper means to that end.
John B. Walker

To finish the moment, to find the journey's end in every step of the road, to live the greatest number of good hours, is wisdom. *Ralph Waldo Emerson*

The wise man, even when he holds his tongue, says more than the fool when he speaks.
Thomas Fuller

The wisdom of the ignorant somewhat resembles the instinct of animals; it is diffused only in a very narrow sphere, but within the circle it acts with vigor, uniformity, and success. *Oliver Goldsmith*

To profit from good advice requires more wisdom than to give it. *John C. Collins*

The wisdom of this world is foolishness with God.
I Corinthians 3:19

The intellect of the wise is like glass; it admits the light of heaven and reflects it. *August W. Hare*

The foundation of all foundations, the pillar supporting all wisdoms, is the recognition of the reality of God.
Moses Maimonides

Happy is the man that findeth wisdom, and the man that getteth understanding. *Proverbs 3:13*

Living in an age of extraordinary events and revolutions, I have learned from thence this truth, which I desire might be communicated to posterity: that all is vanity which is not honest, and that there is no solid wisdom but in real piety. *John Evelyn*

The height of human wisdom is to bring our tempers down to our circumstances and to make a calm within, under the weight of the greatest storm without.
Daniel Defoe

The most certain sign of wisdom is a continual cheerfulness; her state is like that of things in the regions above the moon, always clear and serene.
Michel de Montaigne

The wise man walks with God, surveys far on the endless line of life; values his soul, thinks of eternity; both worlds considers, and provides for both; with reason's eye his passions guards; abstains from evil; lives on hope—on hope, the fruit of faith; looks upward, purifies his soul, expands his wings, and mounts into the sky; passes the sun, and gains his Father's house, and drinks with angels from the fount of bliss. *Robert Pollok*

Wisdom is knowing what to do next; virtue is doing it.
David Starr Jordan

That which before us lies in daily life,
Is the prime wisdom.
John Milton

The sublimity of wisdom is to do those things living which are to be desired when dying.
Jeremy Taylor

The invariable mark of wisdom is to see the miraculous in the common. *Ralph Waldo Emerson*

The clouds may drop down titles and estates;
Wealth may seek us; but wisdom must be sought.
Edward Young

Wisdom allows nothing to be good that will not be so forever; no man to be happy but he that needs no other happiness than what he has within himself; no man to be great or powerful that is not master of himself.
Lucius Annaeus Seneca

Wisdom is the right use of knowledge. To know is not to be wise. Many men know a great deal, and are all the greater fools for it. There is no fool so great a fool as a knowing fool. But to know how to use knowledge is to have wisdom. *Charles H. Spurgeon*

The growth of wisdom may be gauged accurately by the decline of ill-temper.   *Friedrich Wilhelm Nietzsche*

Wisdom denotes the pursuing of the best ends by the best means.   *Frances Hutcheson*

> Wisdom is ofttimes nearer when we stoop
> Than when we soar.
>   *William Wordsworth*

Wisdom does not show itself so much in precept as in life—in firmness of mind and a mastery of appetite. It teaches us to do as well as to talk; and to make our words and actions all of a color.   *Lucius Annaeus Seneca*

Wisdom is divided into two parts; (a) having a great deal to say, and (b) not saying it.
   Anonymous

> Wisdom is not finally tested in the schools,
> Wisdom cannot be passed from one having
>   it to another not having it,
> Wisdom is of the soul, is not susceptible of
>   proof, is its own proof.
>   *Walt Whitman*

The Art of Kindness

I shall pass through this world but once. Anything, therefore, that I can do, or any kindness that I can show to any human being, let me do it now. Let me not defer it or neglect it, for I shall not pass this way again!
Etienne de Grallet

In her tongue is the law of kindness.
Proverbs 31:26

>Have you had a kindness shown?
> Pass it on;
>'Twas not given for thee alone,
> Pass it on;
>Let it travel down the years,
>Let it wipe another's tears,
>'Till in Heaven the deed appears,
> Pass it on.
Henry Burton

Ask thyself, daily, to how many ill-minded persons thou hast shown a kind disposition.
Marcus Antoninus

Kind words are the music of the world. They have a power which seems to be beyond natural causes, as if they were some angel's song which had lost its way and come on earth. It seems as if they could almost do what in reality God alone can do—soften the hard and angry hearts of men. No one was ever corrected by a sarcasm—crushed, perhaps, if the sarcasm was clever enough, but drawn nearer to God, never.
Frederick W. Faber

Kindness is the beginning and the end of the law.
Hebrew proverb

Make a rule, and pray to God to help you to keep it, never, if possible, to lie down at night without being able to say: "I have made one human being at least a little wiser, or a little happier, or at least a little better this day." *Charles Kingsley*

Wherever there is a human being there is a chance for a kindness. *Lucius Annaeus Seneca*

A word of kindness is seldom spoken in vain, while witty sayings are as easily lost as the pearls slipping from a broken string. *George Dennison Prentice*

The ministry of kindness is a ministry which may be achieved by all men, rich and poor, learned and illiterate. Brilliance of mind and capacity for deep thinking have

rendered great service to humanity, but by themselves they are impotent to dry a tear or mend a broken heart.
Anonymous

Little deeds of kindness, little words of love,
Help to make earth happy like the heaven above.
Julia A. Fletcher Carney

Each one of us is bound to make the little circle in which he lives better and happier. Bound to see that out of that small circle the widest good may flow. Each may have fixed in his mind the thought that out of a single household may flow influences that shall stimulate the whole commonwealth and the whole civilized world.
A. P. Stanley

'Twas a thief said the last kind word to Christ:
Christ took the kindness and forgave the theft.
Robert Browning

He who confers a favor should at once forget it, if he is not to show a sordid, ungenerous spirit. To remind a man of a kindness conferred on him, and to talk of it, is little different from reproach. *Demosthenes*

The heart benevolent and kind
The most resembles God.
Robert Burns

Kindness is the golden chain by which society is bound together. *Johann Wolfgang von Goethe*

The early Church unleashed a flood of kindness in a world of racial strife; the modern Church has too often unleashed a flood of resolutions.
Christianity Today

> Kind hearts are more than coronets,
> And simple faith than Norman blood.
> *Alfred, Lord Tennyson*

Kindness seems to come with a double grace and tenderness from the old. It seems in them the hoarded and long purified benevolence of years, as if it had survived and conquered the baseness and selfishness of the ordeal it had passed, as if the winds which had broken the form, had swept in vain across the heart, and the frosts which had chilled the blood, and whitened the thin locks, had no power over the warm tide of the affections.
Edward G. Bulwer-Lytton

The greatest thing a man can do for his heavenly Father is to be kind to some of his other children.
Henry Drummond

Kind looks, kind words, kind acts, and warm handshakes —these are secondary means of grace when men are in trouble and are fighting their unseen battles.
John Hall

The kindest are those who forgive and forget.
Megiddo message

Since trifles make the sum of human things,
And half our misery from our foibles springs;
Since life's best joys consist in peace and ease,
And few can save or serve, but all may please;
Let the ungentle spirit learn from thence,
A small unkindness is a great offense.
Hannah More

Whoever gives a small coin to a poor man has six blessings bestowed upon him, but he who speaks a kind word to him obtains eleven blessings.
The Talmud

He hath a tear for pity, and a hand open as day for melting charity. *Shakespeare*

He that will not give some portion of his ease, his blood, his wealth, for others' good, is a poor, frozen churl.
Joanna Baillie

Kind words produce their own image in men's souls; and a beautiful image it is. They soothe and quiet and comfort the hearer. They shame him out of his sour, morose, unkind feelings. We have not yet begun to use kind words in such abundance as they ought to be used.
Blaise Pascal

It is one of the beautiful compensations of life that no man can sincerely try to help another, without helping himself. Both man and womankind belie their nature when they are not kind. *Gamaliel Bailey*

Kindness in ourselves is the honey that blunts the sting of unkindness in another. *Walter Savage Landor*

The happiness of life may be greatly increased by small courtesies in which there is no parade, whose voice is too still to tease, and which manifest themselves by tender and affectionate looks, and little kind acts of attention. *Laurence Sterne*

Kindness is the only charm permitted to the aged; it is the coquetry of white hair. *Octave Feuillet*

Half the misery of human life might be extinguished if men would alleviate the general curse they lie under by mutual offices of compassion, benevolence, and humanity. *Joseph Addison*

The drying up of a single tear, has more of honest fame, than shedding seas of gore. *Lord Byron*

The last, best fruit which comes to late perfection, even in the kindliest soul, is tenderness toward the hard, forbearance toward the unforbearing, warmth of heart toward the cold, philanthropy toward the misanthropic. *Jean Paul Richter*

When death, the great reconciler, has come, it is never our tenderness that we repent of, but our severity.
George Eliot

What we do for ours while we have them, will be precisely what will render their memory sweet to the heart when we no longer have them.
Frédéric Godet

> So many gods, so many creeds,
>   So many paths that wind and wind,
>   While just the art of being kind
> Is all the sad world needs.
Ella Wheeler Wilcox

Christ:
Teacher of Mankind

For as in Adam all die, even so in Christ shall all be made alive.
I Corinthians 15:22

As the print of the seal on the wax is the express image of the seal itself, so Christ is the express image, the perfect representation of God.
St. Ambrose

God never gave a man a thing to do, concerning which it were irreverent to ponder how the Son of God would have done it.
George Macdonald

Man stands at the apex of the visible creation amid the vast eternities of time and space. Before him rises the significant figure of the Christ. No human life compares with the bright and beautiful history of this young Galilean teacher. Greater than Confucius or the Buddha, more persuasive than the dreams of Plato or the arguments of Aristotle, his words have had more effect upon history than the marching of the armies of Alexander or the conquests of Caesar. The famous men in the records of the race pale beside him.
Herbert Parrish

Christ is God clothed with human nature.
Benjamin Whichcote

A man who can read the New Testament and not see that Christ claims to be more than a man, can look all over the sky at high noon on a cloudless day and not see the sun. *William E. Beiderwolf*

The nature of Christ's existence is mysterious, I admit; but this mystery meets the wants of man. Reject it and the world is an inexplicable riddle; believe it, and the history of our race is satisfactorily explained.
Napoleon Bonaparte

> Into the woods my Master went,
> Clean forspent, forspent,
> Into the woods my Master came,
> Forspent with love and shame.
> But the olives they were not blind to him,
> The little gray leaves were kind to him;
> The thorn-tree had a mind to him,
> When into the woods he came.
> *Sidney Lanier*

Christ changed sunset into sunrise.
Clement of Alexandria

The name of Christ—the one great word—well worth all languages in earth or heaven.
Gamaliel Bailey

Jesus Christ the same yesterday, and today, and for ever.
Hebrews 13:8

Jesus Christ is the outstanding personality of all time.... No other teacher—Jewish, Christian, Buddhist, Mohammedan—is *still* a teacher whose teaching is such a guidepost for the world we live in. Other teachers may have something basic for an Oriental, an Arab, or an Occidental; but every act and word of Jesus has value for all of us. He became the Light of the World. Why shouldn't I, a Jew, be proud of that? *Sholem Asch*

This is part of the glory of Christ as compared with the chiefest of his servants that he alone stands at the absolute center of humanity, the one completely harmonious man, unfolding all which was in humanity, equally and fully on all sides, the only one in whom the real and ideal met and were absolutely one. He is the absolute and perfect truth, the highest that humanity can reach; at once its perfect image and supreme Lord.
Alice French

> Jesus shall reign where e'er the sun
> Does his successive journeys run;
> His kingdom stretch from shore to shore
> Till moons shall wax and wane no more.
> *Isaac Watts*

Nothing will do except righteousness; and no other conception of righteousness will do except Christ's conception of it. *Matthew Arnold*

> The best of men
> That e'er wore earth about him was a sufferer,
> A soft, meek, patient, humble, tranquil spirit,
> The first true gentleman that ever breath'd.
> Thomas Dekker

I find the name of Jesus Christ written on the top of every page of modern history.
George Bancroft

> The Lord from Heaven,
> Born of a village girl, carpenter's son,
> Wonderful, Prince of Peace, the mighty God.
> Alfred, Lord Tennyson

It is not difficult to see one vital significance of Jesus Christ: he has given us the most glorious interpretation of life's meaning that the sons of men have ever had. The fatherhood of God, the friendship of the Spirit, the sovereignty of righteousness, the law of love, the glory of service, the coming of the kingdom, the eternal hope—there never was an interpretation of life to compare with that.
Harry Emerson Fosdick

We preach Christ crucified, unto the Jews a stumblingblock, and unto the Greeks foolishness.
I Corinthians 1:23

> Now he is dead, far hence he lies
> In the lorn Syrian town;

And on his grave, with shining eyes,
The Syrian stars look down.
Matthew Arnold

When Jesus utters a word, he opens his mouth so wide that it embraces all Heaven and earth, even though that word be but in a whisper. *Martin Luther*

If Christ is not divine, every impulse of the Christian world falls to a lower octave, and light and love and hope decline. *Henry Ward Beecher*

Earth grows into heaven, as we come to live and breathe in the atmosphere of the incarnation. Jesus makes heaven wherever he is. *Frederick W. Faber*

In the best sense of the word, Jesus was a radical. . . . His religion has been so long identified with conservatism —often with conservatism of the obstinate and unyielding sort—that it is almost startling for us sometimes to remember that all of the conservatism of his own times was against him; that it was the young, free, restless, sanguine, progressive part of the people who flocked to him.
Phillips Brooks

He is a path, if any be misled;
  He is a robe, if any naked be;
If any chance to hunger, he is bread;
  If any be a bondman, he is free;
  If any be but weak, how strong is he!

To dead men life is he, to sick men health;
To blind men sight, and to the needy wealth;
A pleasure without loss, a treasure without stealth.
Giles Fletcher

Jesus gave history a new beginning. In every land he is at home: everywhere men think his face is like their best face, and like God's face. His birthday is kept across the world. His death-day has set a gallows against every city skyline. Who is he?
George A. Buttrick

Jesus came not to hush the natural music of men's lives, nor to fill it with storm and agitation, but to retune every silver chord in that "harp of a thousand strings" and to make it echo with the harmonies of heaven.
Frederic W. Farrar

If Christ is the wisdom of God and the power of God in the experience of those who trust and love him, there needs no further argument of his divinity.
Henry Ward Beecher

The Christian faith is firmly rooted in the incarnation, in the conviction that, "God was in Christ, reconciling the world unto himself." To believe in Christ is to believe that God has come to earth to dwell with men. . . . In Jesus, we meet the living. Jesus is more than a religious genius or a holy man or a spiritual pioneer. To believe in Christ is to believe that the living God has come.
Earle W. Crawford

> Perhaps the Christian volume is the theme,
>   How guiltless blood for guilty man was shed,
> How he who bore in heaven the second name
>   Had not on earth whereon to lay his head.
>
> Robert Burns

The unique impression of Jesus upon mankind—whose name is not so much written as ploughed into the history of the world—is proof of the subtle virtue of this infusion. Jesus belonged to the race of prophets. He saw with open eyes the mystery of the soul. One man was true to what is in you and me. He, as I think, is the only soul in history who has appreciated the worth of man.

Ralph Waldo Emerson

The purest among the strong and the strongest among the pure, Christ lifted with his wounded hands empires from their hinges and changed the stream of ages.

Jean Paul Richter

> Speak low to me, my Saviour, low and sweet
> From out the hallelujahs, sweet and low,
> Lest I should fear and fall, and miss thee so
> Who art not missed by any that entreat.
>
> Elizabeth Barrett Browning

The sages and heroes of history are receding from us, and history contracts the record of their deeds into a narrower and narrower page. But time has no power over the name and deeds and words of Jesus Christ.

William E. Channing

Mine eyes have seen the glory of the coming of the Lord;
He is trampling out the vintage where the grapes of wrath are stored;
He hath loosed the fateful lightning of his terrible swift sword; His truth is marching on.

Julia Ward Howe

Home:
Citadel of Happiness

A hundred men may make an encampment, but it takes a woman to make a home. *Chinese proverb*

Every bird likes its own nest best. *Randle Cotgrave*

Anyone can build an altar; it requires a God to provide the flame. *Anybody can build a house; we need the Lord for the creation of a home.* A house is an agglomeration of brick and stones, with an assorted collection of manufactured goods; a home is the abiding-place of ardent affection, of fervent hope, of genial trust. There is many a homeless man who lives in a richly furnished house. There is many a fifteen-pound house in the crowded street which is an illuminated and beautiful home. The sumptuously furnished house may only be an exquisitely sculptured tomb; the scantily furnished house may be the very hearthstone of the eternal God. *John H. Jowett*

A dining room table with children's eager, hungry faces around it, ceases to be a mere dining room table, and becomes an altar. *Simeon Strunsky*

Home is home, be it never so homely.
English proverb

A successful marriage is an edifice that must be rebuilt every day. *André Maurois*

Be it ever so humble, there's no place like home.
John H. Payne

> Happy the man, whose wish and care
> A few paternal acres bound,
> Content to breathe his native air,
> In his own ground.
> *Alexander Pope*

It will be great to go to the moon. But earth never invented anything better than coming home, provided home is a center of affection where parents love each other and their children intelligently, and where children admire and respect their parents and want to grow up to be like them. *Erwin D. Canham*

A good home implies good living, which is also a means and a token of true culture, since without good living there can be no good thinking, and—I speak it reverently—no good praying; for mind and soul must have something healthy to go upon. *J. P. Thompson*

Home is where the heart is. *Anonymous*

Hospitality consists in a little fire, a little food, and an immense quiet. — *Ralph Waldo Emerson*

Every house where love abides and friendship is a guest, is surely home, and home, sweet home; for there the heart can rest. — *Henry Van Dyke*

> O dream of joy, is this indeed
> The lighthouse top I see?
> Is this the hill? is this the kirk?
> Is this mine own countree?
> — *Samuel Taylor Coleridge*

A palace without affection is a poor hovel, and the meanest hut with love in it is a palace for the soul. — *Robert G. Ingersoll*

Home, the spot of earth supremely blest, a dearer, sweeter spot than all the rest. — *Robert Montgomery*

Perhaps you have a mother, likewise a sister too,
Perhaps you have a sweetheart to weep and mourn for you.
If this be your condition I advise you to never roam,
I advise you by experience you had better stay at home.
— *Anonymous*

During the last war, London parents shipped as many children as possible into the country where they would be physically safe from air bombardments. Studies made after the war showed that children who remained in London with their parents suffered less, physically and emotionally, than did the children sent to the country for safety. The true security was found to be family unity, not physical safety. *Henry C. Link*

He is the happiest, be he king or peasant, who finds peace in his home. *Johann Wolfgang von Goethe*

The poorest man may in his cottage bid defiance to all the force of the Crown. It may be frail, its roof may shake; the wind may blow through it; the storms may enter, the rain may enter, but the king of England cannot enter; all his forces dare not cross the threshold of the ruined tenement. *William Pitt*

To most men their early home is no more than a memory of their early years. The image is never marred. There's no disappointment in memory, and one's exaggerations are always on the good side. *George Eliot*

> The beauty of the house is order;
> The blessing of the house is contentment;
> The glory of the house is hospitality;
> The crown of the house is godliness.
> *Anonymous*

The happiness of the domestic fireside is the first boon of Heaven; and it is well it is so, since it is that which is the lot of the mass of mankind. *Thomas Jefferson*

Hard indeed, in a world which has come to feel that it is more important to have an automobile to get away from home with, than to have a home which you might like to stay in. *Katharine F. Gerould*

The greatest, most formidable force in the life of a child, with no second competitor, is his home. A leading European university spent a quarter of a million dollars to formally establish this fact. This is approximately how the child's waking time is divided: The public school has him 16% of his time. The church 1% (if he is consistent in his attendance). The home has him 83% of his time.
Howard Hendricks

The sober comfort, all the peace which springs
From the large aggregate of little things;
On these small cares of daughter, wife or friend,
The almost sacred joys of home depend.
Hannah More

This fond attachment to the well-known place whence first we started into life's long race, maintains its hold with such unfailing sway, we feel it e'en in age, and at our latest day. *William Cowper*

The stately homes of England,
How beautiful they stand!
Amidst their tall ancestral trees,
O'er all the pleasant land.
Felicia Hemans

Men are free when they are in a living homeland, not when they are straying and breaking away.
D. H. Lawrence

> A house is built of logs and stone,
> Of tiles and posts and piers;
> A home is built of loving deeds
> That stand a thousand years.
> *Victor Hugo*

The best security for civilization is the dwelling, and upon proper and becoming dwellings depends more than anything else the improvement of mankind. Such dwellings are the nursery of all domestic virtues, and without a becoming home the exercise of those virtues is impossible. *Benjamin D'Israeli*

We need not power or splendor; wide hall or lordly dome; the good, the true, the tender, these form the wealth of home. *Sarah Josepha Hale*

On the banks of the James River, a husband erected a tombstone in memory of his wife, one of those 100 maidens who had come to Virginia in 1619 to marry the lonely settlers. The stone bore this legend: "She touched the soil of Virginia with her little foot and the wilderness became a home." *Eudora R. Richardson*

The final culmination of this vast and varied republic will be the production and perennial establishment of millions of comfortable city homesteads and moderate-sized farms, healthy and independent, single separate ownership, fee simple, life in them complete but cheap, within reach of all. *Walt Whitman*

Our home joys are the most delightful earth affords, and the joy of parents in their children is the most holy joy of humanity. It makes their hearts pure and good, it lifts men up to their Father in heaven.
Johann Pestalozzi

> The family is like a book—
> The children are the leaves,
> The parents are the covers
> That protecting beauty gives.
>
> At first the pages of the book
> Are blank and purely fair,
> But Time soon writeth memories
> And painteth pictures there.
> *Anonymous*

Through all the seas of all thy world, slam-bangin' home again. *Rudyard Kipling*

Six things are requisite to create a "happy home." Integrity must be the architect, and tidiness the upholsterer. It must be warmed by affection, lighted up with cheerfulness; and industry must be the ventilator, renewing the atmosphere and bringing in fresh salubrity day by day; while over all, as a protecting canopy and glory, nothing will suffice except the blessing of God.
James Hamilton

The family is the spiritual atom of the atomic age.
Ralph W. Sockman

There is no home that is not twice as beautiful as the most beautiful city. *West African proverb*

To Adam paradise was home. To the good among his descendants, home is paradise.
August W. Hare

> If there be righteousness in the heart,
>   There will be beauty in the character,
> If there be beauty in the character,
>   There will be harmony in the home.
>
> If there be harmony in the home,
>   There will be order in the nation.
> If there be order in the nation,
>   There will be peace in the world.
>
> *Chinese proverb*

There is a magic in that little word, home; it is a mystic circle that surrounds comforts and virtues never known beyond its hallowed limits.
Robert Southey

There is no synthetic replacement for a decent home life. Our high crime rate, particularly among juveniles, is directly traceable to a breakdown in moral fiber, to the disintegration of home and family life. Religion and home life are supplementary. Each strengthens the other. It is

seldom that a solid and wholesome home life can be found in the absence of religious inspiration.
J. Edgar Hoover

Weep no more, my lady;
  Oh, weep no more today!
We will sing one song for the old Kentucky home,
  For the old Kentucky home, far away.
Stephen C. Foster

When home is ruled according to God's word, angels might be asked to stay with us, and they would not find themselves out of their element.
Charles H. Spurgeon

Two persons who have chosen each other out of all the species, with the design to be each other's mutual comfort and entertainment, have, in that action, bound themselves to be good-humored, affable, discreet, forgiving, patient, and joyful, with respect to each other's frailties and perfections, to the end of their lives.
Joseph Addison

The kindest and the happiest pair
Will find occasion to forbear;
And something, every day they live,
To pity, and perhaps forgive.
William Cowper

Whatever woman may cast her lot with mine, should any ever do so, it is my intention to do all in my power to make her happy and contented; and there is nothing I can imagine that would make me more unhappy than to fail in the effort. *Abraham Lincoln*

Where we love is home,
Home that our feet may leave, but not our hearts.
Oliver Wendell Holmes

You can no more measure a home by inches, or weigh it by ounces, than you can set up the boundaries of a summer breeze, or calculate the fragrance of a rose. Home is the love which is in it. *Edward Whiting*

If solid happiness we prize,
Within our breast this jewel lies,
  And they are fools who roam.
The world has nothing to bestow;
From our own selves our joys must flow,
  And that dear hut, our home.
Nathaniel Cotton

Pathways to God

I am Alpha and Omega, the beginning and the ending, saith the Lord God, who is, and who was, and who is to come, the Almighty. *Revelation 1:8*

This is one of the names which we give to that eternal, infinite, and incomprehensible being, the creator of all things, who preserves and governs every thing by his almighty power and wisdom, and who is the only object of our worship. *Alexander Cruden*

Men may tire themselves in a labyrinth of search and talk of God; but if we would know him indeed, it must be from the impressions we receive of him; and the softer our hearts are, the deeper and livelier those will be upon us. *William Penn*

At the foot of every page in the annals of nations may be written, "God reigns." Events as they pass away proclaim their original; and if you will but listen reverently, you

may hear the receding centuries, as they roll into the dim distances of departed time, perpetually changing "Te Deum Laudamus" (We praise Thee, O God) with all the choral voices of the countless congregations of the age.
George Bancroft

An old mystic says somewhere, "God is an unutterable sigh in the innermost depths of the soul." With still greater justice, we may reverse the proposition, and say the soul is a never ending sigh after God.
Theodore Christlieb

As the very atoms of the earth and the stars of the sky seek harmony with the system which binds them in a cosmic unity, so the souls of men seek harmony with the Spirit which makes them one.
John H. Holmes

I say, the acknowledgement of God in Christ
Accepted by the reason, solves for thee
All questions in the earth and out of it.
Robert Browning

We should give God the same place in our hearts that he holds in the universe. If we have God in all things while they are ours, we shall have all things in God when they are taken away. There is something in the nature of things which the mind of man, which reason, which human power cannot effect, and certainly that which produces this must be better than man. What can this be but God?
Marcus Tullius Cicero

There is no substitute for first-hand experience in the spiritual life. We must believe the explorers of the high places of the unseen world when they tell us that they have been there, and found what they sought. But they cannot really tell us what they found; if we wish to see what they have seen, we must live as they have lived.
William R. Inge

God moves in a mysterious way
   His wonders to perform;
He plants his footsteps in the sea
   And rides upon the storm.
William Cowper

God is a circle whose center is everywhere, and its circumference nowhere. *Empedocles*

Practical prayer is harder on the soles of your shoes than on the knees of your trousers.
Austin O'Malley

Thou hast made us for thyself, O God, and the heart of man is restless until it finds its rest in thee. *St. Augustine*

God's thoughts, his will, his love, his judgments are all man's home. To think his thoughts, to choose his will, to

love his loves, to judge his judgments, and thus to know that he is in us, is to be at home.
George Macdonald

The vastness of God's creation should ever keep us humble. The new telescope at Mt. Palomar enables man to photograph planets over one billion light years away. This distance in miles amounts to a total of 186,000 (miles per second) × 60 seconds × 60 minutes × 24 hours × 365 days × 1,000,000,000 (years). How many billions of planets there are, no one can guess. One astronomer, when asked how he could believe in a God, replied, "I keep enlarging my idea of God."
Obert C. Tanner

> Earth's crammed with heaven,
> And every common bush afire with God.
> And only he who sees takes off his shoes,
> The rest sit round and pluck blackberries.
> *Elizabeth Barrett Browning*

He who bridles the fury of the billows, knows also to put a stop to the secret plans of the wicked. Submitting to his holy will, I fear God; I have no other fear.
Jean Baptiste Racine

To know the mighty works of God; to comprehend his wisdom and majesty and power; to appreciate, in degree, the wonderful working of his laws, surely all this must be a pleasing and acceptable mode of worship to the Most High to whom ignorance can not be more grateful than knowledge.
Copernicus

If I stoop
Into a dark tremendous sea of cloud,
It is but for a time; I press God's lamp
Close to my breast; its splendour, soon or late,
Will pierce the gloom: I shall emerge one day.
Robert Browning

How often we look upon God as our last and feeblest resource! We go to him because we have nowhere else to go. And then we learn that the storms of life have driven us, not upon the rocks, but into the desired haven.
George Macdonald

The greatest question of our time is not communism versus individualism, not Europe versus America, not even the East versus the West: it is whether man can bear to live without God. *Will Durant*

I had rather believe all the fables in the Talmud and the Koran, than that this universal frame is without a mind.
Francis Bacon

God is working his purpose out as year succeeds to year,
God is working his purpose out and the time is drawing near;
Nearer and nearer draws the time, the time that shall surely be,
When the earth shall be filled with the glory of God as the waters cover the sea.
Arthur C. Ainger

In all his dispensations God is at work for our good. In prosperity he tries our gratitude; in mediocrity, our contentment; in misfortune, our submission; in darkness, our faith; under temptation, our steadfastness, and at all times, our obedience and trust in him. God governs the world, and we have only to do our duty wisely, and leave the issue to him. *John Jay*

> When all thy mercies, O my God,
>   My rising soul surveys,
> Transported with the view I'm lost,
>   In wonder, love and praise.
> *Joseph Addison*

It is one of my favorite thoughts, that God manifests himself to mankind in all wise, good, humble, generous, great and magnanimous men. *John C. Lavater*

In all thine actions think that God sees thee, and in all his actions labor to see him. That will make thee fear him, and this will move thee to love him. The fear of God is the beginning of knowledge, and the knowledge of God is the perfection of love. *Francis Quarles*

Let the chain of second causes be ever so long, the first link is always in God's hand. *George Lavington*

Live near to God, and so all things will appear to you little in comparison with eternal realities.
R. M. McCheyne

Nature is too thin a screen; the glory of the omnipresent God bursts through everywhere.
Ralph Waldo Emerson

They that deny a God, destroy man's nobility; for clearly man is of kin to the beasts by his body, and if he be not of kin to God by his spirit, he is a base and ignoble creature.
Francis Bacon

The very word "God" suggests care, kindness, goodness; and the idea of God in his infinity, is infinite care, infinite kindness, infinite goodness. We give God the name of good: it is only by shortening it that it becomes God.
Henry Ward Beecher

There is a God in science, a God in history, and a God in conscience, and these three are one.
Joseph Cook

The whole world is a phylactery, and everything we see is an item of the wisdom, power, or goodness of God.
Sir Thomas Browne

To escape from evil we must be made, as far as possible,

like God; and this resemblance consists in becoming just, and holy, and wise.
Plato

What is there in man so worthy of honor and reverence as this, that he is capable of contemplating something higher than his own reason, more sublime than the whole universe—that Spirit which alone is self-subsistent, from which all truth proceeds, without which is no truth?
Friedrich H. Jacobi

> Flower in the crannied wall,
> I pluck you out of the crannies
> I hold you here, root and all, in my hand,
> Little flower—but if I could understand
> What you are, root and all, and all in all,
> I should know what God and man is.
> *Alfred, Lord Tennyson*

Quest for Life's Meaning

Life is warfare, and the sojourn of a stranger in a strange land.
Marcus Aurelius

> So live that when thy summons come to join
> The innumerable caravan which moves
> To that mysterious realm where each shall take
> His chamber in the silent halls of death,
> Thou goest not, like the quarry-slave at night,
> Scourged to his dungeon, but sustained and soothed
> By an unfaltering trust, approach thy grave
> Like one that wraps the drapery of his couch
> About him, and lies down to pleasant dreams.
> *William Cullen Bryant*

After a teacher had told his students how they should play the game of life, one puzzled student asked: "But how can we play the game when we don't know where the goal posts are?"
Charles L. Wallis

Ships that pass in the night and speak each other in passing;
Only a signal shown and a distant voice in the darkness;

So on the ocean of life we pass and speak one another,
Only a look and a voice; then darkness again and silence.
Henry Wadsworth Longfellow

Every man's life is a fairy-tale written by God's fingers.
Hans Christian Andersen

Hope writes the poetry of the boy, but memory that of the man. Man looks forward with smiles, but backward with sighs. Such is the wise providence of God. The cup of life is sweetest at the brim, the flavor is impaired as we drink deeper, and the dregs are made bitter that we may not struggle when it is taken from our lips. Let us love life and feel the value of it, that we may fill it with Christ. *Adolphe Monod*

Amid two seas, on one small point of land,
Wearied, uncertain, and amazed we stand.
Matthew Prior

Because we can synthesize rubber, span the earth with sound, and spin wool from peanuts, we think we know the answers to all the riddles which have puzzled philosophers since time began. But there comes a moment when man wearies of the things he has won; when he suspects with bewilderment and dismay that there is another purpose, some profound and eternal purpose in his being. It is then he discovers that beyond the kingdom of the world there exists a kingdom of the soul.
A. J. Cronin

Dost thou love life? Then do not squander time, for that is the stuff life is made of.   *Benjamin Franklin*

A little gleam of time between two eternities; no second chance to us forever more!   *Thomas Carlyle*

A man has made at least a start on discovering the meaning of human life when he plants shade trees under which he knows full well he will never sit.
Elton Trueblood

    Ah! somehow life is bigger after all
    Than any painted angel could we see
    The God that is within us!
Oscar Wilde

A wisp of fog betwixt us and the sun;
A call to battle, and the battle done
Ere the last echo dies within our ears;
A rose choked in the grass; an hour of fears;
The gusts that past a darkening shore do beat
The burst of music down an unlistening street.
Lizette Woodworth Reese

Fanaticism consists in redoubling your effort when you have forgotten your aim.   *George Santayana*

    Life! we've been long together
  Through pleasant and through cloudy weather:
    'Tis hard to part when friends are dear;

>   Perhaps 'twill cost a sigh, a tear;
>   Then steal away, give little warning,
>   Choose thine own time,
>   Say not Good-night, but in some brighter clime
>   Bid me Good-morning.
>
> *Anna L. Barbauld*

The life of man on earth is a warfare.

Job 7:1

> If I can stop one heart from breaking,
> I shall not live in vain;
> If I can ease one life the aching,
> Or cool one pain,
> Or help one fainting robin
> Unto his nest again,
> I shall not live in vain.
>
> *Emily Dickinson*

When life is true to the poles of nature, the streams of truth will roll through us in song.

Ralph Waldo Emerson

> A little rule, a little sway,
> A sunbeam in a winter's day,
> Is all the proud and mighty have
> Between the cradle and the grave.
>
> *John Dyer*

Luther Burbank fell in love with plants; Edison fell in love with invention; Ford fell in love with motor cars; Kettering fell in love with research; John Patterson fell in love with salesmanship; the Wright brothers fell in love with airplanes. Someone has truly said: "Be careful what you set your heart on for it will surely come true." The men who harness their hearts to mighty tasks often see their dreams become realities. *Anonymous*

>Our lives are albums written through
>With good or ill, with false or true;
>And as the blessed angels turn
>   The pages of our years,
>God grant they read the good with smiles,
>   And blot the ill with tears!
>
>*John Greenleaf Whittier*

Brother, I have watched men; their insect cares and giant projects—their godlike plans and their mouselike employments—their eager race after happiness; this one trusting to the swiftness of his horse, another to the nose of his ass, a third to his own legs; this checkered lottery of life, on which so many stake their innocence and Heaven to snatch a prize, and blanks are all they draw; for they find to their disappointment that there was no prize in the wheel. *Johann Christoph Friedrich von Schiller*

>Life is an arrow—therefore you must know
>What mark to aim at, how to use the bow.
>Then draw it to the head and let it go!
>
>*Henry Van Dyke*

>Life, believe, is not a dream,
>   So dark as sages say;

> Oft a little morning rain
> Foretells a pleasant day!
>
> *Charlotte Brontë*

> Does the road wind up-hill all the way?
>   Yes, to the very end.
> Will the day's journey take the whole long day?
>   From morn to night, my friend.
>
> *Christina Rossetti*

Men need nothing so much in these modern days as they need a working philosophy of life, an adequate way to live. Loosed from their moorings that have held life, many are now adrift. They have thrown overboard the chart, compass, steering wheel, and the consciousness of destination. They are free from everything except rocks and storms.

E. Stanley Jones

We live in deeds, not years: in thoughts, not breaths;
In feelings, not in figures on a dial.
We should count time by heart-throbs. He most lives
Who thinks most, feels the noblest, acts the best.

Philip J. Bailey

Perhaps it would be a good idea, fantastic as it sounds, to muffle every telephone, stop ever motor and halt all activity for an hour some day to give people a chance to ponder for a few minutes on what it is all about, why they are living and what they really want.

John Truslow Adams

O misery of men! O blinded fools! in what dark mazes, in what dangers we walk this little journey of our life!
Lucretius

There is in nature what is within reach and what is beyond reach. He who is unaware of the distinction may waste himself in lifelong toil trying to get at the inaccessible without ever getting close to truth. But he who knows it and is wise will stick to what is accessible; and in exploring this region in all directions and confirming his gains he will even push back the confines of the inaccessible. *Johann Wolfgang von Goethe*

We sleep, but the loom of life never stops; and the pattern which was weaving when the sun went down is weaving when it comes up to-morrow.
Henry Ward Beecher

A mighty maze, but not without a plan.
Alexander Pope

Life is the faculty of spontaneous activity, the awareness that we have powers. *Immanuel Kant*

Human existence is girt round with mystery: the narrow region of our experience is a small island in the midst of a boundless sea. To add to the mystery, the domain of our earthly existence is not only an island of infinite space, but also in infinite time. The past and the future

are alike shrouded from us: we neither know the origin of anything which is, nor its final destination.
John Stuart Mill

The utmost span of a man's life is a hundred years. Half of it is spent in night, and of the rest half is lost by childhood and old age. Work, grief, longing and illness make up what remains.
Bhartrihari

In our sad condition, our only consolation is the expectation of another life. Here below all is incomprehensible.
Martin Luther

Life, as Cowley seems to say, ought to resemble a well-ordered poem; of which one rule generally received is, the the exordium should be simple, and should promise little.
Samuel Johnson

Life is an apprenticeship to constant renunciations, to the steady failure of our claims, our hopes, our powers, our liberty.
Henri F. Amiel

Life is as tedious as a twice-told tale,
Vexing the dull ear of a drowsy man.
Shakespeare

Life is but a day:
A fragile dewdrop on its perilous way
From a tree's summit.
John Keats

Life, as we call it, is nothing but the edge of the boundless ocean of existence where it comes on soundings.
Oliver Wendell Holmes

Out, out, brief candle!
Life's but a walking shadow, a poor player
That struts and frets his hour upon the stage
And then is heard no more; it is a tale
Told by an idiot, full of sound and fury
Signifying nothing.
Shakespeare

Life, like a dome of many-colored glass,
Stains the white radiance of eternity.
Percy Bysshe Shelley

Life is a long lesson in humility.
James M. Barrie

These are the thoughts of mortals, this is the end and sum of all their designs: a dark night and an ill guide, a boisterous sea and a broken cable, a hard rock and a rough wind. *Jeremy Taylor*

Life is a festival only to the wise. Seen from the nook and chimney-side of prudence, it wears a ragged and dangerous front. *Ralph Waldo Emerson*

Life is terribly deficient in form. Its catastrophes happen in a wrong way and to the wrong people. There is a grotesque horror about its comedies, and its tragedies seem to culminate in farce. *Oscar Wilde*

Still seems it strange, that thou shouldst live for ever?
Is it less strange, that thou shouldst live at all?
This is a miracle, and *that* no more.
Edward Young

My life is not an apology, but a life. It is for itself and not for a spectacle. I much prefer that it should be of a lower strain, so it be genuine and equal, than that it should be glittering and unsteady.
Ralph Waldo Emerson

Life consists in penetrating the unknown, and fashioning our actions in accord with the new knowledge thus acquired. *Count Leo N. Tolstoy*

Why are we so fond of a life that begins with a cry and ends with a groan? *Mary, Countess of Warwick*

Thus we build on the ice, thus we write on the waves of the sea; the roaring waves pass away, the ice melts, and away goes our palace, like our thoughts.
J. C. Von Herder

Life . . . is a combat without grandeur, without happiness, fought in solitude and silence.
Romain Rolland

What shall we call this undermin'd state,
This narrow isthmus 'twixt two boundless oceans,
That whence we came, and that to which we tend?
George Lillo

Tell me not in mournful numbers,
Life is but an empty dream.
Henry Wadsworth Longfellow

To suffer and to endure is the lot of humankind. Let them strive as they may, they will never summon up enough strength and cunning to throw off the ills and troubles which beset them. *Pope Leo XIII*

We are all like vessels tossed on the bosom of the deep; our passions are the winds that sweep us impetuously onward; each pleasure is a rock; the whole of life is a wide ocean. *Pietro Metastasio*

What is the life of man? Is it not to shift from side to side, from sorrow to sorrow, to button up one cause of vexation and unbutton another?
Laurence Sterne

One moment of a man's life is a fact so stupendous as to take the lustre out of all fiction.
Ralph Waldo Emerson

Were it offered to my choice, I should have no objection to a repetition of the same life from its beginning, only

asking the advantages authors have in a second edition to correct some faults of the first.
Benjamin Franklin

Thanks in old age, thanks ere I go.
For health, the midday sun, the impalpable air, for life, mere life,
For precious ever-lingering memories (of you my mother dear, you, father, you, brothers, sisters, friends),
For all my days, not those of peace alone, the days of war the same.
Walt Whitman

The main of life is composed of small incidents and petty occurrences; of wishes for objects not remote, and grief for disappointments of no fatal consequence; of insect vexations which sting us and fly away, impertinences which buzz a while about us, and are heard no more; of meteorous pleasures which dance before us and are dissipated; of compliments which glide off the soul like other music, and are forgotten by him that gave and him that received them. *Samuel Johnson*

Little self-denials, little honesties, little passing words of sympathy, little nameless acts of kindness, little silent victories over favorite temptations—these are the silent threads of gold which, when woven together, gleam out so brightly in the pattern of life that God approves.
Frederic W. Farrar

Faith Gives Meaning to Life

Faith is the substance of things hoped for, the evidence of things not seen. *Hebrews 11:1*

Without faith, we are as stained glass windows in the dark. *Anonymous*

Faith and works are like the light and heat of a candle; they cannot be separated. Faith without works is like a bird without wings; though she may hop about on earth, she will never fly to heaven. But when both are joined together, then doth the soul mount up to her eternal rest. *Joseph Beaumont*

For faith is the beginning and the end is love, and God is the two of them brought into unity. After these comes whatever else makes up a Christian gentleman. *St. Ignatius of Antioch*

Fear builds prison walls around a man and bars him in with dreads, anxieties and timid doubts. Faith is the great liberator from prison walls. Fear paralyzes, faith empowers; fear disheartens, faith encourages; fear sickens, faith heals; fear puts hopelessness at the heart of life, while faith sees beyond the horizon and rejoices in its God. *Lewis L. Dunnington*

All I have seen teaches me to trust the Creator for all I have not seen. *Ralph Waldo Emerson*

Faith makes all evil good to us, and all good better; unbelief makes all good evil, and all evil worse. Faith laughs at the shaking of the spear; unbelief trembles at the shaking of a leaf, unbelief starves the soul; faith finds food in famine, and a table in the wilderness. In the greatest danger, faith says, "I have a great God." When outward strength is broken, faith rests on the promises. In the midst of sorrow faith draws the sting out of every trouble, and takes out the bitterness from every affliction.
Richard Cecil

Faith declares what the senses do not see, but not the contrary of what they see. It is above them, not contrary to them. *Blaise Pascal*

As human beings, we are so made that we cannot help living in two worlds, the "is" and the "ought," the actual and the ideal. Now the power which reaches out into the "ought" and transforms it into the "is" which lays hold upon the possible and of it makes the actual, is creative faith. *Harry Emerson Fosdick*

A simple, childlike faith in a Divine Friend solves all the problems that come to us by land or sea.
Helen Keller

Under the influence of the blessed Spirit, faith produces holiness, and holiness strengthens faith. Faith, like a fruitful parents, is plenteous in all good works; and good works, like dutiful children, confirm and add to the support of faith. Faith in an all-seeing and personal God, elevates the soul, purifies the emotions, sustains human dignity, and lends poetry, nobility, and holiness to the commonest state, condition, and manner of life.
Juan Valera

A living Christianity is necessary to the world. Faith must be actual, practical, existential faith. To believe in God must mean to live in such a manner that life could not possibly be lived if God did not exist. For the practical believer, gospel justice, gospel attentiveness to everything human must inspire not only the deeds of the saints, but the structure and institutions of common life, and must penetrate to the depths of terrestrial existence.
Jacques Maritain

Dark as my path may seem to others, I carry a magic light in my heart. Faith, the spiritual strong searchlight, illumines the way. Although sinister doubts lurk in the shadow, I walk unafraid toward the Enchanted Wood where the foliage is always green, where life and death are one in the presence of the Lord.
Helen Keller

At the summit of every noble human endeavor, you will find a steeple pointing toward God.
Mack Stokes

Faith lights us through the dark to Deity; faith builds a bridge across the gulf of death, to break the shock that nature cannot shun, and lands thought smoothly on the further shore. *Edward Young*

My faith, Lord, cries to thee, the faith that thou hast given me, that thou hast inbreathed in me, through the humanity of thy son and by the ministry of thy preacher.
St. Augustine

> My life is but the weaving
> Between my God and me.
> I only choose the colors
> He weaveth steadily.
> Sometimes he weaveth sorrow
> And I in foolish pride,
> Forget he sees the upper
> And I the under side.
> *Anonymous*

Faith is the daring of the soul to go farther than it can see. *William N. Clarke*

Faith is illuminative, not operative; it does not force obedience, though it increases responsibility; it heightens guilt, it does not prevent sin; the will is the source of action. *Cardinal John Henry Newman*

Faith reels not in the storm of warring words,
She brightens at the clash of "Yes" and "No,"
She sees the best that glimmers thro' the worst,
She feels the sun is hid but for a night,
She spies the summer thro' the winter bud,
She tastes the fruit before the blossom falls,
She finds the fountain where they wail'd "Mirage!"
Alfred, Lord Tennyson

Christian faith is a grand cathedral, with divinely pictured windows. Standing without, you can see no glory, nor can imagine any, but standing within every ray of light reveals a harmony of unspeakable splendors.
Nathaniel Hawthorne

For, from the beginning of the world,
How few of us have heard the silver of thy creed
Or paid our hearts for hours of emptiness
With gold of thy belief?
Thomas Merton

Life is an adventure of faith, if we are to be victors over it, not victims of it. Faith in the God above us, faith in the little infinite soul within us, faith in life and in our fellow souls. Without faith, the plus quality, we cannot really live. *Joseph F. Newton*

Fear knocked at the door. Faith answered. No one was there. *Inscription at Hind's Head Inn, Bray, England*

This is eternal life, that they may know thee, the only true God (John 17:3). This supernatural knowledge is now entered into by faith, which believes, through infused light, truths exceeding our natural wits.
St. Thomas Aquinas

Among all my patients in the second half of life—that is to say, over thirty-five—there has not been one whose problem in the last resort was not that of finding a religious outlook on life. It is safe to say that every one of them fell ill because he had lost that which the living religions of every age have given to their followers, and none of them has been really healed who did not regain his religious outlook. *Dr. Carl Jung*

Belief is a truth held in the mind; faith is a fire in the heart. *Joseph F. Newton*

Great souls have great faith. However, the faith that holds has spiritual qualities. The stable man has that intangible confidence in himself with capacities to be and to do, a recognition of God who may transform and empower his life, and a determined effort to realize man's highest ideals. *Anonymous*

>   Through this dark and stormy night
>   Faith holds a feeble light
>   Up the blackness streaking;
>   Knowing God's own time is best,
>   In a patient hope I rest
>   For the full day-breaking!
> John Greenleaf Whittier

Faith is to believe what we do not see, and the reward of this faith is to see what we believe.
St. Augustine

> Faith is not merely praying
> Upon your knees at night;
> Faith is not merely straying
> Through darkness into light;
> Faith is not merely waiting
> For glory that may be.
> Faith is the brave endeavor,
> The splendid enterprise,
> The strength to serve, whatever
> Conditions may arise.
Anonymous

No ray of sunlight is ever lost, but the green which it wakes into existence needs time to sprout, and it is not always granted to the sower to live to see the harvest. All work that is worth anything is done in faith.
Albert Schweitzer

Faith is the ear of the soul.
Clement of Alexandria

Faith and love are apt to be spasmodic in the best minds. Men live on the brink of mysteries and harmonies into which they never enter, and with their hand on the door-latch they die outside. *Ralph Waldo Emerson*

Humanity will live by the faith and the hope, the love

and the suffering, of a smaller number of men . . . who say: "Nevertheless and in spite of everything, and whatever may come, I believe." *Pierre Van Paassen*

> If faith produce no works, I see
> That faith is not a living tree.
> Thus faith and works together grow;
> No separate life they e'er can know:
> They're soul and body, hand and heart:
> What God hath joined, let no man part.
> *Hannah More*

Saints are persons who make it easier for others to believe in God. *Nathan Soderblom*

For as the body without the spirit is dead, so faith without works is dead also. *St. James 2:17*

The notion that faith is going to help me to live "successfully" or to attain the kind of peace of mind that leaves me unruffled no matter how many refugees sleep on the streets of Hong Kong is far from the heart of our religious tradition. *Janet Harbison*

> We have but faith: we cannot know,
>   For knowledge is of things we see;
>   And·yet we trust it comes from thee,
> A beam in darkness: let it grow.
> *Alfred, Lord Tennyson*

We think we believe, but is our faith really awake, or is it lying bed-ridden in some dormitory of our souls?
William R. Inge

> I need wide spaces in my heart
> Where Faith and I can go apart
> And grow serene.
> Life gets so choked by busy living,
> Kindness so lost in fussy giving
> That Love slips by unseen.
>
> *Anonymous*

On the wall of a cellar in Cologne, where a number of escaped prisoners hid out for the duration, there was found this inscription: "I believe in the sun, even when it is not shining. I believe in love, even when feeling it not. I believe in God, even when he is silent."
Louis Binstock

Man must be arched and buttressed from within, else the temple wavers to the dust.
Marcus Aurelius

The tragedy of the world is that men have given first-class loyalty to second-class causes, and these causes have betrayed them.
Lynn H. Hough

> Faith of our fathers, holy faith,
> We will be true to thee till death.
>
> *Frederick W. Faber*

What I admire in Columbus is not his having discovered a world, but his having gone to search for it on the faith of an opinion.   *A. Robert Jacques Turgot*

The space of the whole universe is emptied . . .
And frightening when there is no God.
Zalman Shneor

Faith is a kind of winged intellect. The great workmen of history have been men who believed like giants.
Charles H. Parkhurst

In every seed to breathe the flower,
In every drop of dew
To reverence a cloistered star
Within the distant blue;
To wait the promise of the bow
Despite the cloud between,
Is Faith, the fervid evidence
Of loveliness unseen.
John H. Tabb

Man is not naturally a cynic; he wants pitifully to believe, in himself, in his future, in his community and in the nation in which he is a part.
Louis Bromfield

I know not where his islands lift
Their fronded palms in air;

I only know I cannot drift
Beyond his love and care.
John Greenleaf Whittier

Faith in order, which is the basis of science, cannot reasonably be separated from faith in an ordainer, which is the basis of religion. *Asa Gray*

Pessimism may often be a poison, and sometimes a medicine, but never a food.
G. K. Chesterton

If ye have faith as a grain of mustard seed, ye shall say unto this mountain, Remove hence to yonder place; and it shall remove; and nothing shall be impossible unto you.
St. Matthew 17:20

Faith goes up the stairs that love has made and looks out of the windows which hope has opened.
Charles H. Spurgeon

Faith and works are as necessary to our spiritual life as Christians, as soul and body are to our life as men; for faith is the soul of religion, and works, the body.
Arthur W. Colton

Faith is not a stained-glass word reserved only for religious use, though it is essential to religion because it is essential to life. It is not something we can see on every street-corner, but we dare not cross the street without it. . . . If faith were removed for one day, our whole way of life would collapse. *V. Carney Hargroves*

There is a limit where the intellect fails and breaks down, and this limit is where the questions concerning God, and freewill, and immortality arise.
Immanuel Kant

Faith is a certain image of eternity. All things are present to it—things past, and things to come; it converses with angels, and antedates the hymns of glory. Every man that hath this grace is as certain there are glories for him, if he perseveres in duty, as if he had heard and sung the thanksgiving song for the blessed sentence of doomsday. *Jeremy Taylor*

Skepticism has not founded empires, established principles, or changed the world's heart. The great doers of history have always been men of faith.
Edwin H. Chapin

It is faith among men that holds the moral elements of society together, as it is faith in God that binds the world to his throne. *William M. Evarts*

Let us have faith that right makes might, and in that faith, let us to the end, dare to do our duty, as we understand it. *Abraham Lincoln*

There are no tricks in plain and simple faith.
Shakespeare

There never was found in any age of the world, either philosopher or sect, or law, or discipline which did so highly exalt the public good as the Christian faith.
Sir Francis Bacon

It is cynicism and fear that freeze life; it is faith that thaws it out, releases it, sets it free.
Harry Emerson Fosdick

To believe in something not yet proved and to underwrite it with our lives: it is the only way we can keep the future open. Man, surrounded by facts, permitting himself no surprise, no intuitive flash, no great hypothesis, no risk, is in a locked cell. Ignorance cannot seal the mind and imagination more securely.
Lillian Smith

> They never fail who light
> Their lamp of faith at the unwavering flame
> Burnt for the altar service of the Race
> Since the beginning.
> *Elsa Barker*

Science has sometimes been said to be opposed to faith, and inconsistent with it. But all science, in fact, rests on a basis of faith, for it assumes the permanence and uniformity of natural laws, a thing which can never be demonstrated.
Tryon Edwards

Take courage, soul!
Hold not thy strength in vain!
With faith o'ercome the steeps
Thy God hath set for thee.
Beyond the Alpine summits of great pain
Lieth thine Italy.

Rose T. Cooke

Whoever sees 'neath winter's field of snow
The silent harvest of the future grow,
God's power must know.
The heart that looks on when the eyelids close,
And dares to live his life in spite of woes,
God's comfort knows.

John Tyndall

Life Beyond the Grave

For this corruptible must put on incorruption, and this mortal must put on immortality.
I Corinthians 15:53

They do it to obtain a corruptible crown; but we an incorruptible.
I Corinthians 9:25

Everything science has taught me, and continues to teach me, strengthens my belief in the continuity of our spiritual existence after death.
Werner von Braun

"Good-night! Good-night!" as we so oft have said,
Beneath this roof at midnight, in the days
That are no more, and shall no more return.
Thou hast but taken up thy lamp and gone to bed;
I stay a little longer, as one stays
To cover up the embers that still burn.
Henry Wadsworth Longfellow

Manifestly the soul is as immortal as the moral order which inhabits it.
Joseph Fort Newton

And though after my skin worms destroy this body, yet in my flesh shall I see God.

Job 19:26

Both free enterprise and the labor movement at their best believe in the worth of the individual. But such a faith is nonsense if men are cheap candles blown out at death, or drops of water absorbed into some vague ocean of being. Thus any real faith in personality rests on faith in the life everlasting. *George A. Buttrick*

I believe in my survival after death. Like many others before me, I have experienced "intimations of immortality." I can no more explain these than the brown seed can explain the flowering tree. Deep in the soil in time's mid-winter, my very stirring and unease seem a kind of growing pain toward June. *Robert Hillyer*

Immortality is the bravest gesture of our humanity toward the unknown. It is always a faith, never a demonstration. *Gaius G. Atkins*

Life is a narrow vale between the cold and barren peaks of two eternities. We strive in vain to look beyond the heights. We cry aloud, and the only murmur is the echo of our wailing cry. From the voiceless lips of the unreplying dead there comes no word. But in the night of Death, Hope sees a star, and listening love can hear the rustle of a wing. *Robert G. Ingersoll*

Nature is the most thrifty thing in the world; she never

wastes anything; she undergoes change, but there's no annihilation. The essence remains.

Thomas Binney

Believing as I do that man in the distant future will be a far more perfect creature than he now is, it is an intolerable thought that he and all other sentient beings are doomed to complete annihilation after such long-continued slow progress. To those who fully admit the immortality of the human soul, the destruction of our world will not appear so dreadful.

Charles Darwin

He that raised up Christ from the dead shall also quicken their mortal bodies by his Spirit that dwelleth in you.

Romans 8:11

> The stars look down on the earth,
> The stars look down on the sea.
> The stars look up to the infinite God,
> The stars look down on me.
> The stars will live for a million years,
> For a million years and a day.
> But God and I will live and love
> When the stars have passed away.
>
> *Harry K. Zeller, Jr.*

As the mother's womb holds us for ten months, making us ready, not for the womb itself, but for life, just so, through our lives, we are making ourselves ready for another birth. . . . Therefore look forward without fear to

that appointed hour, the last hour of the body, but not of the soul. . . . That day, which you fear as being the end of all things, is the birthday of your eternity.
Lucius Annaeus Seneca

I know only scientifically determined truth, but I am going to believe what I wish to believe, what I cannot help but believe. I expect to meet this dear child in another world.
Louis Pasteur at the bedside of his dying daughter

> Were a star quenched on high,
> For ages would its light,
> Still travelling downward from the sky,
> Shine on our mortal sight.
> So when a great man dies,
> For years beyond our ken,
> The light he leaves behind him lies
> Upon the paths of men.
> *Henry Wadsworth Longfellow*

Immortality is the glorious discovery of Christianity.
William E. Channing

> Hence in a season of calm weather
>   Though inland far we be,
> Our Souls have sight of that immortal sea
>   Which brought us hither,
>   Can in a moment travel thither,
> And see the Children sport upon the shore,
> And hear the mighty waters rolling evermore.
> *William Wordsworth*

My flesh shall rest in hope. *Acts 2:26*

God created man to be immortal, and made him to be an image of his own eternity.
Apocrypha: Wisdom of Solomon

> Alas for him who never sees
> The stars shine through his cypress-trees!
> Who, hopeless, lays his dead away,
> Nor looks to see the breaking day
> Across the mournful marbles play!
> Who hath not learned, in hours of faith,
>   The truth to flesh and sense unknown,
> That Life is ever lord of Death,
>   And Love can never lose its own!
> *John Greenleaf Whittier*

I feel my immortality o'ersweep all pains, all tears, all time, all fears, and like the eternal thunder of the deep, peal to my ears this truth: "Thou livest forever."
Lord Byron

Immortality—twin sister of Eternity. *J. G. Holland*

I am the resurrection, and the life: He that believeth in me, though he were dead, yet shall he live.
John 11:25

> Cold in the dust this perished heart may lie,
> But that which warmed it once shall never die!

> That spark unburied in its mortal frame,
> With living light, eternal, and the same.
> *Thomas Campbell*

Not all the subtilties of metaphysics can make me doubt for a moment of the immortality of the soul, and of a beneficent providence. I feel it. I believe it. I desire it. I hope for it. And I will defend it to my last breath.
Jean Jacques Rousseau

> Fool! All that is, at all,
>   Lasts ever, past recall;
> Earth changes, but thy soul and God stand sure:
>   What entered into thee,
>   *That* was, is, and shall be:
> Time's wheel runs back or stops; Potter and clay endure.
> *Robert Browning*

If the father deigns to touch with divine power the cold and pulseless heart of the buried acorn and to make it burst forth from its prison walls, will he leave neglected in the earth the soul of man made in the image of his Creator?
William Jennings Bryan

> For who would lose,
> Though full of pain, this intellectual being,
> Those thoughts that wander through eternity,
> To perish rather, swallow'd up and lost
> In the wide womb of uncreated night,
> Devoid of sense and motion?
> *John Milton*

I have always thought that faith in immortality is proof of the sanity of a man's nature.
Ralph Waldo Emerson

    Dust thou art, to dust returnest,
    Was not spoken of the soul.
Henry Wadsworth Longfellow

In a moment, in the twinkling of an eye, at the last trumpet: for the trumpet shall sound, and the dead shall be raised incorruptible, and we shall be changed.
I Corinthians 15:52

    For tho' from out our bourne of time and place
      The flood may bear me far,
    I hope to see my pilot face to face
      When I have crost the bar.
Alfred, Lord Tennyson

We are like deep sea divers moving slowly and clumsily in the dim twilight of the depths, and we have our work to do. But this is not our element, and the relief of the diver in coming back to fresh air and sunlight and the sight of familiar faces is but a poor picture of the unspeakable delight with which we shall emerge from our necessary imprisonment into the loveliness and satisfaction of our true home. *J. B. Phillips*

    It must be so, Plato, thou reason'st well!
    Else whence this pleasing hope, this fond desire,

This longing after immortality?
Or whence this secret dread, and inward horror,
Of falling into nought? Why shrinks the soul
Back on herself, and startles at destruction?
'T is the divinity that stirs within us;
'T is Heav'n itself that points out an hereafter,
And intimates eternity to man.
Joseph Addison

The belief in the resurrection of Jesus is an act of faith; yes, it is, a faith in the justice, the reasonableness, the goodness, the squareness of the moral universe.
George C. Stewart

Happy he whose inward ear
Angel comfortings can hear,
  O'er the rabble's laughter;
And while hatred's fagots burn,
Glimpses through the smoke discern
  Of the good hereafter.
John Greenleaf Whittier

Let us not lament too much the passing of our friends. They are not dead, but simply gone before us along the road which all must travel.
Antiphanes

I go to prove my soul!
I see my way as birds their trackless way.
I shall arrive! what time, what circuit first,
I ask not: but unless God send his hail

Or blinding fireballs, sleet or stifling snow,
In some time, his good time, I shall arrive.
Robert Browning

I believe in immortality fundamentally, not because I vehemently crave it for myself as an individual, but because its denial seems to me to land the entire race in a hopeless situation and to reduce philosophy to a counsel of despair. *Harry Emerson Fosdick*

Here is my creed. I believe in one God, Creator of the universe. That he governs it by his providence. That he ought to be worshipped. That the most acceptable service we render him is doing good to his other children. That the soul of man is immortal, and will be treated with justice in another life respecting its conduct in this.
Benjamin Franklin

I shall take flight as a bird wings
   Into the infinite blue.
What if my song comes ringing
   Down through the stars and the dew?
Charles L. O'Donnell

Or ever the silver cord be loosed or the golden bowl be broken, or the pitcher be broken at the fountain, or the wheel broken at the cistern. Then shall the dust return to the earth as it was: and the spirit shall return unto God who gave it. *Ecclesiastes 12:6-7*

> Mortal though I be, yea, ephemeral, if but a moment
> I gaze up to the night's starry domain of heaven
> Then no longer on earth I stand; I touch the creator,
> And my lively spirit drinketh immortality.
>
> *Ptolemy*

Let us not be uneasy then about the different roads we may pursue, as believing them the shortest, to that our last abode, but following the guidance of a good conscience, let us be happy in the hope that by these different paths we shall all meet in the end.

Thomas Jefferson

> There is no death. The thing that we call death
> Is but another, sadder name for life,
> Which is itself an insufficient name,
> Faint recognition of that unknown life,
> That power whose shadow is the universe.
>
> *Richard H. Stoddard*

The idea of immortality . . . will continue to ebb and flow beneath the mists and clouds of doubt and darkness as long as love kisses the lips of death. It is the rainbow—hope, shining upon the tears of grief.

Robert G. Ingersoll

No man is prosperous whose immortality is forfeited. No man is rich to whom the grave brings eternal bankruptcy. No man is happy upon whose path there rests but a momentary glimmer of light, shining out between clouds that are closing over him in darkness forever.

Henry Ward Beecher

Our Saviour Jesus Christ, who hath abolished death, and hath brought life and immortality to light through the gospel.
II Timothy 1:10

Is this the end? I know it cannot be,
Our ships shall sail upon another sea;
New islands yet shall break upon our sight,
New continents of love and truth and might.
John W. Chadwick

The universe is a stairway leading nowhere unless man is immortal.
E. Y. Mullins

To look upon the soul as going on from strength to strength, to consider that it is to shine forever with new accessions of glory, and brighten to all eternity; that it will be still adding virtue to virtue, and knowledge to knowledge, carries in it something wonderfully agreeable to that ambition which is natural to the mind of men.
Joseph Addison

The few little years we spend on earth are only the first scene in a divine drama that extends on into eternity.
Edwin Markham

Though it is true that science presents no weighty evidence for life eternal, it is only fair to point out also that science has found no cogent reason for supposing that what is of importance in a man can be buried in a grave. The truth is that science cannot supply a definite answer to this question. Immortality relates to an aspect of life which is not physical, that is, which cannot be detected and measured by any instrument, and to which the application of the laws of science can at best be only a well-considered guess. — *Arthur H. Compton*

The cry of the human for life beyond the grave comes from that which is noblest in the soul of man.
— *Henry van Dyke*

> The stars shall fade away, the sun himself
> Grow dim with age, and nature sink in years,
> But thou shalt flourish in immortal youth,
> Unhurt amidst the wars of elements,
> The wrecks of matter, and the crush of worlds.
> — *Joseph Addison*

There is something beyond the grave; death does not end all, and the pale ghost escapes from the vanquished pyre.
— *Sextus Propertius*

There is nothing innocent or good that dies and is forgotten: let us hold to that faith or none.
— *Charles Dickens*

There is surely a piece of divinity in us, something that was before the elements, and owes no homage to the sun.
— *Sir Thomas Browne*

We cherish the dream and it will not down. We seek and

find warrant for our hope that sometime, somewhere we shall awake in his likeness and be satisfied in that we too behold the dead, small and great, standing before God, conscious, aspiring, resolute, to be dealt with in the ages to come by him who is not the God of the dead but of the living.
Charles R. Brown

> This life is but the passage of a day,
> This life is but a pang and all is over;
> But in the life to come which fades not away
> Every love shall abide and every lover.
> *Christina Rossetti*

The thought of being nothing after death is a burden insupportable to a virtuous man; we naturally aim at happiness and cannot bear to have it confined to our present being.
John Dryden

> If I stoop
> Into a dark tremendous sea of cloud,
> It is but for a time! I press God's lamp
> Close to my breast; its splendour, soon or late,
> Will pierce the gloom: I shall emerge one day.
> *Robert Browning*

We are born for a higher destiny than that of earth. There is a realm where the rainbow never fades, where the stars will be spread before us like islands that slumber on the ocean, where the beings that now pass over before us like shadows will stay in our presence forever.
Edward G. Bulwer-Lytton

We have passed age's icy caves,
And manhood's dark and tossing waves,
And youth's smooth ocean, smiling to betray:
Beyond the glassy gulfs we flee
Of shadow-peopled infancy,
Through death and birth, to a diviner day.
Percy Bysshe Shelley

The future is lighted for us with the radiant colors of hope. Strife and sorrow shall disappear. Peace and love shall reign supreme. The dream of poets, the lesson of priests and prophet, the inspiration of the great musician is confirmed in the light of modern knowledge.
John Fiske

I laugh, for hope hath happy place with me,
If my bark sinks, 'tis to another sea.
William E. Channing

We cannot resist the conviction that this world is for us only the porch of another and more significant temple of the creator's majesty. *Frederick W. Faber*

If then all souls, both good and bad do teach
With general voice, that souls can never die;
'Tis not man's flattering gloss, but nature's speech,
Which, like God's oracles can never lie.
Sir John Davies

Whatever that may be which feels, which has knowledge, which wills, which has the power of growth, it is celestial and divine, and for that reason it must of necessity be eternal. *Marcus Tullius Cicero*

You say, "Where goest thou?" I cannot tell,
And still go on. If but the way be straight
I cannot go amiss: but before me lies
Dawn and the day: the night behind me: that
Suffices me! I break the bounds: I see,
And nothing more, believe and nothing less.
Robert Browning

The Art of Courageous Living

Worry is debilitating. Fear paralyzes the springs of action. The need for a remedy that will release soul and body from the grip of these twin evils is the paramount need of our day. That remedy is the iron virtue of courage. It is the magic alchemist which transforms a person, trembling and scared half to death, into a valiant hero. It enables a person to surmount difficulties, to rise upon the ladder of handicaps, and to turn obstacles into stepping stones.
John A. O'Brien

Conscience is the root of all true courage; if a man would be brave let him obey his conscience.
J. F. Clarke

A stout heart breaks bad luck.
Miguel de Cervantes [Saavedra]

God planted fear in the soul as truly as he planted hope or courage. It is a kind of bell or gong which rings the mind into quick life and avoidance on the approach of danger. It is the soul's signal for rallying.
Henry Ward Beecher

Courage, the highest gift, that scorns to bend
To mean devices for a sordid end.
Courage, an independent spark from Heaven's bright throne,
By which the soul stands raised, triumphant, high, alone.
Great in itself, not praises of the crowd,
Above all vice, it stoops not to be proud.
Courage, the mighty attribute of powers above,
By which those great in war, are great in love,
The spring of all brave acts is seated here,
As falsehoods draw their sordid birth from fear.
George Farquhar

All goes if courage goes. *Sir James M. Barrie*

Of all the qualities of character which provoke the admiration of men, there are few which do so with such spontaneity and universality as that of courage. It makes an appeal to something deep in human nature which neither friend nor foe can resist.

Regardless of the changes in fashion in human conduct, courage is never outmoded. Its appeal is timeless, changeless and universal. If moderation may be said to be the silken thread running through all the virtues, courage may be said to be the foundation of all.
John A. O'Brien

He that raises a large family does, indeed, while he lives to observe them, *stand,* as Watts says, *a broader mark for sorrow;* but then he stands a broader mark for pleasure too. When we launch our little fleet of barks into the ocean, bound to different ports, we hope for each a prosperous voyage! but contrary winds, hidden shoals, storms, and enemies, come in for a share in the disposition of events; and though these occasion a mixture of disappointment, yet, considering the risk where we can make no insurance, we should think ourselves happy if some return with success. *Benjamin Franklin*

Moral courage is a virtue of higher cast and nobler origin than physical. It springs from a consciousness of virtue, and renders a man, in the pursuit or defence of right, superior to the fear of reproach, opposition, or contempt.
S. G. Goodrich

Be strong, and quit yourselves like men . . . and fight.
Samuel 4:9

Like the hardy perennial that shoots forth its blossoms not only amidst the soft zephyrs of May but also amidst the blustery winds of December, courage has blossomed in every season of the race's history and knows no limitations of border or race. It is the monopoly of no race, the heritage of no tribe. Its fatherland is the earth and all men are its potential heirs.
John A. O'Brien

> No longer forward nor behind
> I look in hope or fear;
> But, grateful, take the good I find,
> The best of now and here.
> *John Greenleaf Whittier*

A man who protects and hoards his life may lose it anyhow. Perhaps to protect it is to lose it in the most real sense of the word, for cowardice means spiritual death.
Sherman E. Johnson

Physical courage which despises all danger, will make a man brave in one way; and moral courage, which despises all opinion, will make a man brave in another. The former would seem most necessary for the camp; the latter for the council; but to constitute a great man both are necessary.
Caleb C. Colton

Screw your courage to the sticking-place,
And we'll not fail.
Shakespeare

The only sure way to take fear out of living is to keep a respectful fear of God in our lives, which means to maintain a reverent attitude toward his place and influence in the scheme of things. This brand of fear is a healthy ingredient, a deterrent to want, a spur to courage and confidence, an insurance against loss, a source of comfort and understanding at any age.
Eugene A. Carr

Too much stress cannot be placed upon the fact that prudence and courage walk hand in hand, and are never to be viewed as pulling in opposite directions. The man who takes risks needlessly and without due preparation is not courageous, but rash. Far, then, from acting without the guidance of reason, courage utilizes all the light to

chart its way and then plunges resolutely onward. "Be sure you are right," cautioned Lincoln, "*then* go ahead." His appeal was for courage lighted by reason, the most commendable and fruitful kind of courage.
John A. O'Brien

I dare do all that may become a man:
Who dares do more, is none.
Shakespeare

There's none but fears a future state; and when the most obdurate swear they do not, their trembling hearts belie their boasting tongues. *John Dryden*

He who would acquire fame must not show himself afraid of censure. The dread of censure is the death of genius. *William G. Simms*

True courage is not the brutal force of vulgar heroes, but the firm resolve of virtue and reason.
Paul Whitehead

Courage is generosity of the highest order, for the brave are prodigal of the most precious things.
Caleb C. Colton

Our greatest enemies are not wild beasts or deadly germs but fears that paralise thought, poison the mind, and destroy character. Our only protection against fear is faith.
Ryllis G. Lynip

The results of a scientific investigation of fear, conducted under the direction of the National Research Council, were published in the authoritative *Infantry Journal*. The study shows that fear is nature's method of mobilizing in an all-out way for an all-out emergency: it pulls all the body's resources into a state of preparedness for an ordeal. Fear in the form of prudent concern increases strength and endurance.

There are a few men in every army, the study discloses, who know no fear. Fortunately, just a few. For such individuals are not normal. They would be readily recognized by a psychiatrist as mentally deficient. Their callousness of mind makes them incapable of emotion, and hence incapable of fear; their lack of wholesome inhibitions of prudent fear makes them tend toward mere recklessness. Great accomplishments, calling for sustained courage and intelligence, are achieved by normal men who have learned to subjugate their fear for causes worthwhile.

"They say it takes a guy too dumb to be scared," replied Capt. Joseph J. Foss, when asked what it felt like, thousands of feet high, in a plane with enemy bullets whizzing around him. He had just shot down his twenty-sixth enemy plane over Guadalcanal, equalling Rickenbacker's record in World War I. "But any guy," continued Joe, "that says he isn't scared when Bullets start coming through his plane is a darn liar."

John A. O'Brien

The greatest glory that has ever come to me was to be swallowed up in London, not knowing a soul, with no means of subsistence, and the fun of working till the stars went out.   *Sir James M. Barrie*

> Out of the earth, the rose,
>   Out of the night, the dawn:
> Out of my heart, with all its woes,
>   High courage to press on.
>
> Laura L. Randall

When Francisco Pizzaro was about to undertake his epochal march down the west coast of South America to carve out of the uncharted wilderness a New Spain, he heard that some of his followers were murmuring at the prospect of the dangers before them. Taking his sword, Pizzaro drew a line on the sand from east to west. Then turning toward the south, he said:

"Friends and comrades! On that side are toil, hunger, nakedness, the drenching storm, desertion, and death. On this side, ease and pleasure. There lies Peru with its riches; here, Panama and its poverty. Choose, each man, what best becomes a brave Castilian. For my part I go to the south!"

So saying, he stepped across the line. Thirteen others followed his example, thus showing their willingness to abide the fortunes of their leader, come what may. "Fame," to quote the words of an ancient chronicler, "has commemorated the name of the little band, who thus, in the face of difficulties unexampled in history, with death rather than riches for their reward, preferred all to abandoning their honor, and stood firm by their leader as an example of loyalty to future ages."

John A. O'Brien

> Write on your doors the saying wise and old,
>   "Be bold! be bold!" and everywhere, "Be bold!

Be not too bold!" Yet better the excess
Than the defect; better the more than less;
Better like Hector in the field to die,
Than like a perfumed Paris turn and fly.
Henry Wadsworth Longfellow

True courage is cool and calm. The bravest of men have the least of a brutal, bullying insolence, and in the very time of danger are found the most serene and free.
Anthony A. Shaftsbury

The best way to deal with adversity, afflictions and handicaps is to face them frankly, calmly, realistically. Study them carefully and see how they can be overcome, borne with patience, or transmuted into occasions for growth in mind, heart and soul. The fatal mistake is to seek to ignore them, to bury one's head in the sand. What matters is not what happens to an individual but how he reacts to those happenings. It is what he does to them that counts.

The frank facing of a menacing situation is the first step in removing its fangs. Thinking pays its richest dividends when done in the face of impending danger, adversity or actual affliction. Though facing the tribulation with clarity of vision, adherence to ideals and trust in God, the individual secures the courage to transmute adversity into a stairs on which to scale the heights.
John A. O'Brien

He hath borne himself beyond the promise of his age, doing, in the figure of a lamb, the feats of a lion.
Shakespeare

Shame arises from the fear of men, conscience from the fear of God. *Samuel Johnson*

A ship in harbor is safe, but that is not what ships are built for. *William G. T. Shedd*

True courage is the result of reasoning. Resolution lies more in the head than in the veins; and a just sense of honor and of infamy, of duty and of religion, will carry us farther than all the force of mechanism.
Jeremy Collier

Courage is the best gift of all; courage stands before everything. It is what preserves our liberty, safety, life, and our homes and parents, our country and children. Courage comprises all things: a man with courage has every blessing. *Titus M. Plautus*

For fourteen years I have not had a day of real health. I have wakened sick and gone to bed weary, yet I have done my work unflinchingly. I have written in bed and out of bed, written in hemorrhages, written in sickness, written torn by coughing, written when my head swam for weakness, and I have done it all for so long that it seems to me I have won my wager and recovered my glove. Yet the battle still goes on: ill or well is a trifle so long as it goes. I was made for a contest, and the Powers-That-Be have willed that my battlefield shall be the dingy, inglorious one of the bed and the medicine-bottle. *Robert Louis Stevenson*

That courage is poorly housed which dwells in the numbers. The lion never counts the herd that is about him, nor weighs how many flocks he has to scatter.
Aaron Hill

Let's do it after the high Roman fashion,
And make death proud to take us.
Shakespeare

There is a virtuous fear which is the effect of faith, and a vicious fear which is the product of doubt and distrust. The former leads to hope as relying on God, in whom we believe; the latter inclines to despair, as not relying upon God, in whom we do not believe. Persons of the one character fear to lose God; those of the other character fear to find him.
Blaise Pascal

However mean your life is, meet it and live it; do not shun it and call it hard names.
Henry David Thoreau

The brave man is not he who feels no fear, for that were stupid and irrational; but he whose noble soul subdues its fear, and bravely dares the danger nature shrinks from.
Joanna Baillie

Courage, the footstool of the virtues, upon which they stand.
Robert Louis Stevenson

Virtue is bold, and goodness never fearful.
Shakespeare

Someone once asked James J. Corbett what was the most important thing a man must do to become a champion. He replied, "Fight one more round." The Duke of Wellington said that the British soldiers at the Battle of Waterloo were not braver than Napoleon's soldiers, but they were only braver five minutes longer. That made the difference between victory and defeat.
Anonymous

> Oh, fear not in a world like this,
> And thou shalt know erelong,
> Know how sublime a thing it is
> To suffer and be strong.
Henry Wadsworth Longfellow

God give me the courage to face a fact, though it slay me.
Thomas Huxley

Courage in strife is common enough; even the dogs have it. But the courage which can face the ultimate defeat of a life of good will, . . . that is different, that is victory.
H. M. Tomlinson

Fear is one of the passions of human nature of which it is impossible to divest it. You remember the Emperor Charles V, when he read upon the tombstone of a Spanish

nobleman, "Here lies one who never knew fear," wittily said, "Then he never snuffed a candle with his fingers."
>> Samuel Johnson

Ran on embattled armies clad in iron,
And, weaponless himself,
Made arms ridiculous.
>> John Milton

That most sublime courage I have ever witnessed has been among that class too poor to know they possessed it, and too humble for the world to discover it.
>> Josh Billings

For who gets wealth, that puts not from the shore?
Danger hath honour; great designs, their fame;
Glory doth follow, courage goes before.
>> Samuel Daniel

He who will not reason, is a bigot; he who cannot is a fool; and he who dares not, is a slave.
>> William Drummond

The brave man seeks not popular applause,
Nor, overpowr'd with arms, deserts his cause;
Unsham'd, though foil'd, he does the best he can;
Force is of brutes, but honour is of man.
>> John Dryden

It is good to remember that the tea kettle, although up to its neck in hot water, continues to sing.
Anonymous

He's truly valiant, that can wisely suffer
The worst that man can breathe.
Shakespeare

When the going gets tough, the tough get going.
Knute Rockne

Who has not courage should have legs.
John Ray

If we take the generally accepted definition of bravery as a quality which knows not fear, I have never seen a brave man. All men are frightened. The more intelligent they are, the more they are frightened. The courageous man is the man who forces himself, in spite of his fear, to carry on. Discipline, pride, self-respect, self-confidence, and the love of glory are attributes which will make a man courageous even when he is afraid.
George S. Patton, Jr.

None but the brave deserve the fair.
John Dryden

It is when we all play safe that we create a world of utmost insecurity.
Dag Hammarskjold

> We have hard work to do, and loads to lift;
> Shun not the struggle—face it; 'tis God's gift.
>
> Maltbie Babcock

You cannot run away from a weakness; you must sometime fight it out or perish. And if that be so, why not now, and where you stand?

Robert Louis Stevenson

The greatest test of courage on the earth is to bear defeat without losing heart. *Robert G. Ingersoll*

I love the man who can smile in trouble, who can gather strength from distress, and grow brave by reaction. 'Tis the business of little minds to shrink, but he whose heart is firm, and whose conscience approves his conduct, will pursue his principles unto death.

Thomas Paine

> You cannot choose your battlefield,
>   The gods do that for you,
> But you can plant a standard
>   Where a standard never flew.
>
> Nathalia Crane

One ought never to turn one's back on a threatened danger and try to run away from it. If you do that, you will double the danger. But if you meet it promptly and without flinching, you will reduce the danger by half. Never run away from anything. Never!

Winston Churchill

True courage is to do without witnesses everything that one is capable of doing before all the world.
François Duc de la Rochefoucauld

The soul little suspects its own courage. We have had to tear men's bodies to pieces, to burn, crush, strangle and crucify them to find that last wonderful drop of courage. Take even a common man, the commonest, and beat and bruise him enough and you will see his soul rise God-like.
Frank Crane

Presence of mind and courage in distress,
Are more than armies to procure success.
John Dryden

Our nation was built by men who took risks—pioneers who were not afraid of the wilderness; brave men who were not afraid of failure; scientists who were not afraid of truth; thinkers who were not afraid of progress; dreamers who were not afraid of action.
Brooks Atkinson

What a new face courage puts on everything!
Ralph Waldo Emerson

There is a famous statue in Mexico by Jesus Garcia, entitled "In Spite Of." The sculptor lost his right hand in the midst of his work on the statue. He determined that he would finish it. He learned how to carve with his left hand and finished it, and better, perhaps, than he would

have done with his right hand. For a quality of life had gone into the statue. So they called the statue "In Spite Of."
E. Stanley Jones

To live well in the quiet routine of life; to fill a little space because God wills it; to go on cheerfully with a petty round of little duties, little avocations; to smile for the joy of others when the heart is aching—who does this, his works will follow him. He may not be hero to the world, but he is one of God's heroes.
Anonymous

Who is the bravest hero? He who turns his enemy into a friend.
The Midrash

You should never wear your best trousers when you go out to fight for freedom and truth.
Henrik Ibsen

> Life is mostly froth and bubble,
> Two things stand like stone,
> Kindness in another's trouble,
> Courage in your own.
> *Adam L. Gordon*

Self-Control: A Regal Power

He who reigns himself and rules his passions, desires and fears is more than a king. *John Milton*

Every temptation that is resisted, every noble aspiration that is encouraged, every sinful thought that is repressed, every bitter word that is withheld, adds its little item to the impetus of that great movement which is bearing humanity onward toward a richer life and higher character. *John Fiske*

> In vain he seeketh others to suppress
> Who hath not learned himself first to subdue.
> *Edmund Spenser*

Drunkenness is temporary suicide: the happiness that it brings is merely negative, a momentary cessation of unhappiness. *Bertrand Russell*

If any man will come after me, let him deny himself, and take up his cross, and follow me. *Matthew 16:24*

Do you want to know the man against whom you have most reason to guard yourself? Your looking-glass will give you a very fair likeness of his face.
Richard Whately

If you can command yourself, you can command the world.
Chinese proverb

According to the Book of Genesis, the Creator gave man dominion over the whole wide earth. A mighty big present. But I am not interested in any such super-royal prerogatives. All I desire is dominion over myself—dominion over my thoughts; dominion over my fears; dominion over my mind and over my spirit. And the wonderful thing is that I know that I can attain this dominion to an astonishing degree, any time I want to, by merely controlling my actions, which in turn control my reactions.
Dale Carnegie

He that is slow to anger is better than the mighty; and he that ruleth his spirit than he that taketh a city.
Proverbs 16:32

Self-government is, indeed, the noblest rule on earth; the object of a loftier ambition than the possession of crowns or sceptres. The truest conquest is where the soul is bringing every thought into captivity to the obedience of Christ. The monarch of his own mind is the only real potentate.
John Ciardi

'Tis with our judgments as our watches, none
Go just alike, yet each believes his own.
Alexander Pope

Anybody can become angry—that is easy. But to be angry with the right person, and to the right degree, and at the right time, and for the right purpose, and in the right way—that is not within everybody's power and is not easy. *Aristotle*

One secret act of self-denial, one sacrifice of inclination to duty, is worth all the mere good thoughts, warm feelings, passionate prayers in which idle people indulge themselves. *Cardinal John Henry Newman*

One of the most important, but one of the most difficult things for a powerful mind is, to be its own master. A pond may lie quiet in a plain; but a lake wants mountains to compass and hold it in.
Joseph Addison

There is a great deal of self-denial and manliness in poor and middle-class houses, in town and country, that has not got into literature, and never will, but that keeps the earth sweet. *Ralph Waldo Emerson*

Anger is an acid that can do more harm to the vessel in which it's stored than to anything on which it's poured.
Anonymous

I have had more trouble with myself than with any other man.
                                    Dwight L. Moody

When Alexander had subdued the world, and wept that none were left to dispute his arms, his tears were an involuntary tribute to a monarchy that he knew not, man's empire over himself.
                                    Jane Porter

Anger is a thief that seizes control of man's faculties and uses them blindly and destructively. Usually a man who loses his temper also temporarily loses his ability to think logically.
                                    Lowell Fillmore

Self-denial is the result of a calm, deliberate, invincible attachment to the highest good, flowing forth in the voluntary renunciation of everything inconsistent with the glory of God or the good of our fellow-men.
                                    Gardiner Spring

Anger is a wind which blows out the lamp of the mind.
                                    Robert G. Ingersoll

If you would learn self-mastery, begin by yielding yourself to the One Great Master.
                                    Johann F. Lobstein

Every man is a tamer of wild beasts, and these wild beasts are his passions. To draw their teeth and claws, to muzzle and tame them, to turn them into servants and domestic animals, fuming, perhaps, but submissive—in this consists personal education. *Henri F. Amiel*

One single act performed with true self-denial, in renunciation of the world, is infinitely more of a revival and more of Christianity than 1,000 or 10,000 or 100,000 or 1,000,000 persons, so long as they keep it ambiguous. *Sören Kierkegaard*

Everybody thinks of changing humanity and nobody thinks of changing himself. *Count Leo N. Tolstoy*

Self-reverence, self-knowledge, self-control,
These three alone lead life to sovereign power.
Alfred, Lord Tennyson

In a controversy the instant we feel anger we have already ceased striving for the truth, and have begun striving for ourselves. *Thomas Carlyle*

Self-denial is a kind of holy association with God; and by making him your partner interests him in all your happiness. *Robert Boyle*

In vain do they talk of happiness who never subdued an impulse in obedience to a principle. He who never sacrificed a present to a future good, or a personal to a general one, can speak of happiness only as the blind do of colors.
Horace Mann

Those who wish to transform the world must be able to transform themselves. *Konrad Heiden*

More people are killed by overeating and drinking than by the sword. *Sir William Osler*

The very act of faith by which we receive Christ is an act of utter renunciation of self and all its works, as a ground of salvation. *Mark Hopkins*

> Man who man would be
> Must rule the empire of himself.
> *Percy Bysshe Shelley*

We are very apt to be full of ourselves, instead of Him, that made what we so much value, and but for whom we have no reason to value ourselves. For we have nothing that we can call our own, no, not ourselves; for we are all but tenants, and at will too, of the great Lord of ourselves, and of this great farm, the world we live upon. *William Penn*

The pledge to myself which I have endeavored to keep through the greater part of my life is: I will not allow one prejudiced person or one million or one hundred million to blight my life. I will not let prejudice or any of its attendant humiliations and injustices bear me down to spiritual defeat. My inner life is mine, and I shall defend and maintain its integrity against all the powers of hell. *James W. Johnson*

Whoever will labor to get rid of self, deny himself according to the instruction of Christ, strikes at once at the root of every evil, and finds the germ of every good.
François de Salignac de La Mothe Fénelon

Of what avail are great machines, if the men who mind them are mean? Man's increased command of nature is paltry if it be not accompanied by an increased control of himself. That is the only sort of command relevant to the evolution of man into a higher being.
George Bernard Shaw

People who fly into a rage always make a bad landing.
Will Rogers

What man's mind can create, man's character can control.
Thomas Edison

Two things a man should not be angry at: what he can help, and what he cannot help.
Anonymous

The first and best victory is to conquer self; to be conquered by self is of all things the most shameful and vile.
Plato

Whatever liberates our spirit without giving us self-control is disastrous. *Johann Wolfgang von Goethe*

We are discovering the right things in the wrong order, which is another way of saying that we are learning how to control nature before we have learned how to control ourselves. *Raymond B. Fosdick*

Every personal consideration that we allow, costs us heavenly state. We sell the thrones of angels for a short and turbulent pleasure. *Ralph Waldo Emerson*

The most precious of all possessions, is power over ourselves; power to withstand trial, to bear suffering, to front danger; power over pleasure and pain; power to follow our convictions, however resisted by menace and scorn; the power of calm reliance in scenes of darkness and storms. He that has not a mastery over his inclinations; he that knows not how to resist the importunity of present pleasure or pain, for the sake of what reason tells him is fit to be done, wants the true principle of virtue and industry, and is in danger of never being good for anything. *John Locke*

Laughter:
The Best Medicine

A nation that knows how to laugh at itself is stronger and has greater survival value than one that takes itself with ponderous solemnity; the weakness of Germany, since Bismarck's day, lay not in its arms but in its incapacity to make fun of its own institutions.
Sydney J. Harris

He laughs best who laughs last.
English proverb

A laugh is worth a hundred groans in any market.
Charles Lamb

The man that loves and laughs must sure do well.
Alexander Pope

I am the laughter of the new-born child
On whose soft-breathing sleep an angel smiled.
R. W. Gilder

A man without mirth is like a wagon without springs. He is jolted disagreeably by every pebble in the road.
Henry Ward Beecher

You laugh and you are quite right,
For yours is the dawn of the morning
And God sends you a good night.
Theodore Edward Hook

An onion can make people cry, but there is yet to be invented a vegetable that can make them laugh.
Anonymous

Alas for the worn and heavy soul, if, whether in youth or in age, it has outlived its privilege of spring time and sprightliness.
Nathaniel Hawthorne

You hear that boy laughing? you think he's all fun;
But the angels laugh, too, at the good he has done;
The children laugh loud as they troop to his call,
And the poor man that knows him laughs loudest of all.
Oliver Wendell Holmes

What sunshine is to flowers, smiles are to humanity. They are but trifles, to be sure, but, scattered along life's pathway, the good they do is inconceivable.
Joseph Addison

Laugh and grow fat. *English proverb*

A good laugh is sunshine in a house.
William M. Thackeray

Laugh and the world laughs with you,
  Weep and you weep alone,
For the sad old earth must borrow its mirth,
  But has trouble enough of its own.
Ella Wheeler Wilcox

Life pays a bonus to those who learn that laughter is a vital part of living. It is one of God's richest gifts. The Lord loves a cheerful giver; but he also loves a cheerful— period. And so does everyone else.
Edwin Davis

Laughter should dimple the cheek, and not furrow the brow with ruggedness. *Owen Feltham*

Beware of him who hates the laugh of a child.
John C. Lavater

When laughter is humble, when it is not based on self-esteem, it is wiser than tears. . . . There is no cure for birth and death save to enjoy the interval. The dark background which death supplies brings out the tender colours of life in all their purity.
George Santayana

Are you worsted in a fight?
Laugh it off.

Are you cheated of your right?
   Laugh it off.
Don't make tragedy of trifles,
Don't shoot butterflies with rifles,
   Laugh it off.

Does your work get into kinks?
   Laugh it off.
Are you near all sorts of brinks?
   Laugh it off.
If it's sanity you're after
There's no recipe like laughter,
   Laugh it off.
Henry R. Elliot

Man is distinguished from all other creatures by the faculty of laughter.   *Joseph Addison*

I like the laughter that opens the lips and the heart, that shows at the same time pearls and the soul.
Victor Hugo

I'd rather laugh, a bright-haired boy,
Than reign, a gray-beard king.
Oliver Wendell Holmes

You've all seen the machine a physician uses to take a patient's blood pressure. It indicates something about physical health. Someday, perhaps, someone will invent a laugh-pressure machine to show how sick or how healthy a sense of humor is. That will really indicate a lot about *mental* health.   *Murray Banks*

The day most wholly lost is the one on which one does not laugh. *Nicolas Chamfort*

I am persuaded that every time a man smiles, but much more when he laughs, it adds something to this fragment of life. *Laurence Sterne*

When the green woods laugh with the voice of joy,
And the dimpling stream runs laughing by;
When the air does laugh with our merry wit,
And the green hill laughs with the noise of it.
William Blake

Laughter is a green semaphore on the road of human relationship; it is a hand in the darkness, a whisper of courage in the storm. *Douglas Meador*

The cause of laughter is simply the sudden perception of the incongruity betwen a concept and the real object. *Arthur Schopenhauer*

Laughter is a most healthful exertion; it is one of the greatest helps to digestion with which I am acquainted; and the custom prevalent among our forefathers, of exciting it at table by jesters and buffoons, was founded on true medical principles. *Christoph W. Hufeland*

Frame your mind to mirth and merriment
Which bar a thousand harms and lengthen life.
Shakespeare

Laughter is the cipher-key wherewith we decipher the whole man. *Thomas Carlyle*

Man could direct his ways by plain reason, and support his life by tasteless food, but God has given us wit, and flavor, and brightness, and laughter to enliven the days of man's pilgrimage, and to charm his pained steps o'er the burning marle. *Sydney Smith*

> A laugh is just like sunshine,
>   It freshens all the day,
> It tips the peak of life with light,
>   And drives the clouds away;
> The soul grows glad that hears it,
>   And feels its courage strong;
> A laugh is just like sunshine
>   For cheering folks along.
>   *Anonymous*

If we consider the frequent reliefs we receive from laughter, and how often it breaks the gloom which is apt to depress the mind, one would take care not to grow too wise for so great a pleasure of life. *Joseph Addison*

Strange, when you come to think of it, that of all countless fools who have lived on this planet not one is known in history or in legend as having died of laughter.
 Max Beerbohm

No man who has once heartily laughed can be altogether and irreclaimably depraved. *Thomas Carlyle*

I have always noticed that deeply and truly religious persons are fond of a joke, and I am suspicious of those who aren't. *Alfred N. Whitehead*

Next to a good soul-stirring prayer is a good laugh, when it is promoted by what is pure in itself and in its grotesque application. *Samuel A. Mutchmore*

Fate used me meanly; but I looked at her and laughed,
That none might know how bitter was the cup I quaffed.
Along came Joy, and paused beside me where I sat,
Saying, "I came to see what you were laughing at."
Ella Wheeler Wilcox

One good, hearty laugh is a bombshell exploding in the right place, while spleen and discontent are a gun that kicks over the man who shoots it off. *DeWitt Talmage*

Smiles are as catchin' as the measles and a whole lot more pleasant. *Harvey Hamlyn*

O, glorious laughter! thou man-loving spirit, that for a time doth take the burden from the weary back, that doth lay salve to the weary feet, bruised and cut by flints and shards. *Douglas Jerrold*

It takes thirty-four muscles to frown, and only thirteen to smile. Why make the extra effort?
Anonymous

The laughter of girls is, and ever was, among the delightful sounds of earth.
Thomas De Quincey

The laughter of man is the contentment of God.
Eugene P. Bertin

Laughter is an integral part of life, one that we could ill afford to lose. If I were asked what single quality every human being needs more than any other, I would answer, the ability to laugh at himself. When we see our own grotesqueries, how droll our ambitions are, how comical we are in almost all respects, we automatically become more sane, less self-centered, more humble, more wholesome. To laugh at ourselves we have to stand outside ourselves, and that is an immense benefit. Our puffed-up pride and touchy self-importance vanish; a clean and sweet humility begins to take possession of us. We are on the way to growing a soul.
A. Powell Davies

There is the laughter which is born out of the pure joy of living, the spontaneous expression of health and energy, the sweet laughter of the child. This is a gift of God. There is the warm laughter of the kindly soul which heartens the discouraged, gives health to the sick and comfort to the dying. . . . There is, above all, the laughter that comes from the eternal joy of creation, the joy of expressing the inner riches of the soul, laughter that triumphs over pain and hardship in the passion for an enduring ideal, the joy of bringing the light of happiness, of truth and beauty into a dark world. This is divine laughter par excellence.
J. E. Boodin

Smile a smile. While you smile, another smiles,
And soon there's miles and miles of smiles,
And life's worth while if you but smile.
Anonymous

Nothing on earth can smile but man. Gems may flash reflected light, but what is a diamond-flash compared to an eye-flash and a mirth-flash? Flowers cannot smile; this is a charm that even they cannot claim. It is the prerogative of man; it is the color which love wears, and cheerfulness, and joy—these three. It is a light in the windows of the face by which the heart signifies it is at home and waiting. A face that cannot smile is like a bud that cannot blossom, and dries up on the stalk. Laughter is day, and sobriety is night, and a smile is the twilight that hovers gently between both, more bewitching than either.
Henry Ward Beecher

'Tis easy enough to be pleasant,
When life flows along like a song;
But the man worth while is the one who will smile
When everything goes dead wrong.
Ella Wheeler Wilcox

Hope Must Never Die

When you say a situation or a person is hopeless, you are slamming the door in the face of God.
Charles L. Allen

A religious hope does not only bear up the mind under her sufferings, but makes her rejoice in them.
Joseph Addison

Youth fades; love droops; the leaves of friendship fall;
A mother's secret hope outlives them all.
Oliver Wendell Holmes

Auspicious hope, in thy sweet garden grow wreaths for each toil, a charm for every woe.
Thomas Campbell

Hope writes the poetry of the boy, but memory that of the man. Man looks forward with smiles, but backward with sighs. Such is the wise providence of God. The cup of life is sweetness at the brim—the flavor is impaired as we drink deeper, and the dregs are made bitter that we may not struggle when it is taken from our lips.
Ralph Waldo Emerson

Cling to the flying hours; and yet let one pure hope, one great desire, like song on dying lips be set, that ere we fall in scattered fire our hearts may lift the world's heart higher. *Edmund W. Gosse*

Blessed is the man that trusteth in the Lord, and whose hope the Lord is. *Jeremiah 17:7*

Eternity is the divine treasure house, and hope is the window, by means of which mortals are permitted to see, as through a glass darkly, the things which God is preparing. *William Mountford*

>Behind the cloud the starlight lurks,
>   Through showers the sunbeams fall;
>For God, who loveth all his works,
>   Has left his hope for all.
>   *John Greenleaf Whittier*

Under the storm and the cloud today, and today the hard peril and pain—tomorrow the stone shall be rolled away, for the sunshine shall follow the rain. *Joaquin Miller*

>Know then, whatever cheerful and serene
>Supports the mind, supports the body too:
>Hence, the most vital movement mortals feel
>Is hope, the balm and lifeblood of the soul.
>   *John Armstrong*

Hope is like the sun, which, as we journey toward it, casts the shadow of our burden behind us.
Samuel Smiles

I laugh, for hope hath happy place with me,
If my bark sinks, 'tis to another sea.
William E. Channing

Had mankind nothing to expect beyond the grave, their best faculties would be a torment to them; and the more considerate and virtuous they were, the greater concern and grief they would feel from the shortness of their prospects. *John Balguy*

Everything that is done in the world is done by hope. No husbandman would sow one grain of corn if he hoped not it would grow up and become seed; no bachelor would marry a wife if he hoped not to have children; no merchant or tradesman would set himself to work if he did not hope to reap benefit thereby.
Martin Luther

Hope, of all passions, most befriends us here; joy has her tears, and transport has her death; hope, like a cordial, innocent though strong, man's heart at once inspirits and serenes, nor makes him pay his wisdom for his joys.
Edward Young

Life with Christ is an endless hope, without him a hopeless end. *Anonymous*

He that would undermine the foundations of our hope for eternity, seeks to beat down the column which supports the feebleness of humanity. If the mere delay of hope deferred makes the heart sick, what will the death of hope—its final and total disappointment—despair, do to it?
W. Nevins

If the cross is the measure of God's respect for man's freedom, then we can take new hope that freedom will survive all man's attempts to destroy it.
D. R. Davies

Hope is a lover's staff; walk hence with that, and manage it against despairing thoughts.
Shakespeare

The resurrection of Jesus Christ is our hope today. It is our assurance that we have a living Saviour to help us live as we should now, and that when, in the end, we set forth on that last great journey, we shall not travel an uncharted course, but rather we shall go on a planned voyage—life to death to eternal living.
Raymond MacKendree

Hope is the best part of our riches. What sufficeth it that we have the wealth of the Indies in our pockets, if we have not the hope of heaven in our souls?
Christian N. Bovee

Today well-lived . . . makes every tomorrow a vision of Hope.
Anonymous

It is worth a thousand pounds a year to have the habit of looking on the bright side of things.
Samuel Johnson

In all my wanderings round this world of care,
In all my griefs—and God has given my share—
I still had hopes my latest hours to crown,
Amidst these humble bowers to lay me down.
Oliver Goldsmith

Man is, properly speaking, based upon hope; he has no other possession but hope; this world of his is emphatically the place of hope.
Thomas Carlyle

Now the God of hope fill you with all joy and peace in believing, that ye may abound in hope, through the power of the Holy Ghost.
Romans 15:13

The good man's hope is laid far, far beyond the sway of tempests, or the furious sweep of mortal desolation.
H. K. White

Land of Hope and Glory, Mother of the Free,
How shall we extol thee, who are born of thee?
Wider still and wider shall thy bounds be set;
God, who made thee mighty, make thee mightier yet.
Arthur C. Benson

True hope is swift, and flies with swallow's wings; kings it makes gods, and meaner creatures kings.
Shakespeare

The worldly Hope men set their Hearts upon
Turns ashes, or it prospers; and anon,
  Like snow upon the Desert's dusty Face,
Lighting a little hour or two, is gone.
Omar Khayyám

Religion is the mother of dreams. Over the gray world, ruined by deluge, and death, it has sought ever, and found the arching rainbow of hope.
Albert E. Haydon

We shall nobly save or meanly lose the last, best hope of earth.   *Abraham Lincoln*

So, when dark thoughts my boding spirit shroud,
Sweet Hope; celestial influence round me shed
Waving thy silver pinions o'er my head.
John Keats

What is hope? Hope is *wishing* for a thing to come true; faith is *believing* that it will come true. Hope is wanting something so eagerly that, in spite of all the evidence that you're not going to get it, you go right on wanting it. And the remarkable thing about it is that this very act of hoping produces a kind of strength of its own.
Norman Vincent Peale

That divinest hope, which none can know of
Who have not laid their dearest in the grave.
Thomas L. Beddoes

The word which God has written on the brow of every man is Hope.
Victor Hugo

> The praise of those who sleep in earth,
> The pleasant memory of their worth,
> The hope to meet when life is past,
> Shall heal the tortured mind at last.
> *William Cullen Bryant*

Friendship Enriches Life

Love and friendship exclude each other.
Jean de la Bruyere

A faithful friend is a strong defense: and he that hath found such an one hath found a treasure.
Ecclesiastes 6:14

Before us is a future all unknown, a path untrod;
Beside us a friend well loved and known—
   That friend is God.
Anonymous

A friend may well be reckoned the masterpiece of Nature.
Ralph Waldo Emerson

Friendships are fragile things, and require as much care in handling as any other fragile and precious thing.
Randolph S. Bourne

A true friend is one soul in two bodies.
Aristotle

Friendship is Love without his wings!
>
> *Lord Byron*

A man cannot speak to his son but as a father, to his wife but as a husband, to his enemy but upon terms; whereas a friend may speak as the case requires, and not as it sorteth with the person. *Francis Bacon*

"A friend is the one who comes in when the whole world has gone out." Even as David thanked God for Jonathan and praised him in well-remembered lines, so have we abundant reasons to thank God today for friends and to resolve to keep these friendships in constant repair.
>
> *Edgar DeWitt Jones*

> But Friendship in its greatest Height,
> A constant, rational Delight,
> On Virtue's Basis fix'd to last,
> When Love's Allurements long are past;
> Which gently warms, but cannot burn;
> He gladly offers in return.
>
> *Jonathan Swift*

False friendship, like the ivy, decays and ruins the walls it embraces; but true friendship gives new life and animation to the object it supports. *Richard E. Burton*

All men have their frailties; and whoever looks for a friend without imperfections, will never find what he

seeks. We love ourselves notwithstanding our faults, and we ought to love our friends in like manner.
Cyrus the Great

Friendship is a sheltering tree.
Samuel Taylor Coleridge

A friend is a person with whom I may be sincere. Before him I may think aloud. *Ralph Waldo Emerson*

> I have *friends* in Spirit Land,
> Not shadows in a shadowy band,
> Not *others* but *themselves* are they,
> And still I think of them the same
> As when the Master's summons came.
John Greenleaf Whittier

Of all the means which wisdom uses to ensure happiness throughout the whole of life, by far the most important is the acquisition of friends. *Epicurus*

The loss of a friend is like that of a limb; time may heal the anguish of the wound, but the loss cannot be repaired.
Robert Southey

As widowers proverbially marry again, so a man with the habit of friendship always finds new friends. My old age judges more charitably and thinks better of mankind than my youth ever did. I discount idealization, I forgive one-

sidedness, I see that it is essential to perfection of any kind. And in each person I catch the fleeting suggestion of something beautiful, and swear eternal friendship with that.
George Santayana

> Should auld acquaintance be forgot,
> And never brought to min'?
> Should auld acquaintance be forgot,
> And days o' lang syne?
>
> *Robert Burns*

Friendship is the allay of our sorrows, the ease of our passions, the discharge of our oppressions, the sanctuary to our calamities, the counsellor of our doubts, the clarity of our minds, the emission of our thoughts, the exercise and improvement of what we meditate.
Jeremy Taylor

Friendship is the gift of the gods, and the most precious boon to man. *Benjamin D'Israeli*

If a man does not make a new acquaintance, as he advances through life, he will soon find himself left alone. A man, Sir, should keep his friendship in constant repair.
Samuel Johnson

It is great to have friends when one is young, but indeed it is still more so when you are getting old. When we are young, friends are, like everything else, a matter of course. In the old days we know what it means to have them. *Edvard Grieg*

Blessed are they who have the gift of making friends, for it is one of God's best gifts. It involves many things, but above all, the power of going out of one's self, and appreciating whatever is noble and loving in another.
Thomas Hughes

Come back! ye friendships long departed!
That like o'erflowing streamlets started,
And now are dwindled, one by one,
To stony channels in the sun!
Come back! ye friends, whose lives are ended,
Come back, with all that light attended,
Which seemed to darken and decay
When ye arose and went away!
Henry Wadsworth Longfellow

A woman's friendship borders more closely on love than man's. Men affect each other in the reflection of noble or friendly acts; whilst women ask fewer proofs and more signs and expressions of attachment.
Samuel Taylor Coleridge

A man that hath friends must shew himself friendly: and there is a friend that sticketh closer than a brother.
Proverbs 27:6

Friendship is the shadow of the evening, which strengthens with the setting sun of life.
Jean de La Fontaine

> Fame is the scentless sunflower,
>   with gaudy crown of gold;
> But friendship is the breathing
>   rose, with sweets in every fold.
> *Oliver Wendell Holmes*

Divides a friendship long confirm'd by age?
Alexander Pope

A friend is, as it were, a second half.
Marcus Tullius Cicero

God evidently does not intend us all to be rich, or powerful or great, but he does intend us all to be friends.
Ralph Waldo Emerson

We learn our virtues from the friends who love us; our faults from the enemy who hates us. We cannot easily discover our real character from a friend. He is a mirror, on which the warmth of our breath impedes the clearness of the reflection.
Jean Paul Richter

> Cherish friendship in your breast,
> New is good, but old is best;
> Make new friends, but keep the old;
> Those are silver, these are gold.
> *Joseph Parry*

> For friendship, of itself a holy tie,
> Is made more sacred by adversity.
> *John Dryden*

A true friend unbosoms freely, advises justly, assists readily, adventures boldly, takes all patiently, defends courageously, and continues a friend unchangeably.
William Penn

A true friend is the gift of God, and he only who made hearts can unite them. *Robert South*

The lintel low enough to keep out pomp and pride; the threshold high enough to turn deceit aside; the doorband strong enough from robbers to defend: this door will open at a touch to welcome every friend.
Henry Van Dyke

Friends are needed both for joy and for sorrow.
Yiddish proverb

>Fast as the rolling seasons bring
>   The hour of fate to those we love,
>Each pearl that leaves the broken string
>   Is set in Friendship's crown above.
>As narrower grows the earthly chain,
>   The circle widens in the sky;
>These are our treasures that remain.
>   But those are stars that beam on high.
>*Oliver Wendell Holmes*

Friends are generally of the same sex, for when men and women agree, it is only in their conclusions; their reasons are always different. *George Santayana*

Insomuch as any one pushes you nearer to God, he or she is your friend.
Anonymous

No one can lay himself under obligation to do a wrong thing. Pericles, when one of his friends asked his services in an unjust cause, excused himself, saying, "I am a friend only as far as the altar."
Thomas Fuller

Do not keep the alabaster boxes of your love and tenderness sealed up until your friends are dead. Fill their lives with sweetness. Speak approving, cheering words while their ears can hear them and while their hearts can be thrilled by them.
Henry Ward Beecher

> Friendship, peculiar boon of Heaven,
> The noble mind's delight and pride,
> To men and angels only given,
> To all the lower world denied.
> *Samuel Johnson*

Friendship, gift of Heaven, delight of great souls; friendship, which kings, so distinguished for ingratitude, are unhappy enough not to know.
Voltaire

By friendship you mean the greatest love, the greatest usefulness, the most open communication, the noblest sufferings, the severest truth, the heartiest counsel, and the greatest union of minds of which brave men and women are capable.
Jeremy Taylor

Old friends are best. King James used to call for his old shoes; they were the easiest for his feet.
John Selden

If you have a friend worth loving,
    Love him! Yes, and let him know
That you love him, ere life's evening
    Tinge his brow with sunset glow,
Why should good words ne'er be said
    Of a friend—till he is dead?

Scatter thus your seeds of kindness
    All enriching as you go
Leave them! Trust the Harvest-Giver;
    He will make each seed to grow.
And until the happy end,
    Your life shall never lack a friend.
Anonymous

Friendship is like rivers, and the strand of seas, and the air, common to all the world; but tyrants, and evil customs, wars, and want of love, have made them proper and peculiar.
Jeremy Taylor

Friendship is the hobby-horse of all the moral rhetoricians; it is nectar and ambrosia to them.
Immanuel Kant

I have loved my friends as I do virtue, my soul, my God.
Sir Thomas Browne

Thou mayest be sure that he that will in private tell thee

of thy faults, is thy friend, for he adventures thy dislike, and doth hazard thy hatred; there are few men that can endure it, every man for the most part delighting in self-praise, which is one of the most universal follies that bewitcheth mankind. *Sir Walter Raleigh*

He who has a thousand friends has not a friend to spare,
And he who has one enemy will meet him everywhere.
Ralph Waldo Emerson

O Friendship, flavor of flowers! O Lively sprite of life!
O sacred bond of blissful peace, the stalworth staunch of strife.
Nicholas Grimald

A friend in need is a friend indeed.
English proverb

Friendship with the evil is like the shadow in the morning, decreasing every hour; but friendship with the good is like the evening shadows, increasing till the sun of life sets. *Johann Gottfried von Herder*

The most powerful and the most lasting friendships are usually those of the early season of our lives, when we are most susceptible of warm and affectionate impressions. The connection into which we enter in any after-period decrease in strength as our passions abate in heat; and there is not, I believe, a single instance of a vigorous friendship that ever struck root in a bosom chilled by years. *Sir Thomas Fitzosborne*

The test of friendship is its fidelity when every charm of fortune and environment has been spent away, and the bare, undraped character alone remains; if love still holds steadfast, and the joy of companionship survives in such an hour, the fellowship becomes a beautiful prophecy of immortality.
Hamilton W. Mabie

Nature and religion are the bands of friendship, excellence and usefulness are its great endearments.
Jeremy Taylor

Fly, my friends, with treacherous speed,
  Melt as snow before the sun;
Leave me at my greatest need,
  Leave me to my God alone.
Charles Wesley

The Christian should never complain of his hard fortune while he knows that Christ is his friend.
Anonymous

It is one of the severest tests of friendship to tell your friend his faults. So to love a man that you cannot bear to see a stain upon him, and to speak painful truth through loving words, that is friendship.
Henry Ward Beecher

The highest compact we can make with our fellow is: Let there be truth between us two forevermore.... It is

sublime to feel and say of another, I need never meet, or speak, or write to him; we need not reinforce ourselves or send tokens of remembrance; I rely on him as on myself; if he did thus or thus, I know it was right.
Ralph Waldo Emerson

Histories are more full of examples of the fidelity of dogs than of friends. *Alexander Pope*

Sudden friendship, sure repentance. *John Ray*

The glory of Friendship is not the outstretched hand, nor the kindly smile, nor the joy of companionship; it is the spiritual inspiration that comes to one when he discovers that someone else believes in him and is willing to trust him with his friendship. *Ralph Waldo Emerson*

True friendship's laws are by this rule express'd,
Welcome the coming, speed the parting guest.
Homer

Green be the turf above thee,
Friend of my better days!
None knew thee but to love thee,
Nor named thee but to praise.
Fitz-Greene Halleck

To lose an old friend is as the loss of a bead from life's rosary; or to drop a jewel into the depths of a turbulent sea. *Douglas Meador*

To have known true friends is to have warmed one's hands at the central fire of life. . . . As I look back I would not ask for wealth or power; I would ask only for the supreme gift of friends. That I have had in full measure. It has given me a sense of fellowship that has given to life and happiness beyond the power of sorrow to destroy. *Harold J. Laski*

True friendship is a plant of slow growth, and must undergo and withstand the shocks of adversity, before it is entitled to the appellation. *George Washington*

O friendship! of all things the most rare, and therefore most rare because most excellent, whose comfort in misery is always sweet, and whose counsels in prosperity are ever fortunate. *John Lyly*

The best way for a child to learn to fear God is to know a real Christian. The best way for a child to learn to pray is to live with a father and mother who know a life of friendship with God, and who truly pray.
Johann Heinrich Pestalozzi

There is no man that imparteth his joys to his friends, but he joyeth the more; and no man that imparteth his griefs to his friend, but he grieveth the less. *Francis Bacon*

I find friendship to be like wine, raw when new, ripened with age, the true old man's milk and restorative cordial. *Thomas Jefferson*

We are all travellers in the wilderness of this world, and the best that we find in our travels is an honest friend.
Robert Louis Stevenson

Forsake not an old friend, for the new is not comparable unto him.
Ecclesiastes 9:10

Those friends thou hast, and their adoption tried,
Grapple them to thy soul with hoops of steel;
But do not dull thy palm with entertainment
Of each new-hatched, unfledg'd comrade.
Shakespeare

What is a great blessing is a friend with a heart so trusty you may safely bury your secrets in it, whose conscience you may fear less than your own, who can relieve your cares by his conversation, your doubts by his counsels, your sadness by his good humor, and whose very looks give you comfort.
Lucius Annaeus Seneca

I am complaisant towards friends, and put up patiently with all their ill humors, but I never take much pains to please them when they visit me, and I am never much disquieted by their absence.
François Duc de La Rochefoucauld

The holy passion of Friendship is of so sweet and steady and loyal and enduring a nature that it will last through a whole life-time, if not asked to lend money.
Mark Twain

To God, thy country, and thy friend be true.
Henry Vaughan

Granting that we had both the will and the sense to choose our friends well, how few of us have the power. Nearly all our associations are determined by chance, or necessity; and restricted within a narrow circle.
John Ruskin

> From quiet homes and first beginning
> Out to the undiscoveréd ends
> There's nothing worth the wear of winning
> But laughter and the love of friends.
Hillaire Belloc

There is no better way to become well-mannered than to associate with people who have good manners. There is no better way to learn a language than to live with people who speak it. There is no better way to become honest than to live with honest people. There is no better way to attain dignity, poise, moral excellence, self-control than to live with people who have these qualities. He who walks with wise men shall be wise.
Henry Colestock

Honest men esteem and value nothing so much in this world as a real friend. Such a one is as it were another self, to whom we impart our most secret thoughts, who partakes of our joy, and comforts us in our affliction; add to this, that his company is an everlasting pleasure to us.
Bidpai [Pilpay]

I have followed blindly where adventure's star was
    gleaming,
Heark'ning to a haunting longing deep within my breast.
Many lands have known my spirit's restless, endless
    dreaming
As I hunted for the something that would satisfy my
    quest.

Half across the world and back, adventure's star but
    led me
Through strife and peril and hardship in some far off
    foreign land.
But, returning empty-handed, when the last faint hope
    had fled me
I found it in the hollow of my first born baby's hand.

Louis Lafayette

How Love Helps You

There is no fear in love; but perfect love casts out fear, because fear brings punishment. And he who fears is not perfected in love. Let us therefore love, because God first loved us.
I John 4:18

He who loves God brings God and the world together.
Martin Buber

As every lord giveth a certain livery to his servants, love is the very livery of Christ. Our Saviour, who is the Lord above all lords, would have his servants known by their badge, which is love.
Bishop Hugh Latimer

All loves should be simply stepping-stones to the love of God. So it was with me; and blessed be his name for his great goodness and mercy.
Plato

Love is to the moral nature what the sun is to the earth.
Honoré de Balzac

Ah, how skillful grows the hand
That obeyeth Love's command!
It is the heart, and not the brain,
That to the highest doth attain,
And he who followeth Love's behest
Far excelleth all the rest!
Henry Wadsworth Longfellow

We love a girl for very different things than understanding. We love her for her beauty, her youth, her mirth, her confidingness, her character with its faults, caprices, and God knows what other inexpressible charms; but we do not love her understanding. Her mind we esteem if it is brilliant, and it may greatly elevate her in our opinion; nay, more, it may enchain us when we already love. But her understanding is not that which awakens and inflames our passions. *Johann Wolfgang von Goethe*

Nature is fine in love: and where 'tis fine,
It sends some precious instance of itself
After the thing it loves.
Shakespeare

A man loved by a beautiful and virtuous woman carries with him a talisman that renders him invulnerable; everyone feels that such a one's life has a higher value than that of others. *George Sand*

He who, silent, loves to be with us—he who loves us in our silence—has touched one of the keys that ravish hearts. *John Caspar Lavater*

Oh, the world's a curious compound, with its honey and its gall,
With its cares and bitter crosses, but a good world after all,
An' a good God must have made it—leastways, that is what I say,
When a hand is on my shoulder in a friendly sort of way.
James Whitcomb Riley

Kindness is a language which the blind can read and the deaf can understand. *John A. O'Brien*

When death has dropped the curtain we shall hear no more applause and, although we fondly dream that it will continue after we have left the stage, we do not realize how quickly it will die away in silence while the audience turns to look at the new actor and the next scene. Our position in society will be filled as soon as it is vacated, and our name remembered only for a moment, except, please God, by a few who have learned to love us not because of fame, but because we have helped them and done them some good. *Henry Van Dyke*

I sought my soul
   But my soul I could not see
I sought my God,
   But my God eluded me.
I sought my brother,
   And I found all three.
Author unknown

Love is always building up. It puts some line of beauty

on every life it touches. It gives new hope to discouraged ones, new strength to those who are weak. It helps the despairing to rise and start again. It makes life seem more worth while to everyone into whose eyes it looks. Its words are benedictions. Its every breath is full of inspiration.
Author unknown

I love you for what you are, but I love you yet more for what you are going to be.
I love you not so much for your realities as for your ideals. I pray for your desires that they may be great, rather than for your satisfactions, which may be so hazardously little.
A satisfied flower is one whose petals are about to fall. The most beautiful rose is one hardly more than a bud wherein the pangs and ecstasies of desire are working for larger and finer growth.
Not always shall you be what you are now.
You are going forward toward something great. I am on the way with you and therefore I love you.
Carl Sandburg

When the one man loves the one woman and the one woman loves the one man, the very angels leave heaven and come and sit in that house and sing for joy.
Brahma

Let those about to enter into wedlock pray diligently for divine help, so that they may make their choice in accordance with Christian prudence, not led by the blind and unrestrained impulse of lust, nor by any desire for riches, nor by any other base influence, but by a true and noble love and sincere affection for the future partner.
Pope Pius XI

We receive love—from our children as well as others—not in proportion to our demands or sacrifices or needs, but roughly in proportion to our own capacity to love. And our capacity to love depends, in turn, upon our prior capacity to be persons in our own right. To love means, essentially, to give; and to give requires a maturity of self-feeling. Love is shown in the statement of Spinoza's . . . that truly loving God does not involve a demand for love in return. It is the attitude referred to by the artist Joseph Bender: "To produce art requires that the artist be able to love—that is to give without thought of being rewarded."
Rollo May

A man may be a miser of his wealth; he may tie up his talent in a napkin; he may hug himself in his reputation; but he is always generous in his love. Love cannot stay at home; a man cannot keep it to himself. Like light, it is constantly traveling. A man must spend it, must give it away.
Alexander Macleod

Man is like a child in a family. He can tolerate much deprivation, much sickness, even much pain, if only he be securely at home, sure of belonging, confident of being loved. But if these central assurances are lacking, then food and shelter and toys in abundance can leave him empty and insecure in the center of his life. So it is with man in his world.
Angus Dun

Like the water in the boiler, the depth of our spiritual existence is impossible to measure without a gauge. Outward appearances are not always accurate. But there is one truthful measure and that measure is love.
Juanita A. Morrison

A man that is deeply in love with himself will probably succeed in his suit owing to lack of rivals.
Austin O'Malley

I would give up all my genius, and all my books, if there were only some woman, somewhere, who cared whether or not I came home late for dinner.
Ivan Turgenev

Love covers a multitude of sins. When a scar cannot be taken away, the next kind office is to hide it. Love is never so blind as when it is to spy faults. It is like the painter, who, beginning to draw the picture of a friend having a blemish in one eye, would picture only the other side of his face.
Robert South

I have seen almost all the beautiful things God has made; I have enjoyed almost every pleasure that He has planned for man; and yet as I look back I see standing out above all the life, that has gone, about four or five short experiences when the love of God reflected itself in some poor imitation, some small act of love of mine, and these seem to be the things which alone of all one's life abide. Everything else in all our lives is transitory. Every other good is visionary. But the acts of love which no man knows about, or can ever know about—they never fail.
Henry Drummond

In all the crowded universe
There is but one stupendous word: Love.
There is no tree that rears its crest,

No fern or flower that cleaves the sod
Nor bird that sings above its nest,
But tries to speak this word of God.
Josiah Gilbert Holland

Bitterness imprisons life; love releases it. Bitterness paralyzes life; love empowers it. Bitterness sours life; love sweetens it. Bitterness sickens life; love heals it. Bitterness blinds life; love anoints its eyes.
Harry Emerson Fosdick

>   Time
>   is
> Too slow for those who wait,
> Too swift for those who fear,
> Too long for those who grieve,
> Too short for those who rejoice,
> But for those who love, time is
>   Eternity.
>   Hours fly,
>   Flowers die,
>   New days,
>   New ways,
>   Pass by.
>   Love stays.

*Anonymous: Inscription
on a sundial at the
University of Virginia,
Charlottesville*

As fair art thou, my bonny lass,
   So deep in luve am I:

And I will luve thee still, my dear,
  Till a' the seas gang dry.
Till a' the seas gang dry, my dear,
  And the rocks melt wi' the sun,
I will luve thee still, my dear,
  While the sands o' life shall run.
Robert Burns

There is nothing holier, in this life of ours, than the first consciousness of love—the first fluttering of its silken wings.   *Henry Wadsworth Longfellow*

Love is swift, sincere, pious, pleasant, gentle, strong, patient, faithful, prudent, long-suffering, manly, and never seeking her own; for wheresoever a man seeketh his own, there he falleth from love.   *Thomas à Kempis*

A person once said to me that he could make nothing of love, except that it was friendship accidentally combined with desire. Whence I concluded that he had never been in love. For what shall we say of the feeling which a man of sensibility has towards his wife with her baby at her breast? How pure from sensual desire! Yet how different from friendship!   *Samuel Taylor Coleridge*

Ask not of me, love, what is love?
Ask what is good of God above,
Ask of the great sun what is light,
Ask what is darkness of the night.
Ask sin of what may be forgiven,
Ask what is happiness of Heaven,

Ask what is folly of the crowd,
Ask what is fashion of the shroud.
Ask what is sweetness of thy kiss,
Ask of thyself what beauty is.
Philip J. Bailey

Love is not love
Which alters when it alteration finds,
Or bends with the remover to remove:
O, no! it is an ever-fixed mark
That looks on tempests and is never shaken;
It is a star to every wandering bark.
Shakespeare

Love is not blind; that is the last thing it is. Love is bound; and the more it is bound the less it is blind.
G. K. Chesterton

He who loves his neighbor must needs also love above all else love itself. But *God is love; and he that dwelleth in love, dwelleth in God.* Therefore he must needs above all else love God.
St. Augustine

The soul is called to go up to God by the elevator of love, not to climb the rough stairway of fear.
St. Thérèse of Lisieux

Love is not getting, but giving; not a wild dream of pleasure, and a madness of desire—oh, no, love is not that—it is goodness, and honor, and peace and pure living.
Henry Van Dyke

Two shall be born, the whole wide world apart, . . .
And bend each wandering step to this one end—
That, one day, out of darkness, they shall meet
And read life's meaning in each other's eyes.
And two shall walk some narrow way of life, . . .
And yet, with wistful eyes that never meet . . .
They seek each other all their weary days
And die unsatisfied—and this is Fate!
Susan Marr Spalding

Somewhere there waiteth in this world of ours
   For one lone soul another lonely soul,
Each choosing each through all the weary hours,
   And meeting strangely at one sudden goal,
Then blend they, like green leaves with golden flowers,
   Into one beautiful perfect whole;
And life's long night is ended, and the way
Lies open onward to eternal day.
Edwin Arnold

Our hearts have been made for Thee, O God, and they shall never rest until they rest in Thee.
St. Augustine

   The night has a thousand eyes,
      And the day but one;
   Yet the light of the bright world dies
      With the set of sun.

   The mind has a thousand eyes,
      And the heart but one;

Yet the light of a whole life dies
　　　　When love is done.
　　　　　　　　　　Francis W. Bourdillon

Some night when stars no longer shine
　In Heaven's far-flung tapestry,
When Pleiades no longer line
　The mantle of the southern skies,
You'll know, my dear, the awful mystery
　Of love that flames and burns but never dies.

But does not ev'ry flame go out?
　You ask. Does not there come at last
An end to ev'rything? Why doubt
　That love will rocket in the skies
And pass like flaming comets far apart?
　My answer, dear: The voice within my heart.
　　　　　　　　　　John A. O'Brien

The Companionship of Good Books

A man ought to read just as inclination leads him; for what he reads as a task will do him little good. A young man should read five hours in a day, and so may acquire a great deal of knowledge.   *Samuel Johnson*

Books are the legacies that a great genius leaves to mankind, which are delivered down from generation to generation, as presents to the posterity of those who are yet unborn.   *Joseph Addison*

A good book is the precious life-blood of a master-spirit, embalmed and treasured up on purpose to a life beyond life.   *John Milton*

All that Mankind has done, thought, gained or been, it is lying as in magic preservation in the pages of Books. They are the chosen possession of men.   *Thomas Carlyle*

A book is like a garden carried in the pocket.
Arab proverb

Books are sepulchres of thought.
Henry Wadsworth Longfellow

If thou wouldst profit by thy reading, read humbly, simply, honestly, and not desiring to win a reputation for learning. *Thomas à Kempis*

Books are delightful when prosperity happily smiles; when adversity threatens, they are inseparable comforters. They give strength to human compacts, nor are grave opinions brought forward without books. Arts and sciences, the benefits of which no mind can calculate, depend upon books. *Richard Aungervyle [De Bury]*

Books are the legacies that a great genius leaves to mankind. *Joseph Addison*

But the images of men's wits and knowledges remain in books, exempted from the wrong of time, and capable of perpetual renovation. *Francis Bacon*

Books are the true levellers. They give to all, who will faithfully use them, the society, the spiritual presence, of the best and greatest of our race.
William Ellery Channing

I love to lose myself in other men's minds.
When I am not walking, I am reading;
I cannot sit and think. Books think for me.
Charles Lamb

In science, read by preference the newest works; in literature, the oldest. The classic literature is always modern.
Edward G. Bulwer-Lytton

O, let my books be then the eloquence
And dumb presagers of my speaking breast;
Who plead for love and look for recompense
More than that tongue that more hath more express'd.
Shakespeare

My books are friends that never fail me.
Thomas Carlyle

The books that charmed us in youth recall the delight ever afterwards; we are hardly persuaded there are any like them, any deserving equally our affections. Fortunate if the best fall in our way during this susceptible and forming period of our lives.
A. Bronson Alcott

Books are the bees which carry the quickening pollen from one to another mind.
James Russell Lowell

Leaving us heirs to amplest heritages
Of all the best thoughts of the greatest sages,
And giving tongues unto the silent dead!
Henry Wadsworth Longfellow

Reading maketh a full man, conference a ready man, and writing an exact man. *Francis Bacon*

He ate and drank the precious words,
   His spirit grew robust;
He knew no more that he was poor,
   Nor that his frame was dust.
He danced along the dingy days,
   And this bequest of wings
Was but a book. What liberty
   A loosened spirit brings!
Emily Dickinson

Books have always a secret influence on the understanding; we cannot at pleasure obliterate ideas: he that reads books of science, though without any desire fixed of improvement, will grow more knowing; he that entertains himself with moral or religious treatises will imperceptibly advance in goodness. *Samuel Johnson*

The foolishest book is a kind of leaky boat on a sea of wisdom; some of the wisdom will get in anyhow.
Oliver Wendell Holmes

Books are like individuals; you know at once if they are going to create a sense within the sense, to fever, to madden you in blood and brain, or if they will merely leave you indifferent, or irritable, having unpleasantly disturbed sweet intimate musings as might a draught from an open window. *George Moore*

In books lies the soul of the whole Past Time; the articulate audible voice of the Past, when the body and material substance of it has altogether vanished like a dream. *Thomas Carlyle*

The greatest part of a writer's time is spent in reading, in order to write; a man will turn over half a library to make one book. *Samuel Johnson*

No matter what his rank or position may be, the lover of books is the richest and the happiest of the children of men. *John Alfred Langford*

He hath never fed of the dainties that are bred of a book; he hath not eat paper, as it were; he hath not drunk ink: his intellect is not replenished; he is only an animal, only sensible in the duller parts. *Shakespeare*

If a book come from the heart, it will contrive to reach other hearts; all art and authorcraft are of small amount to that. *Thomas Carlyle*

I go into my library, and all history unrolls before me. I breathe the morning air of the world while the scent of Eden's roses yet lingered in it, while it vibrated only to the world's first brood of nightingales, and to the laugh of Eve. I see the pyramids building; I hear the shoutings of the armies of Alexander. *Alexander Smith*

It is chiefly through books that we enjoy intercourse with superior minds, and these invaluable means of communication are in the reach of all. In the best books, great men talk to us, give us their most precious thoughts, and pour their souls into ours. *William Ellery Channing*

Oh, that mine adversary had written a book.
Job 31:35

I armed her against the censures of the world; showed her that books were sweet unreproaching companions to the miserable, and that if they could not bring us to enjoy life, they would at least teach us to endure it.
Oliver Goldsmith

Of making many books there is no end; and much study is a weariness of the flesh. *Ecclesiastes 12:12*

> That place that does contain
> My books, the best companions, is to me
> A glorious court, where hourly I converse
> With the old sages and philosophers;

And sometimes, for variety, I confer
With kings and emperors, and weigh their counsels.
Francis Beaumont and John Fletcher

I conceive that books are like men's souls, divided into sheep and goats. Some few are going up, and carrying us up, heavenward; calculated, I mean, to be of priceless advantage in teaching, in forwarding the teaching of all generations. Others, a frightful multitude, are going down, down; doing ever the more and the wider and the wilder mischief. *Thomas Carlyle*

Some books are to be tasted, others to be swallowed, and some few to be chewed and digested.
Francis Bacon

There are many virtues in books, but the essential value is the adding of knowledge to our stock by the record of new facts, and, better, by the record of intuitions which distribute facts, and are the formulas which supersede all histories. *Ralph Waldo Emerson*

These are the masters who instruct us without rods and ferules, without hard words and anger, without clothes or money. If you approach them, they are not asleep; if, investigating, you interrogate them, they conceal nothing; if you mistake them, they never grumble; if you are ignorant, they cannot laugh at you.
Richard Aungervyle [De Bury]

That is a good book which is opened with expectation, and closed with profit. *A. Bronson Alcott*

They are for company the best friends, in doubts counsellors, in damps comforters, time's perspective, the home-traveler's ship or horse, the busy man's best recreation, the opiate of idle weariness, the mind's best ordinary, nature's garden, and the seed-plot of immortality.
Bulstrode Whitelocke

The first time I read an excellent book, it is to me just as if I had gained a new friend. When I read over a book I have perused before, it resembles the meeting with an old one. *Oliver Goldsmith*

   Books, we know,
Are a substantial world, both pure and good:
Round these, with tendrils strong as flesh and blood,
Our pastime and our happiness will grow.
William Wordsworth

Prayer:
Man's Link with God

Prayer is the acknowledgement of God's supreme dominion over us and our dependence upon him. Since we are indebted to God for the faculties of our minds and bodies, we must give him the worship of both. In other words, we must worship our Creator with both our intellects and our bodies. Otherwise we are shortchanging him.
John A. O'Brien

God dwells far off from us, but prayer brings him down to earth, and links his power with our efforts.
Madame Gasparin

Prayer has marked the trees across the wilderness of a sceptical world to direct the traveler in distress and all paths lead to a single light. *Douglas Meador*

Prayer should be the key of the morning and the lock of the night. *Owen Feltham*

The effectual fervent prayer of a righteous man availeth much. *St. James 5:6*

Pray as if everything depended on God, and work as if everything depended upon man.
St. Augustine

Prayer is not a substitute for work; it is a desperate effort to work further and to be efficient beyond the range of one's powers. *George Santayana*

It is good for man to open his mind to wonder and awe. Without science we are helpless children. But without a deep religion, we are blundering fools, reeling in our new and terrible cocksureness into one disaster after another.
J. B. Priestley

> Prayer is the burden of a sigh,
>   The falling of a tear,
> The upward glancing of an eye
>   When none but God is near.
James Montgomery

Ask, and it shall be given you; seek, and you shall find; knock, and it shall be opened unto you.
St. Matthew 7:7

> My words fly up, my thoughts remain below:
> Words without thoughts never to heaven go.
Shakespeare

When you pray, you must not be like the hypocrites; for they love to stand and pray in the synagogues and at the street corners, that they may be seen by men. Truly, I say to you, they have their reward. But when you pray, go into your room and shut the door and pray to your Father who is in secret; and your Father who sees in secret will reward you. *St. Matthew 6:5-6*

Prayer is not the easy way out. Prayer is not an easy way of getting things done for us. So many people think of prayer as a kind of magic, a kind of talisman, a kind of divine Aladdin's lamp in which in some mysterious way we command the power of God to work for us. Prayer must always remain quite ineffective, unless we do everything we can to make our own prayers come true. It is a basic rule of prayer that God will never do for us what we can do for ourselves. Prayer does not do things for us; it enables us to do things for ourselves.
William Barclay

None can pray well but he that lives well.
Thomas Fuller

> Prayer is a bridge, whereof the span
> Is rooted in the heart of man,
> And reaches, without pile or rod,
> Unto the Great White Throne of God.
> *William Wordsworth*

Prayer, as the first, second, and third element of the Christian life, should open, prolong, and conclude each day. The first act of the soul in early morning should be a draught at the heavenly fountain. It will sweeten the

taste for the day. A few moments with God at that calm and tranquil season, are of more value than much fine gold. And if you tarry long so sweetly at the throne, you will come out of the closet as the high priest of Israel came from the awful ministry at the altar of incense, suffused all over with the heavenly fragrance of that communion.
Henry Ward Beecher

More things are wrought by prayer
Than this world dreams of.
Wherefore, let thy voice
Rise like a fountain for me night and day.
For what are men better than sheep or goats
That nourish a blind life within the brain,
If, knowing God, they lift not hands of prayer
Both for themselves and those who call them friends?
For so the whole round earth is every way
Bound by gold chains about the feet of God.
Alfred, Lord Tennyson

I have been driven many times to my knees by the overwhelming conviction that I had nowhere else to go. My own wisdom, and that of all about me, seemed insufficient for the day.
Abraham Lincoln

Prayer is the most powerful form of energy one can generate. The influence of prayer on the human mind and body is as demonstrable as that of secreting glands. Prayer is a force as real as terrestrial gravity. It supplies us with a steady flow of sustaining power in our daily lives.
Alexis Carrel

I believe I should have been swept away by the flood of French infidelity, if it had not been for one thing, the remembrance of the time when my sainted mother used to make me kneel by her side, taking my little hands in hers, and caused me to repeat the Lord's Prayer.
John Randolph

The finest fruit of serious learning should be the ability to speak the word God without reserve or embarrassment. And it should be spoken without adolescent resentment, rather with some sense of communion, with reverence and with joy. *Nathan M. Pusey*

Prayer ardent opens heaven, lets down a stream of glory on the consecrated hour of man, in audience with the Deity; who worships the great God, that instant joins the first in heaven, and sets his foot on hell.
Edward Young

The sovereign cure for worry is prayer.
William James

'Tis heaven alone this is given away; it is only God may be had for the asking. *James Russell Lowell*

God warms his hands at man's heart when he prays.
John Masefield

Prayer is the preface to the book of Christian living; the text of the new life sermon; the girding on of the armor

for battle; the pilgrim's preparation for his journey. It must be supplemented by action or it amounts to nothing.
A. Phelps

The man who says his prayers in the evening is a captain posting his sentries. After that, he can sleep.
Charles Baudelaire

All the duties of religion are eminently solemn and venerable in the eyes of children. But none will so strongly prove the sincerity of the parent; none so powerfully awaken the reverence of the child; none so happily recommend the instruction he receives, as family devotions, particularly those in which petitions for the children occupy a distinguished place.
Timothy Dwight

Prayer digs the channels from the reservoir of God's boundless resources to the tiny pools of our lives.
E. Stanley Jones

Holy, humble, penitent, believing, earnest, persevering prayer is never lost; it always prevails to the accomplishment of the thing sought, or that with which the suppliant will be better satisfied in the end, according to the superior wisdom of his heavenly father, in which he trusts. *Robert Kelly Weeks*

Conviction brings a silent, indefinable beauty into faces made of the commonest human clay; the devout worshiper at any shrine reflects something of its golden glow, even as the glory of a noble love shines like a sort of light from a woman's face. *Honoré de Balzac*

The greater thy business is, by so much the more thou hast need to pray for God's good-speed and blessing upon it, seeing it is certain nothing can prosper without his blessing. The time spent in prayer never hinders, but furthers and prospers a man's journey and business: therefore, though thy haste be never so much, or thy business never so great, yet go not about it, nor out of thy doors, till thou hast prayed. *Lewis Bayly*

Prayer is the very soul and essence of religion and therefore prayer must be the very core of the life of man, for no man can live without religion. *Mohandas K. Gandhi*

To a certain extent, God gives to the prayerful control of himself, and becomes their willing agent; and when the time comes when all mysteries are solved, and the record of all lives is truthfully revealed, it will probably be seen that not those who astonished the world with their own powers, but those who quietly, through prayer, used God's power, were the ones who made the world move forward. *Edward Payson Roe*

To pray together, in whatever tongue or ritual, is the most tender brotherhood of hope or sympathy that men can contract in this life. *Madame de Stael*

Genius, without religion, is only a lamp on the outer gate of a palace; it may serve to cast a gleam of light on those that are without, while the inhabitant is in darkness.
Hannah More

    He prayeth well who loveth well
    Both man and bird and beast.
    He prayeth best who loveth best
    All things, both great and small;
    For the dear God who loveth us
    He made and loveth all.
Samuel Taylor Coleridge

If radio's slim fingers can pluck a melody
From night and toss it over continent or sea;
If the petaled notes of a violin
Are blown across a mountain or a city's din;
If songs like crimson roses are culled from thin blue air,
Why should mortals wonder that God hears prayer?
Frank Kane

Prayer is the pillow of religion.   *Arab proverb*

God hears no more than the heart speaks; and if the heart be dumb, God will certainly be deaf.
Thomas Benton Brooks

Prayer is a sincere, sensible, affectionate pouring out of the soul to God, through Christ in the strength and assistance of the Spirit, for such things as God has promised.
John Bunyan

> Prayer is the little implement
> Through which men reach
> Where presence is denied them.
> *Emily Dickinson*

Every time you pray, if your prayer is sincere, there will be new feeling and new meaning in it which will give you fresh courage, and you will understand that prayer is an education. *Feodor Dostoevski*

> Two went to pray? Oh, rather say
> One went to brag, the other to pray;
> One stands up close and treads on high
> Where the other dares not send his eye;
> One nearer to God's altar trod,
> The other to the altar's God.
> *Richard Crashaw*

Prayer is the soul getting into contact with the God in whom it believes. *Harry Emerson Fosdick*

The spectacle of a nation praying is more awe-inspiring than the explosion of an atomic bomb. The force of prayer is greater than any possible combination of man-controlled powers, because prayer is man's greatest means of trapping the infinite resources of God. *J. Edgar Hoover*

> I know not but what methods rare,
> But this I know: God answers prayer.

> I know not if the blessing sought
> Will come in just the guise I thought.
> I leave my prayer to him alone
> Whose will is wiser than my own.
> Eliza M. Hickok

Prayer at its highest is a two-way conversation, and for me the most important part is listening to God's reply.
Frank C. Laubach

There is an "Archimedian" point outside the world which is the little chamber where a true suppliant prays in all sincerity, where he lifts the world off its hinges.
Sören Kierkegaard

Prayer is a strong wall and fortress of the church; it is a goodly Christian weapon.   *Martin Luther*

Prayer is raised to its greatest power; and the prayer of intercession is the noblest and most Christian kind of prayer because in it love and imagination reach their highest and widest range.   *Robert J. McCracken*

Prayer is not only "the practice of the presence of God," it is the realization of his presence.
Joseph Fort Newton

Prayer is the chief agency and activity whereby men align themselves with God's purpose. Prayer does not consist in battering the walls of heaven for personal benefits or the success of our plans. Rather it is the committing of ourselves for the carrying out of his purposes. It is the telephone call to headquarters for orders. It is not bending God's will to ourselves but our will to God's. In prayer, we tap vast resources of spiritual power whereby God can find fuller entrance into the hearts of men.

G. Ashton Oldham

Prayer is not artful monologue
A voice uplifted from the sordid;
It is love's tender dialogue
Between the soul and God.

John Richard Moreland

God answers prayers; sometimes, when hearts are weak,
He gives the very gifts believers seek.
But often faith must learn a deeper rest,
And trust God's silence, when he does not speak;
For he whose name is Love will send the best:
Stars may burn out nor mountain walls endure
But God is true; his promises are sure
    To those who seek.

M. G. Plantz

Though smooth be the heartless prayer, no ear in heaven
  will mind it;
And the finest phrase falls dead, if there is no feeling
  behind it.

Ella Wheeler Wilcox

The efficacy of prayer is not so much to influence the divine counsels as to consecrate human purposes.
John S. Blackie

> Prayer is the soul's sincere desire,
> Uttered or unexpressed,
> The motion of a hidden fire
> That trembles in the breast.
> *James Montgomery*

How to Achieve Success

Nothing succeeds like success. *Alexandre Dumas*

He has achieved success who has lived well, laughed often, and loved much. *Mrs. A. J. Stanley*

The secret of success is constancy to purpose.
Benjamin D'Israeli

'Tis an old lesson; time approves it true,
   And those who know it best, deplore it most;
When all is won that all desire to woo,
   The paltry prize is hardly worth the cost.
Lord Byron

A friend of mine says that every man who takes office in Washington either grows or swells, and when I give a man an office, I watch him carefully to see whether he is swelling or growing. *Woodrow Wilson*

Be studious in your profession, and you will be learned. Be industrious and frugal, and you will be rich. Be sober and temperate, and you will be healthy. Be in general virtuous, and you will be happy. At least, you will, by such conduct, stand the best chance for such consequences. *Benjamin Franklin*

According to the theory of aerodynamics, and as may be readily demonstrated through laboratory tests and wind-tunnel experiments, the bumble bee is unable to fly. This is because the size, weight and shape of its body in relation to the total wing spread make flying impossible. But the bumble bee, being ignorant of these profound scientific truths, goes ahead and flies anyway and manages to make a little honey every day.
Anonymous

>Not in the clamor of the crowded street,
>Not in the shouts and plaudits of the throng,
>But in ourselves, are triumph and defeat.
>*Henry Wadsworth Longfellow*

Firm must be the will, patient the heart, passionate the aspiration, to secure the fulfillment of some high and lonely purpose, when reverie spreads always its bed of roses on the one side, and practical work summons to its treadmill on the other. *Samuel Smiles*

Success is full of promise till men get it; and then it is a last-year's nest from which the birds have flown.
Henry Ward Beecher

I am only one, but I am one. I cannot do everything, but I can do something. And I will not let what I cannot do interfere with what I can do.
Edward Everett Hale

> He started to sing as he tackled the thing
> That couldn't be done, and he did it.
Edgar A. Guest

I divide the world into three classes: the few who make things happen; the many who watch things happen; and the vast majority who have no idea of what happens. We need more people who make things happen.
Nicholas Murray Butler

To stand upon the ramparts and die for our principles is heroic, but to sally forth to battle and win for our principles is something more than heroic.
Franklin D. Roosevelt

A man can be as truly a saint in a factory as in a monastery, and there is as much need of him in the one as in the other.
Robert J. McCracken

Success serves men as a pedestal. It makes them seem greater, when not measured by reflection.
Joseph Joubert

One of the chief reasons for success in life is the ability

to maintain a daily interest in one's work, to have a chronic enthusiasm, to regard each day as important.
William Lyon Phelps

>Not to the swift, the race:
>   Not to the strong, the fight:
>Not to the righteous, perfect grace:
>   Not to the wise, the light.
>But often faltering feet
>   Come surest to the goal;
>And they who walk in darkness meet
>   The sunrise of the soul.
>*Henry Van Dyke*

If you wish success in life, make perseverance your bosom friend, experience your wise counselor, caution your elder brother, and hope your guardian genius.
Joseph Addison

We learn wisdom from failure much more than from success. We often discover what *will* do, by finding out what will not do; and probably he who never made a mistake never made a discovery.
Samuel Smiles

For threescore years I have been analyzing the causes of success and failure. Experience has taught me that financial success, job success, and happiness in human relations are, in the main, the result of (a) physical well-being; (b) constant effort to develop one's personal assets; (c) setting up and working toward a series of life

goals; (d) allowing time for meditation and spiritual regeneration.
Roger W. Babson

'Tis not in mortals to command success,
But we'll do more, Sempronius; we'll deserve it.
Joseph Addison

The great secret of success is to go through life as a man who never gets used up. That is possible for him who never argues and strives with men and facts, but in all experiences retires upon himself, and looks for the ultimate cause of things in himself.
Albert Schweitzer

If you can dream and not make dreams your master;
If you can think and not make thoughts your aim;
If you can meet with Triumph and Disaster
And treat those two impostors just the same; ...
If you can fill the unforgiving minute
With sixty seconds' worth of distance run,
Yours is the Earth and everything that's in it,
And, which is more, you'll be a Man, my son!
Rudyard Kipling

The reason most people do not succeed is that they will not do the things that successful people must do. The successful scientist must follow a formula. The tourist follows a road map. The builder follows a blueprint. The successful cook follows a recipe. ... It is not important that you merely want to succeed, unless you want to badly enough that you are willing to do certain things.
Anonymous

> What though success will not attend on all,
> Who bravely dares must sometimes risk a fall.
> *Tobias G. Smollett*

I have learned that success is to be measured not so much by the position that one has reached in life as by the obstacles which he has overcome while trying to succeed. *Booker T. Washington*

The success of any great moral enterprise does not depend upon numbers. *William Lloyd Garrison*

The greatest obstacle to being heroic is the doubt whether one may not be going to prove one's self a fool; the truest heroism is to resist the doubt, and the profoundest wisdom is to know when it ought to be resisted and when to be obeyed. *Nathaniel Hawthorne*

> Presence of mind and courage in distress
> Are more than armies to procure success.
> *John Dryden*

Nothing will ever be attempted if all possible objections must be first overcome. *Samuel Johnson*

'Tis man's to fight, but Heaven's to give success.
Homer

There are two significant characteristics of every great

life. The first is capacity to make a good beginning and the second is courage to push on to a good ending. One of the saddest things in life is to see a man begin some worthy venture revealing great promise and then to watch him flounder into failure for lack of courage to push on through frustration and disappointment. . . . A life of triumph hinges on a firm faith for rugged times.
Harold B. Walker

Success begins with a fellow's will.
It's all in the state of mind.
Walter D. Wintle

Opportunities do not come with their values stamped upon them. Every one must be challenged. A day dawns, quite like other days; in it a single hour comes, quite like other hours; but in that day and in that hour the chance of a lifetime faces us. To face every opportunity of life thoughtfully and ask its meaning bravely and earnestly, is the only way to meet the supreme opportunities when they come, whether open-faced or disguised.
Maltbie D. Babcock

Take care to get what you like or you will be forced to like what you get. *George Bernard Shaw*

The most powerful weapon on earth is the human soul on fire. *Marshal Ferdinand Foch*

Those things which are not practicable are not desirable. There is nothing in the world really beneficial that does not lie within the reach of an informed understanding and a well-directed pursuit. *Edmund Burke*

>Isn't it strange
>That princes and kings,
>And clowns that caper
>In sawdust rings,
>And common people
>Like you and me
>Are builders for eternity?
>
>Each is given a bag of tools,
>A shapeless mass,
>A book of rules;
>And each must make,
>Ere life is flown,
>A stumbling-block
>Or a stepping-stone.
>
>*R. L. Sharpe*

The talent of success is nothing more than doing what you can do well; and doing well whatever you do, without a thought of fame. *Henry Wadsworth Longfellow*

Success slips away from you like sand through the fingers, like water through a leaky pail, unless success is held tight by hard work, day by day, night by night, year in and year out. Everyone who is not looking forward to going to seed looks forward to working harder and harder and more fruitfully as long as he lasts.
Stuart Sherman

The race is not to the swift, nor the battle to the strong, neither yet bread to the wise, nor yet riches to men of understanding, nor yet favour to men of skill; but time and chance happeneth to them all.
Ecclesiastes 9:11

There is something in each of us that resents restraints, repressions, and controls but we forget that nothing left loose ever does anything creative. No horse gets anywhere until he is harnessed. No steam or gas ever drives anything until it is confined. No Niagara is ever turned into light and power until it is tunneled. No life ever grows great until it is dedicated, focused, disciplined.
Harry Emerson Fosdick

The man who seeks one thing in life, and but one,
May hope to achieve it before life be done;
But he who seeks all things, wherever he goes,
Only reaps from the hopes which around him he sows
A harvest of barren regrets.
Owen Meredith

To have faith where you cannot see; to be willing to work on in the dark; to be conscious of the fact that, so long as you strive for the best, there are better things on the way, this in itself is success. *Katherine Logan*

When a person alibies that he could have amounted to something if it had not been for his race, creed or religion, one should call attention to Epictetus, the slave who lived in the first century in Greece, and became one

of the world's most profound scholars and philosophers. He should be reminded that Disraeli, the despised Jew, became Prime Minister of Great Britain; that Booker T. Washington, who was born in slavery in this country became one of the nation's greatest educators; and that another Negro slave, George Washington Carver, became one of the greatest scientists of his generation. Lincoln, born of illiterate parents in a log cabin in Kentucky, lived to be acclaimed one of the greatest statesmen of all time.
Phil Conley

      The heights by great men reached and kept
      Were not attained by sudden flight,
      But they while their companions slept
      Were toiling upward in the night.
              Henry Wadsworth Longfellow

This is the foundation of success nine times out of ten—having confidence in yourself and applying yourself with all your might to your work.   *Thomas E. Wilson*

The common idea that success spoils people by making them vain, egotistic, and self-complacent is erroneous; on the contrary it makes them, for the most part, humble, tolerant, and kind. Failure makes people bitter and cruel.
W. Somerset Maugham

      Have little care that Life is brief,
      And less that Art is long.
      Success is in the silences
      Though Fame is in the song.
              Bliss Carman

Making Life Worthwhile

How could life annoy me any more?
Life: a lighted window and a closed door.
Clement Wood

Fortune is a prize to be won. Adventure is the road to it. Chance is what may lurk in the shadows at the roadside.
O. Henry

Be such a man, and live such a life,
That if every man were such as you,
And every life a life like yours,
This earth would be God's Paradise.
Phillips Brooks

Many will know the story of the fish in Mammoth Cave, Kentucky. These fish have lived for generations in the dark, so that at last the optic nerve has atrophied and they are quite blind. Similarly Darwin tells us that he lost completely his love of poetry and music, once very strong within him, simply because he ceased to develop it. This is true of all our powers, memory, concentration, capacity for hard work. We must use them or lose them.
Harold Nicolson

Life is a smoke that curls—
  Curls in a flickering skein,
That winds and whisks and whirls,
  A figment thin and vain,
  Into the vast inane.
William Ernest Henley

How small a portion of our life it is that we really enjoy! In youth we are looking forward to things that are to come; in old age we are looking backward to things that are gone past; in manhood, although we appear indeed to be more occupied in things that are present, yet even that is too often absorbed in vague determinations to be vastly happy on some future day when we have time.
Caleb C. Colton

Be thou faithful unto death, and I will give thee a crown of life. *Revelation 2:10*

As yesterday is history, and tomorrow may never come, I have resolved that from this day on, I will do all the business I can honestly, have all the fun I can reasonably, do all the good I can willingly, and save my digestion by thinking pleasantly. *Robert Louis Stevenson*

So long as faith in freedom reigns
  And loyal hope survives,
And gracious charity remains
  To leaven lowly lives;
While there is one untrodden tract
  For intellect or will,

> And men are free to think and act,
> Life is worth living still.
> *Alfred Austin*

If this life be not a real fight, in which something is eternally gained for the universe by success, it is no better than a game of private theatricals from which one may withdraw at will. *William James*

Live every day as if it were your last. Do every job as if you were the boss. Drive as if all other vehicles were police cars. Treat everybody else as if he were you.
Phoenix Flame

A friend of Ivan Turgenev once wrote to him, "It seems to me that to put oneself in the second place is the whole significance of life." To this the great Russian author replied: "It seems to me to discover what to put before oneself in the first place is the whole problem of life."
Robert E. Luccock

> Life is mostly froth and bubble;
> Two things stand like stone:
> KINDNESS in another's trouble,
> COURAGE in your own.
> *Adam Lindsay Gordon*

Life is hardly respectable if it has no generous task, no

duties or affections that constitute a necessity of existence. Every man's task is his life-preserver.
Ralph Waldo Emerson

>From fibers of pain and hope and trouble
>　And toil and happiness, one by one,
>Twisted together, or single or double,
>　The varying thread of our life is spun.
>Hope shall cheer though the chain be galling;
>Light shall come though the gloom be falling;
>Faith will list for the Master calling
>　Our hearts to his rest, when the day is done.
Alonzo B. Bragdon

Let us endeavor so to live that when we come to die, even the undertaker will be sorry.　　*Mark Twain*

>Life's but a means unto an end—that end,
>Beginning, mean and end to all things—God.
Philip J. Bailey

Life is the only real counsellor; wisdom unfiltered through personal experience does not become a part of the moral tissue.　　*Edith Wharton*

He that findeth his life shall lose it: and he that loseth his life for my sake shall find it.　　*St. Matthew 10:39*

The one essential thing is that we strive to have light in ourselves. Our strivings will be recognized by others, and when people have light in themselves, it will shine out from them. Then we get to know each other as we walk together in the darkness, without needing to pass our hands over each other's faces, or to intrude into each other's hearts. *Albert Schweitzer*

> Life is a leaf of paper white
> Whereon each one of us may write
> His word or two, and then comes night.
> *James Russell Lowell*

Life is fruitful in the ratio in which it is laid out in noble action or patient perseverance.
Henry P. Liddon

Many think themselves to be truly God-fearing when they call this world a valley of tears. But I believe they would be more so, if they called it a happy valley. God is more pleased with those who think everything right in the world, than with those who think nothing right. With so many thousand joys, is it not black ingratitude to call the world a place of sorrow and torment?
Jean Paul Richter

A child asked a man to pick a flower for her. That was simple enough. But when she said, "Now put it back," the man experienced a baffling helplessness he never knew before. "How can you explain that it cannot be done?" he asked. "How can one make clear to young people that there are some things which, when once broken, once mutilated, can never be replaced or mended?"
Marcia Borowsky

> Tell me not, in mournful numbers,
>   Life is but an empty dream!
> For the soul is dead that slumbers,
>   And things are not what they seem.
> *Henry Wadsworth Longfellow*

Let your life lightly dance on the edges of time like dew on the tip of a leaf.   *Rabindranath Tagore*

> God asks no man whether he will accept life.
> That is not the choice. You *must* take it.
> The only choice is *how*.
> *Henry Ward Beecher*

Fear not that thy life shall come to an end, but rather fear that it shall never have a beginning.
John Henry Newman

Life is a ladder infinite-stepped, that hides its rungs from human eyes;
Planted its foot in chaos gloom, its head soars high above the skies.
Sir Richard Burton

The web of our life is of a mingled yarn, good and ill together; our virtues would be proud if our faults whipped them not; and our crimes would despair if they were not cherished by our virtues.
Shakespeare

Archbishop Leighton used often to say that if he were to choose a place to die in, it should be an inn; it looking like a pilgrim's going home, to whom this world was all as an inn, and who was weary with the noise and confusion in it . . . And he obtained what he desired, for he died at the Bell Inn in Warwick Lane.
Gilbert Burnet

There once lived a wondrous good and wise man named Socrates. But he gave offense to those who were in power, and they jailed him; told him that he would have to die. Socrates received the news with a smile.

"You should prepare for death," they told him, but he shook his head and kept on smiling. "I have been preparing for death all my life," he said. "In what way?" they asked. And Socrates said, "I have never, secretly or openly, done a wrong to any man."
Quentin Reynolds

Life is a boundless privilege, and when you pay for your ticket, and get into the car, you have no guess what good company you will find there.
Ralph Waldo Emerson

The life of every man is a diary in which he means to write one story, and writes another; and his humblest hour is when he compares the volume as it is with what he hoped to make it. *James M. Barrie*

If we are to survive the atomic age, we must have something to live by, to live on, and to live for. We must stand

aside from the world's conspiracy of fear and hate and grasp once more the great monosyllables of life; faith, hope and love. Men must live by these if they live at all under the crushing weight of history.
O. P. Kretzmann

The art of living successfully consists of being able to hold two opposite ideas in tension at the same time: first, to make long-term plans as if we were going to live forever; and, second, to conduct ourselves daily as if we were going to die tomorrow. *Sydney J. Harris*

Life is a perpetual instruction in cause and effect.
Ralph Waldo Emerson

There is not one life which the Life-giver ever loses out of his sight; not one which sins so that he casts it away; not one which is not so near to him that whatever touches it touches him with sorrow or with joy.
Phillips Brooks

> The One remains, the many change and pass;
> Heaven's light forever shines, earth's shadows fly;
> Life, like a dome of many-coloured glass,
> Stains the white radiance of eternity.
> *Percy Bysshe Shelley*

Every year that I live I am more convinced that the waste of life lies in the love we have not given, the powers we have not used, the selfish prudence which will risk

nothing, and which, shirking pain, misses happiness as well.
John B. Tabb

Life is a mission. Every other definition of life is false, and leads all who accept it astray. Religion, science, philosophy, though still at variance upon many points, all agree in this, that every existence is an aim.
Giuseppe Mezzini

One life; a little gleam of time between two eternities; no second chance for us forever more.
Thomas Carlyle

    Man cannot live by bread alone,
       This has been proven o'er and o'er.
    Yet still men try to satisfy
       The inner life with earthly store.
Anonymous

I am not bound to win but I am bound to be true. I am not bound to succeed but I am bound to live up to what light I have. I must stand with anybody that stands right: stand with him while he is right and part with him when he goes wrong.
Abraham Lincoln

Life is a flame that is always burning itself out, but it catches fire again every time a child is born.
George Bernard Shaw

Though we seem grieved at the shortness of life in gen-

eral, we are wishing every period of it at an end. The minor longs to be at age, then to be a man of business; then to make up an estate, then to arrive at honors, then to retire.
Joseph Addison

I count all that part of my life lost which I spent not in communion with God, or in doing good.
John Donne

To live well we must have a faith fit to live by, a self fit to live with, and a work fit to live for.
Joseph F. Newton

Life is a long lesson in humility.
James M. Barrie

The idea shared by many that life is a vale of tears is just as false as the idea shared by the great majority, the idea to which youth and health and riches incline you, that life is a place of entertainment.
Count Leo N. Tolstoy

Life is the childhood of our immortality.
Johann Wolfgang von Goethe

Live your life each day as you would climb a mountain. An occasional glance toward the summit keeps the goal in mind, but many beautiful scenes are to be observed from each new vantage point. Climb slowly, steadily,

enjoying each passing moment; and the view from the summit will serve as a fitting climax for the journey.
Harold V. Melchert

Life is like playing a violin solo in public and learning the instrument as one goes on.
Samuel Butler the Younger

There is no cure for birth and death save to enjoy the interval. The dark background which death supplies brings out the tender colours of life in all their purity.
George Santayana

Our lives are a manifestation of what we think about God.   *Anonymous*

It is better to light one small candle than to curse the darkness.   *Confucius*

> Our lives are albums written through
> With good or ill, with false or true;
> And as the blessed angels turn
>   The pages of our years,
> God grant they read the good with smiles,
>   And blot the ill with tears!
> *John Greenleaf Whittier*

Little self-denials, little honesties, little passing words of sympathy, little nameless acts of kindness, little silent

victories over favorite temptations—these are the silent threads of gold which, when woven together, gleam out so brightly in the pattern of life that God approves.
Frederic W. Farrar

We have received the world as a legacy which none of us is allowed to impair, but which, on the contrary, every generation is bound to bequeath in a better state to its posterity. *Joseph Joubert*

> Our lives are songs; God writes the words
> And we set them to music at pleasure;
> And the song grows glad, or sweet or sad,
> As we choose to fashion the measure.
> *Ella Wheeler Wilcox*

The great use of life is to spend it for something that outlasts it. *William James*

Man cannot live by bread alone. The making of money, the accumulation of material power, is not all there is to living. Life is something more than these, and the man who misses this truth misses the greatest joy and satisfaction that can come into his life—service for others.
Edward Bok

The only significance of life consists in helping to establish the kingdom of God; and this can be done only by means of the acknowledgements and profession of the truth by each one of us. *Count Leo N. Tolstoy*

Life's greatest achievement is the continual remaking of yourself so that at last you know how to live.
Anonymous

We live in deeds, not years; in thought, not breath;
In feelings, not in figures on a dial.
We should count time by heart-throbs. He most lives
Who thinks most, feels the noblest, acts the best.
Life's but a means unto an end; that end
Beginning, mean, and end of all things: God.
Philip J. Bailey

The lesson of life is to believe what the years and centuries say against the hours. *Ralph Waldo Emerson*

Mankind a future life must have to balance life's unequal lot.
Sir Richard Burton

Nothing in life is to be feared. It is only to be understood.
Marie Curie

Teach me to live that I may dread
The grave as little as my bed.
Thomas Ken

Life is like a camel. You can make it do anything except back up.
Marcelene Cox

Perfect conformity to the will of God is the sole sovereign and complete liberty.
Jean Henri Merle d'Aubigné

Solitude is important to man. It is necessary to his achievement of peace and contentment. It is a well into which he dips for refreshment for his soul. It is his laboratory in which he distills the pure essence of worth from the raw materials of his experiences. It is his refuge when the very foundations of his life are being shaken by disastrous events.
Margaret E. Mulac

The final test of our lives will not be how *much* we have lived but *how* we have lived, not how tempestuous our lives have been, but how much bigger, better and stronger these trials have left us. Not how much money, fame or fortune we have laid up here on earth, but how many treasures we have laid up in heaven!
Megiddo Message

So live that you would not be ashamed to sell the family parrot to the town gossip.
Will Rogers

This is what Christianity is for—to teach men the art of Life. And its whole curriculum lies in one word, "Learn of me."
Anonymous

The art of living consists in keeping earthly step to heavenly music.
Ivan N. Panin

Thy life is no idle dream, but a solemn reality; it is thine own, and it is all thou hast to front eternity with.
Thomas Carlyle

When anyone has offended me, I try to raise my soul so high that the offence cannot reach it.
René Descartes

To live is Christ, and to die is gain.
Philippians 1:21

The poorest day that passes over us is the conflux of two Eternities; it is made up of currents that issue from the remotest past and flow onwards into the remotest future.
Thomas Carlyle

The rule that governs my life is this: Anything that dims my vision of Christ, or takes away my taste for Bible study, or cramps my prayer life, or makes Christian work difficult, is wrong for me, and I must, as a Christian, turn away from it.
J. Wilbur Chapman

The facts of existence are like so much loose type which can be set up into many meanings. One man leaves these facts in chaotic disarrangement, or sets them up into cynical affirmations, and he exists. But another man takes the same facts and by spiritual insight makes them mean glorious things and he lives indeed.
Harry Emerson Fosdick

For life is the mirror of king and slave,
  'Tis just what we are and do;
Then give to the world the best you have,
  And the best will come back to you.
Madeleine Bridges

Religion:
Man's Bond with God

Pure religion and undefiled before God and the Father is this, To give aid to orphans and widows in their tribulation, and to keep oneself unspotted from this world.
St. James 1:27

We are created on this condition, that we pay just and due obedience to God who created us, that we should know and follow him alone. We are bound and tied to God by this *chain of piety;* from which *religion* itself received its name.
Firmianus Lactantius

Every religion is false which in its creed fails to worship one God as source of all things, and in its practice fails to love only God as the end of all.
Blaise Pascal

Religion is the first thing and the last thing, and until a man has found God and been found by God, he begins at no beginning, he works to no end.
H. G. Wells

No religion is a true religion that does not make men tingle to their finger tips with a sense of infinite hazard.
William E. Hocking

A man who is religious, is religious morning, noon, and night; his religion is a certain character, a mould in which his thoughts, words, and actions are cast, all forming parts of one and the same whole.
Cardinal John Henry Newman

God is not dumb, that he should speak no more;
If thou hast wanderings in the wilderness
And find'st not Sinai, 'tis thy soul is poor.
Maria W. Lowell

Art and religion are the soul of our civilization. Go to them, for there love exists and endures.
Frank Lloyd Wright

A cosmic philosophy is not constructed to fit a man; a cosmic philosophy is constructed to fit a cosmos. A man can no more possess a private religion than he can possess a private sun and moon. *G. K. Chesterton*

His religion at best is an anxious wish like that of Rabelais, a great Perhaps. *Thomas Carlyle*

At times in the lonely silence of the night and in rare lonely moments I come upon a sort of communion of myself with Something great that is not myself. Is it perhaps poverty of mind and language which obliges me to say that this universal scheme takes on the effect of a sympathetic person, and my communion a quality of fearless worship. These moments happen and are the supreme fact of my religious life to me, they are the crown of my religious experience.   *H. G. Wells*

All religion is based on the recognition of a superhuman Reality of which man is somehow conscious and towards which he must in some way orientate his life. The existence of the tremendous transcendent reality that we name God is the foundation of all religion in all ages and among all peoples.   *Christopher Dawson*

Men will wrangle for religion; write for it; fight for it; die for it; anything but live for it.
Caleb C. Colton

Religion is the reaching out of one's whole being—mind, body, spirit, emotions, intuitions, affections, will—for completion, for inner unity, for true relation with those about us, for right relation to the universe in which we live. Religion is life, a certain kind of life, life as it should and could be, a life of harmony within and true adjustment without—life, therefore, in harmony with the life of God himself.   *Henry P. Van Dusen*

God has no need for our worship. It is we who need to show our gratitude for what we have received.
St. Thomas Aquinas

No one is so much alone in the universe as a denier of God. With an orphaned heart, which has lost the greatest of fathers, he stands mourning by the immeasurable corpse of nature, no longer moved or sustained by the Spirit of the universe, but growing in its grave; and he mourns, until he himself crumbles away from the dead body. *Jean Paul Richter*

A man cannot be religious without belonging to a particular religion any more than he can talk without using a particular language. *George Santayana*

A religion is not a proposition, but a system; it is a rite, a creed, a philosophy, a rule of duty, all at once; and to accept a religion is neither a simple assent to it nor a complex, neither a conviction nor a prejudice, neither a notional assent nor a real, not a mere act of profession, nor of credence, nor of opinion, nor of speculation, but it is a collection of all these various kinds of assents, at once and together, some of one description, some of another. *Cardinal John Henry Newman*

Sacrifice is the first element of religion, and resolves itself in theological language into the love of God.
James A. Froude

Let your religion be seen. Lamps do not talk, but they do shine. A lighthouse sounds no drum, it beats no gong; yet, far over the waters, its friendly light is seen by the mariner. *Theodore L. Cuyler*

Religion is not a theory, a subjective view, an opinion, but is, objectively, at once a principle, a law, and a fact, and, subjectively, it is, by the aid of God's grace, practical conformity to what is universally true and real.
Orestes Brownson

We do ourselves wrong, and too meanly estimate the holiness above us, when we deem that any act or enjoyment good in itself, is not good to do religiously.
Nathaniel Hawthorne

The question of bread for myself is a material question, but the question of bread for my neighbor is a spiritual question. *Nikolai Berdyaev*

But even in our quiet life I think we can feel the great fact that is the core of all religion. However quiet may be the skies, or however cool the meadows, we always feel that if we did know what they meant the meaning would be something mighty and shattering. About the weakest weed there is still a sensational difference between understanding and not understanding. We stare at a tree in an infinite leisure; but we know all the time that the real difference is between a stillness of mystery and the question is whether it will always continue to be a tree or turn suddenly into something else.
G. K. Chesterton

A man who puts aside his religion because he is going into society, is like one taking off his shoes because he is about to walk upon thorns.
Richard Cecil

Religion has its origins in the depths of the soul and it can be understood only by those who are prepared to take the plunge. *Christopher Dawson*

What I mean by a religious person is one who conceives himself or herself to be the instrument of some purpose in the universe which is a high purpose, and is the motive power of evolution—that is, of a continual ascent in organization and power and life, and extension of life.
George Bernard Shaw

If the providence of God does not preside over human affairs, there is no point in busying oneself about religion.
St. Augustine

If man's religion is of any importance, it is not just a garment of expression of unity with and security in the professed beliefs of a special group. It is rather an attitude of respect for himself, his God, his fellowman, which underwrites all his activity, which is allowed freedom of expression within the limitations of that respect.
Grace D. Yerbury

Religion is not religion until it has become, not only natural, but so natural that nothing else seems natural in its presence; and until the whole being of man says, *Whom have I in heaven but thee, and what on earth in comparison of thee?* and *To whom shall we go if we leave thee?* *Coventry Patmore*

We define religion as the assumption that life has meaning. Religion, or lack of it, is shown not in some intellectual or verbal formulations but in one's total orientation to life. Religion is whatever the individual takes to be his ultimate concern. One's religious attitude is to be found at that point where he has a conviction that there are values in human existence worth living and dying for.
Rollo May

Pessimism says that life is so short that it gives nobody a chance; religion says that life is so short that it gives everybody his final chance.
G. K. Chesterton

Religion should be the motor of life, the central heating plant of personality, the faith that gives joy to activity, hope to struggle, dignity to humility, zest to living.
William Lyon Phelps

Religion admits the heart and the whole man to the witness-box, while science only admits the head, scarcely even the senses. *Robert Hugh Benson*

Your daily life is your temple and your religion.
Kahlil Gibran

Now the human mind needs, if it would be united to God, the guidance of the things of sense; for as the apostle says to the Romans (I:20): *The invisible things of him are clearly seen, being understood by the things that are made.* Hence in divine worship it is necessary to make use of certain corporal acts, so that by their means, as by certain signs, man's mind may be stirred up to those spiritual acts whereby it is knit to God. Consequently religion has certain interior acts which are its chief ones and which essentially belong to it; but it has also external acts which are secondary and which are subordinated to the interior acts. *St. Thomas Aquinas*

The purpose of science is to develop, without prejudice or preconception of any kind, a knowledge of the facts, the laws, and the processes of nature. The even more important task of religion, on the other hand, is to develop the conscience, the ideals, and the aspirations of mankind. *Robert A. Millikan*

Religion always is, and always has been, at the root of every world movement. *Robert Hugh Benson*

True religion is a profound uneasiness about our highest social values. *Reinhold Niebuhr*

The life of a good religious man ought to be eminent in all virtues, that he may be such interiorly as he appears to men in his exterior. *Thomas à Kempis*

Religion too has certain first principles which universal reason or piety has dictated, and these, in the service of God and in training character, contribute to the attainment of blessedness. There is one principle that all reli-

gions have, and that is that there is a God, powerful, wise, good, awe-inspiring, and lovable.
John of Salisbury

Religion is ever, *qua* religion, authoritative and absolute. What constitutes religion is not simply to hold a view and to try and live a life with respect to the unseen and the Deity as possibly or even certainly beautiful or true or good: but precisely that which is over and above this, the holding this view and this life to proceed somehow from God himself, so as to bind my innermost mind and conscience to unhesitating assent. Not simply that I think it, but that in addition I feel bound to think it transforms a thought about God into a religious act.
Baron Friedrich von Hügel

Religion is the sense of ultimate reality, of whatever meaning a man finds in his own existence or the existence of anything else.
G. K. Chesterton

Each cloud-capped mountain is a holy altar;
An organ breathes in every grove;
And the full heart's a Psalter,
Rich in deep hymns of gratitude and love.
Thomas Hood

Humility Becomes Everyone

God resisteth the proud, but giveth grace to the humble.
St. James 4:6

An able yet humble man is a jewel worth a kingdom.
William Penn

A mountain shames a molehill until they are both humbled by the stars.   *Anonymous*

God hath sworn to life on high
Who sinks himself by true humility.
John Keble

Life is a long lesson in humility.
James M. Barrie

God revealed himself in a bush, to teach us that the loftiest may be found in the lowliest.
Eleazar ben Arak

After crosses and losses men grow humbler and wiser.
> Benjamin Franklin

O wad some power the giftie gie us
To see oursel's as ithers see us!
It wad frae monie a blunder free us.
　And foolish notion;
What airs in dress and gait wad lae'e us,
　And ev'n devotion!
> Robert Burns

Everyone is a moon, and has a dark side which he never shows to anybody.
> Mark Twain

Do not consider yourself to have made any spiritual progress, unless you account yourself the least of all men. God walks with the humble; he reveals himself to the lowly; he gives understanding to the little ones; he discloses his meaning to pure minds, but hides his grace from the curious and the proud.
> Thomas à Kempis

That no man will learn anything at all,
Unless he first learn humility.
> Owen Meredith

Everybody makes mistakes; that's why they put erasers on pencils.
> Anonymous

I ate 'umble pie with an appetite.
Charles Dickens

Humble we must be, if to heaven we go:
High is the roof there; but the gate is low:
When e're thou speak'st, look with a lowly eye:
Grace is increased by humility.
Robert Herrick

I do not know, what I may appear to the world; but to myself I seem to have been only like a boy playing on the seashore of knowledge; and diverting myself in now and then finding a smoother pebble or a prettier shell than ordinary, whilst the great ocean of truth lay all undiscovered before me. *Isaac Newton*

Don't let us think that we need to be "stars" in order to shine. It was by the ministry of a candle that the woman recovered her lost piece of silver.
John H. Jowett

To be humble to superiors is duty, to equals courtesy, to inferiors nobleness. *Benjamin Franklin*

How hard it is to confess that we have spoken without thinking, that we have talked nonsense. How many a man says a thing in haste and heat, without fully understanding or half meaning it, and then, because he has said it, holds fast to it, and tries to defend it as if it were true! But how much wiser, how much more admirable and attractive it is when a man has the grace to perceive and acknowledge his mstakes! It gives us assurance that he is capable of learning, of growing, of improving, so that his future will be better than his past.

Henry Van Dyke

The proud man counts his newspaper clippings, the humble man his blessings.   *Fulton J. Sheen*

> The tumult and the shouting dies,
> The captains and the kings depart;
> Still stands thine ancient sacrifice,
> A humble and a contrite heart.

Rudyard Kipling

We have an old saying in Japan that a woman cannot love a man who is truly vain, for there is no crevice in his heart for love to enter and fill up.

Okakura Kakuzo

It is the laden bough that hangs low, and the most faithful Christian who is the most humble.

Anonymous

Humility, like darkness, reveals the heavenly lights.

Henry David Thoreau

Humility is the genuine proof of Christian virtue. Without it we keep all our defects; and they are only crusted over by pride, which conceals them from others, and often from ourselves. *François Duc de la Rochefoucauld*

> Oh! Why should the spirit of mortal be proud?
> Like a swift-fleeing meteor, a fast flying cloud,
> A flash of the lightning, a break of the wave,
> Man passes from life to his rest in the grave.
> *William Knox*

True humility is intelligent self respect which keeps us from thinking too highly or too meanly of ourselves. It makes us mindful of the nobility God meant us to have. Yet it makes us modest by reminding us how far we have come short of what we can be. *Ralph W. Sockman*

If a little knowledge is dangerous, where is the man who has so much as to be out of danger? *Thomas H. Huxley*

> Mountain gorses, do ye teach us . . .
> That the wisest word man reaches
> Is the humblest he can speak?
> *Elizabeth Barrett Browning*

I believe that the first test of a truly great man is his humility. I do not mean by humility, doubt of his own powers. But really great men have a curious feeling that the greatness is not in them, but through them. And they see something divine in every other man. *John Ruskin*

Humility is the altar upon which God wishes us to offer him sacrifices. — *François Duc de la Rouchefoucauld*

Last week I saw a man who had not made a mistake in 4,000 years. He was a mummy in the British Museum. — *H. L. Wayland*

Nothing sets a person so much out of the devil's reach as humility. — *Jonathan Edwards*

The doctrine of human equality reposes on this; that there is no man really clever who has not found that he is stupid. There is no big man who has not felt small. Some men never feel small; but these are the few men who are. — *G. K. Chesterton*

Humility, that low, sweet root,
From which all heavenly virtues shoot. — *Thomas Moore*

When he consults himself man knows that he is great. When he contemplates the universe around him he knows that he is little and his ultimate greatness consists in his knowledge of his littleness. — *Blaise Pascal*

Should you ask me: What is the first thing in religion? I should reply: The first, second, and third thing therein is humility. — *St. Augustine*

I have not the slightest feeling of humility towards the public, or to anything in existence but the Eternal Being, the principle of beauty, and the memory of great men.
John Keats

If thou wouldst find much favor and peace with God and man, be very low in thine own eyes. Forgive thyself little and others much. *Robert Leighton*

True humility is not an abject, groveling, self-despising spirit; it is but a right estimate of ourselves as God sees us. *Tryon Edwards*

The Christian is like the ripening corn; the riper he grows the more lowly he bends his head. *Thomas Guthrie*

The casting down of our spirits in true humility is but like throwing a ball to the ground, which makes it rebound the higher toward heaven. *John Mason*

The saint that wears heaven's brightest crown in deepest adoration bends; the weight of glory bows him down the most when his soul ascends; nearest the throne itself must be the footstool of humility.
James Montgomery

He that is down, needs fear no fall;
He that is low, no pride;
He that is humble ever shall
Have God to be his guide.
John Bunyan

Patience and Perseverance Win the Victory

Be thou faithful unto death, and I will give thee a crown of life.
Revelation 2:10

A phlegmatic insensibility is as different from patience, as a pool from a harbor. Into the one, indolence naturally sinks us; but if we arrive at the other it is by encountering many an adverse wind and rough wave, with a more skillful pilot at the helm than self, and a company under better command than the passions.
Lewis W. Dilwyn

All the performances of human art, at which we look with praise and wonder, are instances of the resistless force of perseverance.
Ben Johnson

Since you will buckle fortune on my back,
To bear her burden, whether I will or no,
I must have patience to endure the load.
Shakespeare

All that I have accomplished, or expect or hope to accomplish, has been and will be by that plodding, patient, persevering process of accretion which builds the antheap, particle by particle, thought by thought, fact by fact.
Elihu Burritt

All men commend patience, although few be willing to practice it. *Thomas à Kempis*

Excellence is never granted to man as the reward of labor. It argues no small strength of mind to persevere in habits of industry without the pleasure of perceiving those advances, which, like the hands of a clock, whilst they make hourly approaches to their point, yet proceed so slowly as to escape observation.
Sir Joshua Reynolds

Even the best must own that patience and resignation are the pillars of human peace on earth.
Edward Young

Beware the fury of a patient man.
John Dryden

And many strokes, though with a little axe, hew down and fell the hardest-timbered oak.
Shakespeare

Enter into the sublime patience of the Lord. Be charitable in view of it. God can afford to wait; why cannot we,

since we have him to fall back upon? Let patience have her perfect work, and bring forth her celestial fruits. The two powers which in my opinion constitute a wise man are those of bearing and forbearing.
Epictetus

At least bear patiently, if thou canst not joyfully.
Thomas à Kempis

I had no special sagacity, only the power of patient thought. I kept the subject constantly before me and waited until the first dawnings opened little by little into the full light. *Sir Isaac Newton*

It is not necessary for all men to be great in action. The greatest and sublimest power is often simple patience.
Horace Bushnell

Patience is the queen of the soul. She is seated on the rock of fortitude. She conquers and is never conquered.
Archbishop Ullathorne

Genius is eternal patience. *Michelangelo*

How poor are they who have not patience! What wound did ever heal but by degrees.
Shakespeare

Be plastered with patience. *William Langland*

When nothing seems to help, I go and look at a stonecutter hammering away at his rock perhaps a hundred times without as much as a crack showing in it. Yet at the hundred and first blow it will split in two, and I know it was not that blow that did it, but all that had gone before.   *Jacob Riis*

I have known twenty persevering girls to one patient one; but it is only the twenty-first one who can do her work, out and out, and enjoy it. Patience lies at the root of all pleasures as well as of all powers.
John Ruskin

Have patience with all the world, but first of all with yourself.   *St. Francis de Sales*

> Learn to wait—life's hardest lesson
> Conned, perchance, through blinding tears;
> While the heart throbs sadly echo
> To the tread of passing years.
>
> Learn to wait—hope's slow fruition:
> Faint not, though the way seems long;
> There is joy in each condition;
> Hearts through suffering may grow strong.
>
> Thus a soul untouched by sorrow
> Aims not at a higher state;
> Joy seeks not a brighter morrow;
> Only sad hearts learn to wait.
> *Anonymous*

Life has such hard conditions that every dear and precious gift, every rare virtue, every genial endowment, love, hope, joy, wit, sprightliness, benevolence, must sometimes be put into the crucible to distil the one elixir —patience.
Gail Hamilton

Let patience grow in your garden alway.
John Heywood

Great works are performed, not by strength, but by perseverance. He that shall walk, with vigor, three hours a a day will pass, in seven years, a space equal to the circumference of the globe.
Samuel Johnson

Never think that God's delays are God's denials. Hold on; hold fast; hold out. Patience is genius.
Comte Georges Louis Leclerc de Buffon

Patience is the companion of wisdom.
St. Augustine

Patience is bitter, but its fruit is sweet.
Jean Jacques Rousseau

Patient waiting is often the highest way of doing God's will.
Jeremy Collier

Patience is the root and guardian of all the virtues.
Pope Gregory I

Genius is only the power of making continuous efforts. The line between failure and success is so fine that we scarcely know when we pass it: so fine that we are often on the line and do not know it. How many a man has thrown up his hands at a time when a little more effort, a little more patience, would have achieved success. As the tide goes clear out, so it comes clear in. In business, sometimes, prospects may seem darkest when really they are on the turn. A little more persistence, a little more effort, and what seemed hopeless failure may turn to glorious success. There is no failure except from within, no really insurmountable barrier save our own inherent weakness of purpose. *Elbert Hubbard*

It's easy finding reasons why other folks should be patient.
George Eliot

Patience is not good, if when you may be free you allow yourself to become a slave.
St. Bernard

Patience and fortitude conquer all things.
Ralph Waldo Emerson

Patience is the key of content. *Mohammed*

Perseverance is a great element of success. If you only knock long enough and loud enough at the gate, you are sure to wake up somebody.
Henry Wadsworth Longfellow

Our real blessings often appear to us in the shape of pains, losses, and disappointments; but let us have patience, and we soon shall see them in their proper figures.
Joseph Addison

The saints are the sinners who keep trying.
Robert Louis Stevenson

Patience! why, it is the soul of peace; of all the virtues, it is nearest kin to heaven; it makes men look like gods. The best of men that ever wore earth about him was a sufferer, a soft, meek, patient, humble, tranquil spirit; the first true gentleman that ever breathed.
Thomas Decker

The road to success is not to be run by seven-leagued boots. Step by step, little by little, bit by bit—that is the way to wealth, that is the way to wisdom, that is the way to glory.
Sir Thomas F. Buxton

Patience is the courage of the conqueror, the strength of man against destiny, of the one against the world, and of the soul against matter. Therefore it is the courage of the gospel; and its importance, in a social view and to races and institutions, cannot be too earnestly inculcated.
Edward G. Bulwer-Lytton

To know how to wait is the great success of success.
Joseph M. De Maistre

The falling drops at last will wear the stones.
Lucretius

They also serve who only stand and wait.
John Milton

Patience is power; with time and patience the mulberry leaf becomes silk. *Chinese proverb*

Trust to God to weave your thread into the great web, though the pattern shows it not yet.
George Macdonald

When you get into a tight place and everything goes against you, till it seems as though you could not hold on a minute longer, never give up then, for that is just the place and time that the tide will turn.
Harriet Beecher Stowe

There is as much difference between genuine patience and sullen endurance, as between the smile of love, and the malicious gnashing of the teeth.
W. S. Plumer

A tree is shown by its fruit, and in the same way those who profess to belong to Christ will be seen by what they do. For what is needed is not mere present profession, but perseverance to the end in the power of faith.
St. Ignatius of Antioch

When Abraham Lincoln was a young man he ran for the legislature of Illinois and was badly swamped. He next entered business, failed and spent seventeen years of his life paying up the debts of a worthless partner.

He was in love with a beautiful young woman to whom he became engaged, and then she died. Later he married a woman who was a constant burden to him. Entering politics again, he was badly defeated for Congress.

He failed to get an appointment to the U.S. Land Office. He was badly defeated for the U.S. Senate. In 1856 he became a candidate for the Vice Presidency and was again defeated. In 1858 he was defeated by Douglas.

One failure after another—bad failures—great setbacks. In the face of all this he eventually became one of the country's greatest men, if not the greatest. When you think of a series of setbacks like this, doesn't it make you feel small to become discouraged, just because you think that you're having a hard time in life?

Anonymous

With patience bear the lot to thee assigned, nor think it chance, nor murmur at the load; for know what man calls fortune, is from God.   *Nicholas Rowe*

>Heaven is not reached at a single bound,
>We build the ladder by which we rise
>From the lowly earth to the vaulted skies,
>And we mount to its summit round by round.
>
>*J. G. Holland*

Conquering Fear, Anxiety, Worry

Why are ye fearful, O ye of little faith.
> *St. Matthew 8:26*

A hundred load of worry will not pay an ounce of debt.
> *George Herbert*

A doctor who had many patients that were in the large income brackets made a study of why they worried so much. Here is what he found: 40 percent of their worries were about things that never happened. Thirty percent were about matters entirely beyond their control. Twelve percent were related to the physical ills which were caused or aggravated by their emotional attitudes. Ten percent were about friends or relatives who were quite able to look after themselves. Only eight percent were about matters that really needed their attention, but worry even in these cases was not the remedy to apply.
> *Anonymous*

Medical authorities inform us that worry, directly or indirectly, takes a larger annual toll of human life than any other disease. It is scarcely too much to assert that if fear were abolished from modern life, the work of the psychotherapist would be nearly gone.

John A. O'Brien

> 'Gainst minor evils let him pray,
>   Who fortune's favour curries.
> For one that big misfortunes slay,
>   Ten die of little worries.

George R. Sims

Anxiety is the rust of life, destroying its brightness and weakening its power. A childlike and abiding trust in Providence is its best preventive and remedy.

Tryon Edwards

How paltry and inconsequential the things that frighten us become, when once we realize that we are in the shadow of the everlasting arms capable of protecting us from every foe.

John A. O'Brien

> Let naught disturb thee,
>   Naught fright thee ever,
> All things are passing
>   God changeth never.
> Patience e'er conquers;
>   With God for thine own
> Thou nothing dost lack.
>   He suffiiceth alone!

Thérèse de Lisieux

It is not work that kills, but worry.

English proverb

A Chicago physician specializing in research on ulcers told recently that his laboratories had been obliged to abandon the use of dogs in their experiments. The fool critters just wouldn't worry, and worry is the thing that makes ulcers and keeps them active. You can inflict an ulcer upon a dog by artificial methods and he will sit down placidly and cure himself by refusing to be bothered about anything. It's just possible that there might be a lesson here for humans!
Lee Ragsdale

> Some strange commotion
> Is in his brain: he bites his lip, and starts;
> Stops on a sudden, looks upon the ground,
> Then lays his finger on his temple; straight
> Springs out into fast gait; then stops again,
> Strikes his breast hard, and anon he casts
> His eye against the moon.
> *Shakespeare*

Borrow trouble for yourself, if that's your nature, but don't lend it to your neighbors.
Rudyard Kipling

Have a constant love for mankind. Carry about no grudges. Don't strike back. The pus pockets of hatred are the favorite breeding ground of strife, irritation and worry.
John A. O'Brien

A large industrial concern discovered that nine out of ten cases of workers' inefficiency were caused by worry.

A life insurance company found that four out of five nervous breakdowns began not in actual events but in worry. A medical clinic's analysis of its patients showed that thirty-five percent of all illnesses on its records started with worry.
Charles M. Crowe

Nothing in the affairs of men is worthy of great anxiety.
Plato

Do not anticipate trouble, or worry about what may never happen. Keep in the sunlight.
Benjamin Franklin

Happy is the man who has broken the chains which hurt the mind, and has given up worrying once and for all.
Ovid

O fond anxiety of mortal men!
How vain and inconclusive arguments
Are those, which make thee beat thy wings below!
Dante Alighieri

If pleasures are greatest in anticipation, just remember that this is also true of trouble.
Elbert Hubbard

It has been well said that no man ever sank under the burden of the day. It is when tomorrow's burden is added to the burden of today that the weight is more than a

man can bear. Never load yourselves, so, my friends. If you find yourselves so loaded, at least remember this: it is your own doing, not God's. He begs you to leave the future to him, and mind the present.
George Macdonald

Love your friends and hate your enemies was the practice of the pagans as it is of unredeemed human nature today. But Christ said: "Love your enemies, do good to them that hate you." It is not easy. But it is the distinctive mark of a true Christian.

It begets the richest premium in peace of mind and true happiness, both in time and in eternity. When Christ said, "Perfect love casteth out fear," he epitomized for all mankind a volume of psychotherapy, which psychiatrists will be but unraveling for centuries to come.
John A. O'Brien

The world is wide
In time and tide,
And God is guide,
  Then, do not hurry.
That man is blest
Who does his best
And leaves the rest,
  Then, do not worry.
Charles F. Deems

How much have cost us the evils that never happened!
Thomas Jefferson

Man, like the bridge, was designed to carry the load of the moment, not the combined weight of a year at once.
William A. Ward

Worry is interest paid on trouble before it becomes due.
William R. Inge

Let us be of good cheer, remembering that the misfortunes hardest to bear are those which never come.
James Russell Lowell

Many of the worries which afflict mankind arise from the recollection of past mistakes or misfortunes. There is a widespread tendency to cry over spilled milk, to lament mistakes long past, which no amount of lamentation can undo. Why worry and fret over past mistakes when such fretting only robs one of the physical and mental strength to solve present problems?
John A. O'Brien

The legs of the stork are long; the legs of the duck are short. You cannot make a stork's legs short, nor a duck's legs long. So why worry?
Chinese proverb

> Some of your hurts you have cured
> And the sharpest you still have survived
> But what torments of grief you endured
> From evils that never arrived.
> *Ralph Waldo Emerson*

Man is born to trouble, as the sparks fly upward.
Job 5:7

He is well along the road to perfect manhood who does not allow the thousand little worries of life to embitter his temper, or disturb his equanimity. An undivided heart which worships God alone, and trusts him as it should, is raised above anxiety for earthly wants.
John Cunningham Geikie

To carry care to bed, is to sleep with a pack on your back.
Thomas C. Halliburton

> Better never trouble Trouble
> Until Trouble troubles you;
> For you only make your trouble
> Double-trouble when you do;
> And the trouble, like a bubble,
> That you're troubling about,
> May be nothing but a cipher
> With its rim rubbed out.
>
> *David Keppel*

The achievement of the supreme values of life challenge us to throw off fear, with its paralyzing effect, scaring us still and making us die many times before our death. It summons us to leave the slum district of the mind, with its black pessimism and haunting fears, and climb to the mountain peaks where the air is fresh and pure, and bathed in the sunlight of heaven. "He has not learned the lesson of life," says Emerson, "who does not every day surmount a fear."
John A. O'Brien

It is not the cares of to-day, but the cares of to-morrow that weigh a man down. For the needs of to-day we have corresponding strength given. For the morrow we are told to trust. It is not ours yet. — *George Macdonald*

Worry affects the circulation, the heart, the glands, the whole nervous system, and profoundly affects the health. I have never known a man who died from overwork, but many who died from doubt. — *Dr. Charles Mayo*

> Build for yourself a strong-box,
>   Fashion each part with care;
> Fit it with hasp and padlock;
>   Put all your troubles there.
> Hide therein all your failures,
>   And each bitter cup you quaff,
> Lock all your heartaches within it,
>   Then sit on the lid and laugh.
> — *J. V. Danner*

One of the most useless of all things is to take a deal of trouble in providing against dangers that never come. How many toil to lay up riches which they never enjoy; to provide for exigencies that never happen; to prevent troubles that never come; sacrificing present comfort and enjoyment in guarding against the wants of a period they may never live to see. — *W. Jay*

Worry distorts our thinking, disrupts our work, disquiets our soul, disturbs our body, disfigures our face, destroys

our poise, depresses our friends, demoralizes our life, defeats our faith and debilitates our energy.
William A. Ward

    I'll not willingly offend,
      Nor be easily offended;
    What's amiss I'll strive to mend,
      And endure what can't be mended.
Isaac Watts

When we borrow trouble, and look forward into the future and see what storms are coming, and distress ourselves before they come, as to how we shall avert them if they ever do come, we lose our proper trustfulness in God. When we torment ourselves with imaginary dangers, or trials, or reverses, we have already parted with that perfect love which casteth out fear.
Henry Ward Beecher

    Worry is an old man with bended head,
    Carrying a load of feathers
    Which he thinks are lead.
Anonymous

Of our troubles we must seek some other cause than God.
Plato

Sufficient to each day are the duties to be done and the trials to be endured. God never built a Christian strong enough to carry to-day's duties and to-morrow's anxieties piled on the top of them. *T. L. Cuyler*

> Oh, a trouble's a ton, or a trouble's an ounce,
>   Or a trouble is what you make it,
> And it isn't the fact that you're hurt that counts,
>   But only how did you take it?
> > — *Edmund Vance Cooke*

All fear is painful, and then it conduces not to safety, is painful without use. Every consideration, therefore, by which groundless terrors may be removed, adds something to human happiness. — *Samuel Johnson*

> Pack up your troubles in your old kit-bag,
>   And smile, smile, smile.
> > — *George Asaf*

Fear is the tax that conscience pays to guilt. — *George Sewell*

Trouble runs off him like water off a duck's back. — *George Herbert*

God planted fear in the soul as truly as he planted hope or courage. It is a kind of bell or gong which rings the mind into quick life and avoidance of the approach of danger. It is the soul's signal for rallying. — *Henry Ward Beecher*

> The troubles of our proud and angry dust
>   Are from eternity, and shall not fail.

> Bear them we can, and if we can we must.
> Shoulder the sky, my lad, and drink your ale.
> *A. E. Housman*

The wise man thinks about his troubles only when there is some purpose in doing so; at other times he thinks about other things. *Bertrand Russell*

Women like to sit down with trouble as if it were knitting.
Ellen Glasgow

> For every evil under the sun,
> There is a remedy or there is none.
> If there is one, try to find it,
> If there is none, never mind it.
> *Anonymous*

Uses of Adversity

Adversity is the trial of principle. Without it a man hardly knows whether he is honest or not.
Henry Fielding

A little boy was leading his sister up a mountain path. "Why," she complained, "it's not a path at all. It's all rocky and bumpy." "Sure," he said, "the bumps are what you climb on." *J. Wallace Hamilton*

Adversity is the first path to truth:
He who hath proved war, storm or woman's rage,
Whether his winters be eighteen or eighty,
Has won the experience which is deem'd so weighty.
Lord Byron

We beseech thee for those who are afflicted and in bonds and in poverty; give rest to each, free them from bonds, bringing them out of poverty; comfort all, thou who art the Comforter and Consoler.
Prayer in the 4th century

A friend loveth at all times, and a brother is born for adversity. *Proverbs 17:17*

Adversity is the diamond dust Heaven polishes its jewels with. *Robert Leighton*

It's a different song when everything's wrong, when you're feeling infernally mortal; when it's ten against one, and hope there is none, buck up, little soldier, and chortle! *Robert W. Service*

As a rule, the game of life is worth playing, but the struggle is the prize. *William R. Inge*

Adversity is sometimes hard upon a man; but for one man who can stand prosperity, there are a hundred that will stand adversity. *Thomas Carlyle*

God measures our affliction to our need.
St. John Chrysostom

Adversity makes men; prosperity, monsters.
French proverb

Behold a worthy sight, to which God . . . may direct his gaze. Behold a thing worthy of a God: a brave man matched in conflict with adversity.
Lucius Annaeus Seneca

Adversity has ever been considered the state in which a man most easily becomes acquainted with himself, then, especially, being free from flatterers. *Samuel Johnson*

A problem is an opportunity in work clothes.
Henry J. Kaiser, Jr.

His overthrow heap'd happiness upon him:
For then, and not till then, he felt himself,
And found the blessedness of being little.
Shakespeare

Many would be willing to have afflictions provided that they be not inconvenienced by them.
St. Francis de Sales

Adversity comes with instruction in his hand.
Welsh proverb

In every failure the wise man will find the seed of success.
W. Clement Stone

And these vicissitudes come best in youth;
For when they happen at a riper age,
People are apt to blame the Fates, forsooth,
And wonder Providence is not more sage.
Adversity is the first path to truth.
Lord Byron

No life is so hard that you can't make it easier by the way you take it.
Ellen Glasgow

It is not what nature does with a man that matters but what he does with nature. *Ray S. Baker*

> Sweet are the uses of adversity;
> Which, like the toad, ugly and venomous,
> Wears yet a precious jewel in his head.
> *Shakespeare*

One and the same violence of affliction proves, purifies and melts the good, and condemns, wastes and casts out the bad. *St. Augustine*

> Daughter of Jove, relentless power,
>   Thou tamer of the human breast,
> Whose iron scourge and torturing hour
>   The bad affright, afflict the best.
> *Thomas Gray*

Come then, affliction, if my Father wills, and be my frowning friend. A friend that frowns is better than a smiling enemy. *Anonymous*

Adversity is a severe instructor, set over us by one who knows us better than we do ourselves, as he loves us better too. He that wrestles with us strengthens our nerves and sharpens our skill. One antagonist is our helper. This conflict with difficulty makes us acquainted with our object, and compels us to consider it in all its relations. It will not suffer us to be superficial. *Edmund Burke*

He who has been delivered from pain must not think he is now free again, and at liberty to take life up as it was before, entirely forgetful of the past. He is now a man whose eyes are open with regard to pain and anguish, and he must help to overcome these two enemies and bring to others the deliverance which he has himself enjoyed. *Albert Schweitzer*

> The good are better made by ill,
> As odours crushed are sweeter still.
> *Samuel Rogers*

The truly loving heart loves God's good pleasure not in consolations only, but, and especially, in afflictions also. *St. Francis de Sales*

Gold is tried in fire, and acceptable men in the furnace of adversity. *Ecclesiastes 2:5*

Different people must contend with different trials, but adversities in some shape or other come to everyone. Life is a procession of people bearing crosses and when one carries his awkwardly he interferes with his fellow-marchers. *R. C. McCarthy*

A smooth sea never made a skillful mariner, neither do uninterrupted prosperity and success qualify for usefulness and happiness. The storms of adversity, like those of the ocean, rouse the faculties, and excite the invention, prudence, skill, and fortitude of the voyager. The martyrs

of ancient times, in bracing their minds to outward calamities, acquired a loftiness of purpose and a moral heroism worth a lifetime of softness and security.
Anonymous

Any one can hold the helm when the sea is calm.
Publilius Syrus

Human life is a state of probation, and adversity is the post of honor in it. *John Hughes*

For a man to rejoice in adversity is not grievous to him who loves; for so to joy is to joy in the cross of Christ.
Thomas à Kempis

No man is more unhappy than the one who is never in adversity; the great affliction of life is never to be afflicted. *Anonymous*

Adversity has the same effect on a man that severe training has on the pugilist—it reduces him to his fighting weight. *Josh Billings*

If thou faint in the day of adversity, thy strength is small.
Proverbs 24:10

I never met with a single instance of adversity which I have not in the end seen was for my good. I have never

heard of a Christian on his deathbed complaining of his afflictions.
Alexander M. Proudfit

Stars may be seen from the bottom of a deep well, when they cannot be discerned from the top of a mountain. So are many things learned in adversity which the prosperous man dreams not of.
Charles H. Spurgeon

Rembrandt's domestic troubles served only to heighten and deepen his art, and perhaps his best canvases were painted under stress of circumstances and in sadness of heart. His life is another proof, if needed, that the greatest truths and beauties are to be seen only through tears. Too bad for the man! But the world—the same ungrateful, selfish world that has always lighted its torch at the funeral pyres of genius—is the gainer.
John C. Van Dyke

In time of prosperity friends will be plenty;
In time of adversity not one in twenty.
James Howell

Let us be patient! These severe afflictions
  Not from the ground arise,
But oftentimes celestial benedictions
  Assume this dark disguise.
Henry Wadsworth Longfellow

The flower that follows the sun does so even in cloudy days.
Robert Leighton

I thank God for my handicaps, for, through them, I have found myself, my work, and my God.
Helen Keller

If adversity purifies me, why not nations?
Jean Paul Richter

Prosperity is the blessing of the Old Testament; adversity of the New, which carrieth the greater benediction and the clearer revelation of God's favor. Prosperity is not without many fears and distastes; adversity not without many comforts and hopes. *Sir Francis Bacon*

The brightest crowns that are worn in heaven have been tried, and smelted, and polished, and glorified through the furnace of tribulation. *E. H. Chapin*

God sometimes puts us on our back so that we may look upward. *Anonymous*

In prosperous times I have sometimes felt my fancy and powers of language flag, but adversity is to me at least a tonic and bracer. *Sir Walter Scott*

Now let us thank th' eternal power, convinc'd
That Heaven but tries our virtue by affliction:
That oft the cloud which wraps the present hour,
Serves but to brighten all our future days!
John Brown

Those who have suffered much are like those who know many languages; they have learned to understand and be understood by all.   *Anne Sophie Swetchine*

There is nothing the body suffers that the soul may not profit by.   *George Meredith*

The virtue of prosperity is temperance; the virtue of adversity is fortitude, which in morals is the more heroical virtue.   *Sir Francis Bacon*

Rightly conceived, time is the friend of all who are in any way in adversity, for its mazy road winds in and out of the shadows sooner or later into sunshine, and when one is at its darkest point one can be certain that presently it will grow brighter.
    Arthur Bryant

It has done me good to be somewhat parched by the heat and drenched by the rain of life.
    Henry Wadsworth Longfellow

The greatest object in the universe, says a certain philosopher, is a good man struggling with adversity; yet there is a still greater, which is the good man that comes to relieve it.   *Oliver Goldsmith*

The only way to meet affliction is to pass through it solemnly, slowly, with humility and faith, as the Israelites

passed through the sea. Then its very waves of misery will divide, and become to us a wall, on the right side and on the left, until the gulf narrows before our eyes, and we land safely on the opposite shore.
Dinah Maria Mulick Craik

I was the son of an immigrant. I experienced bigotry, intolerance and prejudice, even as so many of you have. Instead of allowing these things to embitter me, I took them as spurs to more strenuous effort.
Bernard Baruch

In prosperity, caution; in adversity, patience.
Dutch proverb

With silence only as their benediction,
   God's angels come
Where in the shadow of a great affliction
   The soul sits dumb!
John Greenleaf Whittier

To a brave man, good and bad luck are like his right and left hand. He uses them both.
St. Catherine of Siena

Conscience:
An Inner Voice

Conscience is the judgment of reason concerning the rightness or wrongness of an action here and now to be performed. Distinct from the speculative intellect which deals with abstractions, conscience concerns itself with our obedience or disobedience to clearly apprehended moral laws. The former it approves, the latter it condemns.
John A. O'Brien

A good conscience is a continual Christmas.
Benjamin Franklin

A peace above all earthly dignities, a still and quiet conscience.
Shakespeare

A tender conscience is an inestimable blessing; that is, a conscience not only quick to discern what is evil, but instantly to shun it, as the eyelid closes itself against the mote.
Nehemiah Adams

Conscience and reputation are two things. Conscience is due to yourself, reputation to your neighbor.
St. Augustine

A good conscience is a mine of wealth. And in truth what greater riches can there be, what thing more sweet than a good conscience? *St. Bernard*

Conscience that can see without light sits in the aeropagy and dark tribunal of our hearts, surveying our thoughts and condemning their obliquities.
Thomas Browne

A disciplined conscience is a man's best friend. It may not be his most amiable, but it is his most faithful monitor.
Austin Phelps

A good conscience is the palace of Christ, the temple of the Holy Ghost, the paradise of delight and the standing Sabbath of the Saints. *St. Augustine*

Conscience is the voice of the soul, the passions are the voice of the body. *Jean Jacques Rousseau*

Conscience does not repose on itself, but vaguely reaches forward to something beyond self, and dimly discerns a sanction higher than self for its decisions, as is evidenced in that keen sense of obligation and responsibility which informs them.
Cardinal John Henry Newman

Freedom of conscience is a natural right, both antecedent and superior to all human laws and institutions whatever; a right which laws never gave and which laws never take away.
John Goodwin

A man's own conscience is his sole tribunal, and he should care no more for that phantom "opinion" than he should fear meeting a ghost if he crossed the churchyard at dark.
Edward G. Bulwer-Lytton

Conscience is God's vicegerent on earth and, within the limited jurisdiction given to it, it partakes of his infinite wisdom and speaks in his tone of absolute command. It is a revelation of the being of a God, a divine voice in the human soul, making known the presence of its rightful sovereign, the author of the law of holiness and truth.
Francis Bowen

Conscience is God's presence in man.
Emmanuel Swedenborg

Conscience is the aboriginal vicar of Christ, a prophet in its informations, a monarch in its peremptoriness, a priest in its blessings and anathemas, and, even though the eternal priesthood throughout the Church could cease to be, in it the sacerdotal principle would remain and would have a sway.
Cardinal John Henry Newman

> I feel within me
> A peace above all earthly dignities;
> A still and quiet conscience.
> *Shakespeare*

Every man has a paradise around him till he sins and the angel of an accusing conscience drives him from his Eden. And even then there are holy hours, when this angel sleeps, and man comes back, and with the innocent eyes of a child looks into his lost paradise again, into the broad gates and rural solitudes of nature.
Henry Wadsworth Longfellow

Conscience is a great ledger book in which all our offences are written and registered, and which time reveals to the sense and feeling of the offender.
Sir Richard Burton

He that loses his conscience has nothing left that is worth keeping.
Nicolas Caussin

> O honorable conscience, clear and chaste,
> How small a fault stings thee to bitter smart!
> *Dante Alighieri*

> My conscience is my crown,
>   Contented thoughts my rest;
> My heart is happy in itself;
>   My bliss is in my breast.
> *Robert Southwell*

Conscience, true as the needle to the pole points steadily to the pole-star of God's eternal justice, reminding the soul of the fearful realities of the life to come.
Ezra Hall Gillett

I ever understood an impartial liberty of conscience to be the natural rights of all men. . . . Liberty of conscience is the first step to having a religion.
William Penn

The testimony of a good conscience is the glory of a good man; have a good conscience and thou shalt ever have gladness. A good conscience may bear right many things and rejoices among adversities.
Thomas à Kempis

Governments being, among other purposes, instituted to protect the consciences of men from oppression, it certainly is the duty of rulers not only to abstain from it themselves but, according to their stations, to prevent it in others.   *George Washington*

Yet still there whispers the small voice within,
Heard through Gain's silence, and o'er Glory's din:
Whatever creed be taught or land be trod,
Man's conscience is the oracle of God.
Lord Byron

He will easily be content and at peace, whose conscience is pure.   *Thomas à Kempis*

In matters of conscience that is the best sense which every wise man takes in before he hath sullied his understanding with the designs of sophisters and interested persons.
Jeremy Taylor

The voice of God in man! which without rest
Doth softly cry within a troubled breast;
To all temptations is that soul left free
That makes not to itself a curb of me.
Sir Edward Sherburne

I desire so to conduct the affairs of this administration that if at the end, when I come to lay down the reins of power, I have lost every other friend on earth, I shall at least have one friend left, and that friend shall be down inside of me.
Abraham Lincoln

A good conscience is to the soul what health is to the body; it preserves a constant ease and serenity within us, and more than countervails all the calamities and afflictions that can possibly befall us.
Joseph Addison

If any speak ill of thee, flee home to thine own conscience, and examine thine heart; if thou be guilty, it is a just correction; if not guilty, it is a fair instruction. Make use of both; so shalt thou distil honey out of gall, and out of an open enemy make a secret friend.
Francis Quarles

Oh! Conscience! Conscience! man's most faithful friend,
Him canst thou comfort, ease, relieve, defend;
But if he will thy friendly checks forego,
Thou art, oh! woe for me, his deadliest foe!
George Crabbe

The moral sense, or conscience, is as much a part of man as his leg or arm. It is given to all human beings in a stronger or weaker degree, as force of members is given them in a greater or less degree.
Thomas Jefferson

A person whose conscience tells him at fifty exactly what it told him at twenty has not grown up; he has kept his faculty of moral discernment out of the general development of his mind. We do not always learn the will of God by remembering what he told us yesterday, even when we are sure that we have heard him rightly. Conscience is not memory. It is the power of discerning the moral relation of things.
T. E. Jessop

Let no man be sorry he has done good because others have done evil. If a man has acted right, he has done well, though alone; if wrong, the sanction of all mankind will not justify him.
Henry Fielding

What other dungeon is so dark as one's own heart! What jailer so inexorable as one's own self!
Nathaniel Hawthorne

To endeavor to domineer over conscience is to invade the citadel of heaven. *Charles V*

The great beacon light God sets in all,
The conscience of each bosom.
Robert Browning

The prosperous and beautiful
 To me seem not to wear
The yoke of conscience masterful,
 Which galls me everywhere.
Ralph Waldo Emerson

Fear is the tax that conscience pays to guilt.
George Sewall

I love to think of nature as an unlimited broadcasting station, through which God speaks to us every hour, if we will only tune in. *George Washington Carver*

What conscience dictates to be done, or warns me not to do, this teach me more than hell to shun, that more than Heaven pursue. *Alexander Pope*

Tenderness of conscience is always to be distinguished from scrupulousness. The conscience cannot be kept too sensitive and tender; but scrupulousness arises from bodily or mental infirmity, and discovers itself in a multitude of ridiculous, superstitious, and painful feelings.
Richard Cecil

The conscience is a thousand witnesses.
Richard Taverner

Sell not your conscience; thus are fetters wrought.
What is a slave but one who can be bought?
Arthur Guiterman

Man became the first implement-making creature not later than the beginning of the Ice Age, probably a million years ago. At the same time he became the first weapon-making creature. For perhaps a million years, therefore, he has been improving those weapons; but it is less than five thousand years since man began to feel the power of conscience to such a degree that it became a potent social force.
James H. Breasted

A wounded conscience is able to un-paradise paradise itself.
Thomas Fuller

The torture of a bad conscience is the hell of a living soul.
John Calvin

I am more afraid of my own heart than of the Pope and all his cardinals. I have within me the great Pope, self.
Martin Luther

There is a spectacle more grand than the sea; it is heaven: there is a spectacle more grand than heaven; it is the conscience.
Victor Hugo

Help us to save free conscience from the paw
Of hireling wolves, whose gospel is their maw.
John Milton

According to the state of a man's conscience, so do hope and fear on account of his deeds arise in his mind.
Ovid

The only tyrant I accept in this world is the "still, small voice" within me. *Mohandas Gandhi*

The world stands or falls with the laws of life which Heaven has written in the human conscience.
Pierre Van Paassen

Man's conscience is the supreme judge of what is true or false, good or evil. A person who lives professing a belief he does not hold has lost the only true, the only immutable thing—his conscience. *Dagobert D. Runes*

The conscience, which does not sink its roots in the subsoil of religious faith nor shoot its antennae up beyond the roof of the skies, misses alike the music of divine inspiration and the thunder of divine commands.
John A. O'Brien

Dreamers of Dreams

Dreams in their development have breath,
And tears, and tortures, and the touch of joy.
They leave a weight upon our waking thoughts.
They take a weight from off our waking toils.
They do divide our being; they become
A portion of ourselves as of our time,
And look like heralds of eternity.
Lord Byron

I believe it to be true that dreams are the true interpreters of our inclinations; but there is art required to sort and understand them. *Michel Eyquem de Montaigne*

Dreamers are the architects of greatness. Their brains have wrought all human miracles. . . . Your homes are set upon a land a dreamer found. The pictures on its walls are visions from a dreamer's soul. A dreamer's pain wails from your violin. They are the chosen few—the blazers of the way—who never wear doubt's bandage on their eyes. *Herbert Kaufman*

A crooked street goes past my door, entwining love of
every land;

It wanders, singing, round the world, to Ashkelon and Samarkand.
To roam it is an ecstasy, each mile the easier it seems,
And yet the longest street on earth is this—the Street of Dreams.
Charles Divine

A child, awakened out of a deep sleep, expressed all the crying babies and all the weeping idealists in the world. "Oh, dear," he said, "I have lost my place in my dream."
Lincoln Steffens

>Come to me in my dreams, and then
>By day I shall be well again.
>For then the night will more than pay
>The hopeless longing of the day.
>*Matthew Arnold*

Existence would be intolerable if we were never to dream.
Anatole France

>Back of the job—the dreamer
>Who's making the dream come true.
>*Berton Braley*

A task without a vision is drudgery; a vision without a task is a dream; a task with a vision is victory.
Anonymous

Dreams are but interludes which fancy makes:
When Monarch-Reason sleeps, this mimic wakes;
Compounds a medley of disjointed things,
A mob of cobblers and a court of kings.
John Dryden

Live in contact with dreams, and you will get something of their charm; live in contact with facts, and you will get something of their brutality. I wish I could find a country where the facts were not brutal, and the dreams not unreal. *George Bernard Shaw*

But that a dream can die will be a thrust
Between my ribs forever of hot pain.
Edna St. Vincent Millay

Humanity certainly needs practical men, who get the most out of their work, and, without forgetting the general good, safeguard their own interests. But humanity also needs dreamers, for whom the disinterested development of an enterprise is so captivating that it becomes impossible for them to devote their care to their own material profit. *Marie Curie*

To sleep: perchance to dream: ay, there's the rub;
For in that sleep of death what dreams may come,
When we have shuffled off this mortal coil,
Must give us pause.
Shakespeare

Vision is the Aladdin's lamp of the soul. It is the divine spark that lights the lamp of progress. It is the hand that pushes aside the curtains of night to let the sunrise in. It is vision that guides a log-cabin boy to the presidency of our Republic. Vision gave wings to man, pulled atomic energy from the sun, subdued the forces of nature, making them the soulless and untiring slaves of those whom such powers held in bondage since time began.
Anonymous

For a dreamer lives forever,
And a toiler dies in a day.
John B. O'Reilly

If age is strictly honest with youth it has to tell it things that are not altogether good for youth to take to heart. The experience of the years is largely made up of vanished dreams, deluded hopes and frustrated ambitions. But it is the very dreams, hopes and ambitions of youth that accomplish so many things that age in its wisdom knows to be impossible. Where would the world be if wisdom ruled youth and power rested in age?
Thomas F. Woodlock

Don't tell me what you dream'd last night, for
I've been reading Freud.
Franklin P. Adams

Man knows his littleness; his own mountains remind him; but the dreams of man make up for our faults and failings; for the brevity of our lives, for the narrowness of our scope; they leap over boundaries and are away and away. *Lord Dunsany*

O thou, the Father of us all,
    Whose many mansions wait,
To whose dream welcome each must come
    A child, at Heaven's gate;
In that fair house not made with hands
    Whenever splendor beams,
Out of thy bounty keep for me
    A little room of dreams.
R. U. Johnson

The greatest achievement was at first and for a time a dream. The oak sleeps in the acorn; the bird waits in the egg; and in the highest vision of the soul a waking angel stirs. Dreams are the seedlings of realities. *James Allen*

The chambers in the house of dreams
    Are fed with so divine an air,
That Time's hoar wings grow young therein,
    And they who walk there are most fair.
Francis Thompson

The indelicate hand of necessity is forever leaving its fingerprints on the fragile crystal of dreams. *Douglas Meador*

> I arise from dreams of thee
> In the first sweet sleep of night,
> When the winds are breathing low,
> And the stars are shining bright.
>
> *Percy Bysshe Shelley*

It was a Spring that never came, but we have lived enough to know what we have never had, remains. It is the things we have that go. *Sara Teasdale*

It is not the shrines of the gods, nor the powers of the air, that send the dreams which mock the mind with flitting shadows: each man makes his own dreams.

Gaius Petronius

> And so, his senses gradually wrapt
> In a half sleep, he dreams of better worlds,
> And dreaming hears thee still, O singing lark:
> That singest like an angel in the clouds.
>
> *Samuel Taylor Coleridge*

We grow great by dreams. All big men are dreamers. They see things in the soft haze of a spring day or in the red fire of a long winter's evening. Some of us let these great dreams die, but others nourish and protect them; nurse them through bad days till they bring them to the sunshine and light which comes always to those who sincerely hope that their dreams will come true.

Woodrow Wilson

The eye of man hath not heard, the ear of man hath not seen, man's hand is not able to taste, his tongue to conceive, nor his heart to report, what my dream was.
Shakespeare

And yet, as angels in some brighter dreams
Call to the soul when man doth sleep,
So some strange thoughts transcend our wonted dreams,
And into glory peep.
Henry Vaughan

You see things; and you say "Why?" But I dream things that never were; and I say "Why not?"
George Bernard Shaw

The fisher droppeth his net in the stream,
And a hundred streams are the same as one;
And the maiden dreameth her love-lit dream;
And what is it all, when all is done?
Alice Cary

We are the music-makers,
And we are the dreamers of dreams,
Wandering by lone sea-breakers,
And sitting by desolate streams;
World-losers and world-forsakers,
On whom the pale moon gleams;
Yet we are the movers and shakers
Of the world forever, it seems.
Arthur O'Shaughnessy

The Quest for Happiness

Amusement is the happiness of those that cannot think.
Alexander Pope

Friends, books, a cheerful heart, and conscience clear
Are the most choice companions we have here.
William Mather

Do you wish never to be sad? Live rightly!
Isidorus of Aegae

Happiness in this world, when it comes, comes incidentally. Make it the object of pursuit, and it is never attained. *Nathaniel Hawthorne*

Happiness was born a twin. *Lord Byron*

Civilization, in the real sense of the term, consists not in the multiplication, but in the deliberate and voluntary reduction of wants. This alone promotes real happiness and contentment, and increases the capacity for service.
Mohandas Gandhi

All the world is searching for joy and happiness, but these cannot be purchased for any price in any market place, because they are virtues that come from within and like rare jewels must be polished, for they shine brightest in the light of faith, and in the services of brotherly love.
Lucille R. Taylor

All happiness is in the mind. *H. G. Bohn*

Happiness, like every other emotional state, has blindness and insensibility to opposing facts given it as its instinctive weapon for self-protection against disturbance.
William James

A brook is going somewhere. It is water-on-a-mission. About to present itself to other waters at its destination, it never neglects little wayside opportunities. On its way to make its final offering, it gaily gives itself all along the way. Deer drink of its refreshing coolness with a deep content. Boys of seven years and of seventy probe its pools and eddies with their lures and return home at day's end with the brook's gift of speckled trout. Fish, crustaceans, mollusks, and water insects are given a home in its swirling currents and tranquil pools. From its birth in bubbling springs to its arrival at its final goal the brook is selfless and a happy appearing thing. Service and happiness belong together. *Harold E. Kohn*

How soon a smile of God can change the world!
How we are made for happiness—how work
Grows play, adversity a winning fight!
Robert Browning

Our object in the establishment of the state was not the exceptional happiness of any one class, but the greatest possible happiness of the city as a whole.
Plato

He that keepeth the Law, happy is he.
Proverbs 29:18

A man who finds no satisfaction in himself seeks for it in vain elsewhere. *François Duc de la Rochefoucauld*

Brethren, happiness is *not* our being's end and aim. The Christian's aim is perfection, not happiness; and every one of the sons of God must have something of that spirit which marked his master. *Frederick W. Robertson*

Happy is he that chastens himself.
George Herbert

> If happiness hae not her seat
> And centre in the breast,
> We may be wise, or rich, or great,
> But never can be blest.
> *Robert Burns*

A big dog saw a little dog chasing its tail and asked, "Why are you chasing your tail so?" Said the puppy, "I have mastered philosophy; I have solved the problems of the universe which no dog before me has rightly solved;

I have learned that the best thing for a dog is happiness, and that happiness is my tail. Therefore I am chasing it; and when I catch it I shall have happiness."

Said the old dog, "My son, I, too, have paid attention to the problems of the universe in my weak way, and I have formed some opinions. I, too, have judged that happiness is a fine thing for a dog, and that happiness is in the tail. But I have noticed that when I chase after it, it keeps running away from me, but when I go about my business, it comes after me."
C. L. James

Happy days are here again,
The skies above are clear again,
Let us sing a song of cheer again,
Happy days are here again!
Jack Yellen

Happiness is the legitimate fruitage of love and service. Set happiness before you as an end, no matter what guise of wealth, or fame, or oblivion even, and you will not attain it. But renounce it and seek the pleasure of God, and that instant is the birth of your own.
Arthur S. Hardy

Looking for happiness is like clutching the shadow or chasing the wind.
Japanese proverb

Above all, let us never forget that an act of goodness is in itself an act of happiness. It is the flower of a long inner life of joy and contentment; it tells of peaceful hours and days on the sunniest heights of our soul.
Maurice Maeterlinck

Have your heart right with Christ, and he will visit you often, and so turn weekdays into Sundays, meals into sacraments, homes into temples and earth into heaven.
Charles H. Spurgeon

He who leaves his house in search of happiness pursues a shadow. *S. G. Champion*

Happy is the man whom God correcteth: therefore despise not thou the chastening of the Almighty.
Job 5:17

Few persons realize how much of their happiness is dependent upon their work, upon the fact that they are kept busy and not left to feed upon themselves. Happiness comes most to persons who seek her least, and think least about it. It is not an object to be sought; it is a state to be induced. It must follow and not lead. It must overtake you, and not you overtake it.
John Burroughs

Happiness is the legal tender of the soul.
Robert G. Ingersoll

Mankind are always happier for having been happy; so that, if you make them happy now, you make them happy twenty years hence by the memory of it.
Sydney Smith

Mankind is the artificer of his own happiness.
Henry David Thoreau

Happiness! It is useless to seek it elsewhere than in this warmth of human relations. Our sordid interests imprison us within their walls. Only a comrade can grasp us by the hand and haul us free. *Antoine D. Exupery*

It is interesting to note that even Jefferson never proposed happiness as an inalienable right. Our constitution talks of a right only for the *pursuit* of happiness. Ours for the seeking and winning! Not free. Happiness is the result, the product, of endeavor. Never God-given. Happiness is only God-*permitted*.
Permanized Paper Quarterly

It is neither wealth, nor splendor, but tranquility and occupation, which give happiness.
Thomas Jefferson

There is nothing of permanent value (putting aside a few human affections), nothing that satisfies quiet reflection, except the sense of having worked according to one's capacity and light to make things clear and get rid of cant and shams of all sorts.

A man may lose his strength; he may lose his money; he may lose every earthly thing which he possesses. Yet he may still attain and control his happiness if it stems from service to others.

He who makes service to others his method of obtaining happiness has in his possession something which comes from within his own mind, from within his own soul, and which is controlled largely by his own will or desire. Most other things are beyond control of an individual, and circumstances may deprive him of them.

George E. Mathieu

If an Arab in the desert were suddenly to discover a spring in his tent, and so would always be able to have water in abundance, how fortunate he would consider himself. So, too, when a man, who has a physical being, is always turned toward the outside, thinking that his happiness lies outside him, finally turns inward and discovers that the source is within him, not to mention his discovery that the source is his relation to God.

Sören Kierkegaard

Never believe that anyone who depends upon happiness is happy. *Lucius Annaeus Seneca*

Happiness is that pleasure which flows from the sense of virtue and from the consciousness of right deeds.

Henry Moore

If you observe a really happy man, you will find him building a boat, writing a symphony, educating his son, growing double dahlias or looking for dinosaur eggs in the Gobi Desert. He will not be searching for happiness as if it were a collar button that had rolled under the radiator, striving for it as a goal in itself. He will have become aware that he is happy in the course of living life twenty-four crowded hours of each day.

W. Bertram Wolfe

If I have faltered more or less
In my great task of happiness;
If I have moved among my race
And shown no glorious morning face; . . .
Lord, thy most pointed pleasure take,
And stab my spirit broad awake;
Or, Lord, if too obdurate I,
Choose thou, before that spirit die,
A piercing pain, a killing sin,
And to my dead heart run them in!
Robert Louis Stevenson

Happiness is neither within us only, or without us; it is the union of ourselves with God.
Blaise Pascal

To watch the corn grow or the blossoms set; to draw hard breath over the ploughshare or spade; to read, to think, to love, to pray, are the things that make men happy.
John Ruskin

If a man should ascend alone into heaven and behold clearly the structure of the universe and the beauty of the stars, there would be no pleasure for him in the awe-inspiring sight which would have filled him with delight if he had had someone to whom he could describe what he had seen.
Marcus Tullius Cicero

Mark Antony sought for happiness in love; Brutus in glory; Caesar in dominion; the first found disgrace, the second disgust, the last ingratitude, and each destruction.
Lord Byron

If you ever find happiness by hunting for it, you will find it as the old woman did her lost spectacles—on her own nose all the time. *Josh Billings*

Little deeds of kindness, little words of love,
Help to make earth happy like the heaven above.
Julia A. Fletcher Carney

Happiness is like a sunbeam, which the least shadow intercepts, while adversity is often as the rain of spring. *Chinese proverb*

Let him who would be happy for a day, go to the barber; for a week, marry a wife; for a month, buy him a new horse; for a year, build him a new house; for all his life time, be an honest man. *Thomas Fuller*

The secret of happiness is this: let your interests be as wide as possible, and let your reactions to the things and persons that interest you be as far as possible friendly rather than hostile. *Bertrand Russell*

A contributing factor to happiness is to be able to enjoy the gifts of nature. The poorest man living can enjoy these, for such blessings are free. Everybody can take pleasure in a glorious sunset. You would have to pay a great sum for a painting by a skilled artist. Only the wealthy can afford it, but almost any evening we can look at a brilliant western sky, and each one of us can say, "That's mine!" *David O. McKay*

The hand that in life grips with a miser's clutch, and the ear that refuses to heed the pleading voice of humanity, forfeit the most precious of all gifts of earth and of heaven—the happiness that comes of doing good to others. *Amos G. Carter*

Happiness and virtue rest upon each other; the best are not only the happiest, but the happiest are usually the best. *Edward G. Bulwer-Lytton*

O Happiness! our being's end and aim!
Good, Pleasure, Ease, Content! whate'er thy name.
Alexander Pope

Happy the man who, unknown to the world, lives content with himself in some retired nook, whom the love of this nothing called fame, has never intoxicated with its vain smoke; who makes all his pleasure dependent on his liberty of action, and gives an account of his leisure to no one but himself. *Nicolas Boileau*

God has so constituted our nature that we cannot be happy unless we are, or think we are, the means of good to others. We can scarcely conceive of greater wretchedness than must be felt by him who knows he is wholly useless in the world. *Erskine Mason*

There are briers besetting every path,
Which call for patient care;

There is a cross in every lot,
  And an earnest need for prayer;
But a lowly heart that leans on thee
  Is happy anywhere.
Alice Cary

Happiness is like manna; it is to be gathered in grains, and enjoyed every day. It will not keep; it cannot be accumulated; nor have we got to go out of ourselves or into remote places to gather it, since it has rained down from Heaven, at our very doors.

Seek happiness for its own sake, and you will not find it; seek for duty, and happiness will follow as the shadow comes with the sunshine. *Tryon Edwards*

Reason shows me that if my happiness is desirable and a good, the equal happiness of any other person must be equally desirable. *Henry Sidgwick*

Resigned to Heaven, we may with joy
To any state submit,
And in the world of miseries
Have happiness complete.
Daniel Defoe

Happiness is not found in self-contemplation, it is perceived only when it is reflected from another.
Samuel Johnson

The happiest person is the person who thinks the most interesting thoughts. *Timothy Dwight*

The happiest heart that ever beat
Was in some quiet breast
That found the common daylight sweet,
And left to Heaven the rest.
John V. Cheney

Happiness is the legitimate fruitage of love and service. It never comes and never can come by making it an end, and it is because so many persons mistake here and seek for it directly, instead of loving and serving God, and thus obtaining it, that there is so much dissatisfaction and sorrow.

Set happiness before you as an end, no matter in what guise of wealth, or fame, or oblivion even, and you will not attain it. But renounce it and seek the pleasure of God, and that instant is the birth of your own.
A. S. Hardy

There are three sureties of happiness: good habits, amiability, and forbearance. *Welsh proverb*

Happiness is a perfume you cannot pour on others without getting a few drops on yourself.
Ralph Waldo Emerson

Three things make us happy and content: the seeing eye, the hearing ear, the responsive heart.
Missionary Digest

The sunshine of life is made up of very little beams that are bright all the time. To give up something, when giving up will prevent unhappiness; to yield, when persisting will chafe and fret others; to go a little around rather than come against another; to take an ill look or a cross word quietly, rather than resent or return it—these are the ways in which clouds and storms are kept off, and a pleasant and steady sunshine secured.
John Aiken

O, how bitter a thing it is to look into happiness through another man's eyes!
Shakespeare

If thou art sound in stomach, side, and feet, the riches of a king will add nothing to thy happiness.
Horace

To be happy is easy enough if we give ourselves, forgive others, and live with thanksgiving. No self-centered person, no ungrateful soul can ever be happy, much less make anyone else happy. Life is giving, not getting.
Joseph F. Newton

What happiness is, the Bible alone shows clearly and certainly, and points out the way that leads to the attainment of it. "In Cicero and Plato, and other such writers,"

says Augustine, "I meet with many things acutely said, and things that excite a certain warmth of emotions, but in none of them do I find these words. 'Come unto me, all ye that labor, and are heavy laden, and I will give you rest.'"
Samuel Taylor Coleridge

In vain do they talk of happiness who never subdued an impulse in obedience to a principle. He who never sacrificed a present to a future good, or a personal to a general one, can speak of happiness only as the blind do of colors.
Horace Mann

The only happiness, a brave man ever troubled himself with asking much about, was happiness enough to get his work done.
Thomas Carlyle

That action is best which procures the greatest happiness for the greatest numbers.
Francis Hutcheson

Getters generally don't get happiness; givers get it. You simply give to others a bit of yourself—a thoughtful act, a helpful idea, a word of appreciation, a lift over a rough spot, a sense of understanding, a timely suggestion. You take something out of your mind, garnished in kindness out of your heart, and put it into the other fellow's mind and heart.
Charles H. Burr

We hold these truths to be self-evident: that all men are created equal; that they are endowed by their Creator

with certain inalienable Rights; that among these are Life, Liberty and the Pursuit of Happiness.
The Declaration of Independence

Happiness is the harvest of a quiet eye.
Austin O'Malley

We have no more right to consume happiness without producing it than to consume wealth without producing it. *George Bernard Shaw*

I have now reigned about fifty years in victory or peace, beloved by my subjects, dreaded by my enemies, and respected by my allies. Riches and honors, power and pleasure, have waited on my call, nor does any earthly blessing appear to have been wanting to my felicity. In this situation I have diligently numbered the days of pure and genuine happiness which have fallen to my lot: they amount to fourteen. *Abd-er-Rahman III*

In order that people may be happy in their work, these three things are needed: They must be fit for it: They must not do too much of it: And they must have a sense of success in it. *John Ruskin*

This is the true joy of life—the being used for a purpose recognized by yourself as a mighty one, the being thoroughly worn out before you are thrown to the scrapheap; the being a force of nature instead of a feverish, selfish clod of ailments and grievances.
George Bernard Shaw

The sun and stars that float in the open air;
The apple-shaped earth, and we upon it—
   surely the drift of them is something grand!
I do not know what it is, except that it is grand,
   and that it is happiness.
Walt Whitman

He who harbors a slight will miss the haven of happiness.
Author unknown

The belief that youth is the happiest time of life is founded on a fallacy. The happiest person is the person who thinks the most interesting thoughts, and we grow happier as we grow older. *William L. Phelps*

Unbroken happiness is a bore: it should have ups and downs. *Molière [Jean Baptiste Poquelin]*

In our frantic search for happiness we assume it resides in something that we can possess or manipulate: a spacious home, smart clothes, powerful automobiles or a huge bank account; we think of expensive vacations or costly amusements. We are sorely mistaken. If we have material comforts and at the same time possess happiness, it means that our happiness stems from within ourselves. It resides in something we are, not in what we have.
Kenneth Hildebrand

Most people have the idea that happiness is something that can be manufactured. They do not realize that it can no more be manufactured than wheat or corn can be manufactured. It must grow; and the harvest will be like the seed. It will take every moment that we have lived of life's probation day to think on the true, honest, just, pure and lovely things of life. These are the things that will make us contented. *Author unknown*

In every part and corner of our life, to lose oneself is to be gainer; to forget oneself is to be happy.
Robert Louis Stevenson

Happiness is a rebound from hard work. One of the follies of man is to assume that he can enjoy mere emotion. As well try to eat beauty! Happiness must be tricked. She loves to see men work. She loves sweat, weariness, self-sacrifice. She will not be found in palaces, but lurking in cornfields and factories, and hovering over littered desks. She crowns the unconscious head of the busy child. *David Grayson*

I believe the root of all happiness on this earth to lie in the realization of a spiritual life with a consciousness of something wider than materialism; in the capacity to live in a world that makes you unselfish because you are not overanxious about your personal place; that makes you tolerant because you realize your own comic fallibilities; that gives you tranquility without complacency because you believe in something so much larger than yourself.
Hugh Walpole

One of the finest sides to living is liking people and wanting to share activities in the human enterprise. The greatest pleasures come by giving pleasure to those who live under the same roof. Entering into this human enterprise, feeling oneself a part of the community, is a very important element which generates happiness.
Fred J. Hafling

That person lives in hell who gets what he desires too soon. Whether he finds his happiness in wealth, power, fame or women, or in a combination of all, that happiness will be meaningless if it robs him of his desire. Heaven is a country through which we are permitted to search eagerly and with hope for what we want.
Thomas Dreier

Happiness sneaks in through a door you didn't know you left open.
John Barrymore

Many persons have a wrong idea about what constitutes true happiness. It is not attained through self-gratification, but through fidelity to a worthy purpose.
Helen Keller

The fountain of content must spring up in the mind, and he who has so little knowledge of human nature as to seek happiness by changing anything but his own disposition will waste his life in fruitless efforts and multiply the griefs which he purposes to remove.
Samuel Johnson

The secret of being miserable is to have leisure to bother about whether you are happy or not.
George Bernard Shaw

Happiness is a sunbeam which may pass through a thousand bosoms without losing a particle of its original ray; nay, when it strikes on a kindred heart, like the converged light on a mirror, it reflects itself with redoubled brightness. It is not perfected till it is shared.
Jane Porter

Only one thing I know. The only ones among you who will be really happy are those who will have sought and found how to serve.
Albert Schweitzer

The happy people are those who are producing something; the bored people are those who are consuming much and producing nothing.
William R. Inge

The purpose of life is not to be happy, but to *matter*, to be productive, to be useful, to have it make some difference that you lived at all.
Leo Rosten

Happiness is like coke—something you get as a by-product in the process of making something else.
Aldous Huxley

Success is getting what you want; happiness is wanting what you get.
Author unknown

To me there is in happiness an element of self-forgetfulness. You lose yourself in something outside yourself when you are happy; just as when you are desperately miserable you are intensely conscious of yourself, are a solid little lump of ego weighing a ton.

J. B. Priestley

What right have we to decline to be happy, until we shall have found a world full of superlatives? God only is perfect, and he alone can look for the blessedness that comes from such spotless surroundings. Perfection must be the goal of man; the aim of his soul and mind, inward in thought and feeling, and outward in acts and deeds, but his happiness must not wait for that divine end. The same soul that longs for the absolutely beautiful must feed upon the common in the long meanwhile.

David Swing

Truth Will Make You Free

You shall know the truth, and the truth shall make you free. *John 8:32*

His truth shall be thy shield and buckler. *Psalms 91:4*

And fierce though the fiends may fight, and
  long though the angels hide,
I know that truth and right have the universe
  on their side.
Washington Gladden

Although it may not be always advisable to say all that is true, yet it is never allowable to speak against the truth. *St. Francis de Sales*

Great tranquility of heart is his who cares for neither praise nor blame. *Thomas à Kempis*

A truth that is merely acquired from others only clings to us as a limb added to the body, or as a false tooth, or

a wax nose. A truth we have acquired by our own mental exertions, is like our natural limbs, which really belong to us. This is exactly the difference between an original thinker and the mere learned man.
Arthur Schopenhauer

A judicious silence is always better than truth spoken without charity. Philip Mann

I tell the honest truth in my paper, and I leave the consequence to God. James C. Bennett the Elder

A man has to live with himself, and he should see to it that he always has good company.
Charles Evans Hughes

Honesty of thought and speech and written word is a jewel, and they who curb prejudice and seek honorably to know and speak the truth are the only builders of a better life. John Galsworthy

A lie travels round the world while Truth is putting on her boots. Charles H. Spurgeon

If we would only stop lying, if we would only testify to the truth as we see it, it would turn out at once that there are hundreds, thousands, even millions of men just as we are, who see the truth as we do, are afraid as we are of seeming to be singular by confessing it, and are only waiting, again as we are, for some one to proclaim it. *Count Leo N. Tolstoy*

Do not wish you were like someone else. God made you as you are in order to use you as he planned.
J. C. Macaulay

According to Democritus, truth lies at the bottom of a well, the water of which serves as a mirror in which objects may be reflected. I have heard, however, that some philosophers, in seeking for truth, to pay homage to her, have seen their own image and adored it instead.
Jean Paul Richter

Christianity knows no truth which is not the child of love and the parent of duty. *Phillips Brooks*

If you will be persuaded by me, pay little attention to Socrates, but much more to the truth, and if I appear to you to say anything true, assent to it, but if not, oppose me with all your might, taking good care that in my zeal I do not deceive both myself and you, and like a bee depart, leaving my sting behind.
Socrates

I do the very best I know how; the very best I can; and I mean to keep on doing it to the end. If the end brings me out all right, what is said against me will not amount to anything. If the end brings me out all wrong, then a legion of angels swearing I was right will make no difference. *Abraham Lincoln*

Falsehood is in a hurry; it may be at any moment detected and punished; truth is calm, serene; its judgment is on high; its king cometh out of the chambers of eternity. *Joseph Parker*

Gradually I came to see that I could use the Bible, which had so baffled me, as an instrument for digging out precious truths, just as I could use my hindered, halting body for the high behests of my spirit. *Helen Keller*

My efforts are ever striving toward no other end than, as far as in me lieth, to set the truth before my eyes, to embrace it, and to lay out to good account the small talent that I've received: in order to draw the world away from its old heathenish superstition, to go over to the truth, and to cleave unto it.
Antony Van Leeuwenhoek

If you have anything really valuable to contribute to the world it will come through the expression of your own personality, that single spark of divinity that sets you off and makes you different from every other living creature. *Bruce Barton*

I believe that it is better to tell the truth than a lie. I believe it is better to be free than to be a slave. And I believe it is better to know than be ignorant.
H. L. Mencken

But let the free-winged angel Truth their guarded passes scale,
To teach that right is more than might, and justice more than mail!
> *John Greenleaf Whittier*

The "truths" that come down the ages are like a long string of grasshoppers standing in single file who jump over one another's backs. They continue without pause, always "moving ahead," until they arrive over and over again at the point where they began. And where was that?
> *Benjamin de Casseres*

Great God, I ask thee for no meaner pelf
Than that I may not disappoint myself,
That in my action I may soar as high
As I can now discern with this clear eye.
> *Henry David Thoreau*

General, abstract truth is the most precious of all blessings; without it man is blind, it is the eye of reason.
> *Jean Jacques Rousseau*

God offers to every mind its choice between truth and repose. Take which you please—you can never have both.
> *Ralph Waldo Emerson*

Truth is the beginning of every good thing, both in Heaven and on earth; and he who would be blessed and happy should be from the first a partaker of the truth, for then he can be trusted.
> *Plato*

I hope I shall always possess firmness and virtue enough to maintain what I consider the most enviable of all titles, the character of an Honest Man.
George Washington

It is twice as hard to crush a half-truth as a whole lie.
Austin O'Malley

I do not know what I may appear to the world, but to myself I seem to have been only like a boy playing on the seashore and diverting myself in now and then finding a smoother pebble or a prettier shell than ordinary, whilst the great ocean of truth lay all undiscovered before me. *Sir Isaac Newton*

To love truth for truth's sake is the principal part of human perfection in this world, and the seed-plot of all other virtues. *John Locke*

If I could get the ear of every young man but for one word, it would be this; make the most and best of yourself. There is no tragedy like a wasted life, a life failing of its true end, and turned to a false end.
T. T. Munger

If a thousand old beliefs were ruined in our march to truth we must still march on. *Stopford A. Brooke*

God is truth and light his shadow. *Plato*

There is a common saying amongst us: Say the truth and shame the Devil.
Hugh Latimer

Give me heart, touch with all that live,
And strength to speak my word;
But if that is denied me, give
The strength to live unheard.
Edwin Markham

Keep one thing forever in view, the truth; and if you do this, though it may seem to lead you away from the opinions of men, it will assuredly conduct you to the throne of God.
Horace Mann

Hark! Hark! my soul, angelic songs are swelling
O'er earth's green fields, and ocean's wave-beat shore;
How sweet the truth those blessed strains are telling
Of that new life when sin shall be no more!
Frederick W. Faber

There are certain times when most people are in a disposition of being informed, and 'tis incredible what a vast good a little truth might do, spoken in such seasons.
Alexander Pope

It makes a great difference in the force of a sentence whether a man be behind it or no.
Ralph Waldo Emerson

My way of joking is to tell the truth. It's the funniest joke in the world.
George Bernard Shaw

Once to every man and nation comes the moment to decide
In the strife of Truth with Falsehood, for the good or evil side.
James Russell Lowell

The inquiry of truth, which is the love-making or wooing of it; the knowledge of truth, which is the presence of it; and the belief of truth, which is the enjoying of it, is the sovereign good of human nature.
Francis Bacon

Most of us are like snowflakes trying to be like each other, yet knowing full well that no two snowflakes are ever identical. If we were to devote the same amount of energy in trying to discover the true self that lies buried deep within our own nature, we would all work harmoniously with life instead of forever *fighting* it.
Walter E. Elliott

There is no fit search after truth which does not, first of all, begin to live the truth which it knows.
Horace Bushnell

If the truth shall have made thee free, thou shalt not care for the vain words of men.
Thomas à Kempis

The mind, in discovering truths, acts in the same manner as it acts through the eye in discovering an object; when once any object has been seen, it is impossible to put the mind back to the same condition it was in before it saw it.
Thomas Paine

Honesty is something more than keeping out of jail, living within the law, avoiding trouble with the authorities. Honesty is the pure-gold bullion of integrity. The honest man determines to scrupulously keep the rules of the game. He stands upright, no matter how great the storm that breaks over him. He is fearlessly outspoken. He is courageously true in action and expression. Our country needs honest men today. The man of high integrity does not "have his price." He can never be bought.
Gordon Palmer

Truth is the object of our understanding, as good is of our will; and the understanding can no more be delighted with a lie than the will can choose an apparent evil.
John Dryden

In proportion as we perceive and embrace the truth we do become just, heroic, magnanimous, divine.
William Lloyd Garrison

Truth is strong, next to the Almighty; she needs no policies, nor stratagems, nor licensings to make her victorious; those are the shifts and the defenses that error uses against her power: give her but room, and do not bind her when she sleeps, for then she speaks not true.
John Milton

Let everyone be himself, and not try to be someone else. Let us not torment each other because we are not all alike, but believe that God knew best what he was doing in making us so different. So will the best harmony come out of seeming discords, the best affection out of differences, the best life out of struggle, and the best work will be done when each does his own work, and lets everyone else do and be what God made him for.
James F. Clarke

The greatest homage we can pay to truth is to use it.
Ralph Waldo Emerson

Reason teaches that the truths of divine revelation and those of nature cannot really be opposed to one another, and that whatever is at variance with them must necessarily be false. *Pope Leo XIII*

To all new truths, or renovation of old truths, it must be as in the ark between the destroyed and the about-to-be renovated world. The raven must be sent out before the dove, and ominous controversy must precede peace and the olive-wreath. *Samuel Taylor Coleridge*

The only guide to a man is his conscience; the only shield to his memory is the rectitude and sincerity of his actions. It is very imprudent to walk through life without this shield, because we are often mocked by the failure of our hopes and the upsetting of our calculations; but with this shield, however the fates may play, we march always in the ranks of honour.
Winston Churchill

Truth can hardly be expected to adapt herself to the crooked policy and wily sinuosities of worldly affairs; for truth, like light, travels only in straight lines.
Caleb C. Colton

The most emotionally mature person who ever lived was Jesus, and all the great religions teach the same fundamental truths which we psychiatrists try to drive home to our patients—that life has meaning and responsibilities, and that serving others is as much a part of living as enjoying life's good things. *Robert V. Seliger*

Truth always lags behind, limping along on the arm of time. *Baltasar Gracián*

Many people go throughout life committing partial suicide—destroying their talents, energies, creative qualities. Indeed, to learn how to be good to oneself is often more difficult than to learn how to be good to others.
Joshua L. Liebman

Truth and love are two of the most powerful things in the world; and when they both go together they cannot easily be withstood. *Ralph Cudworth*

If you tell the truth, you have infinite power supporting you; but if not, you have infinite power against you.
General Charles ("Chinese") Gordon

Truth is always strange, stranger than fiction.
Lord Byron

The greatest want of the world is the want of men—men who will not be bought or sold; men who in their inmost souls are true and honest; men who do not fear to call sin by its right name; men whose conscience is as true to duty as the needle to the pole; men who will stand for the right though the heavens fall.
E. G. White

Truth lies in character. Christ did not simply speak the truth; he was truth; truth, through and through; for truth is a thing not of words, but of life and being.
Frederick W. Robertson

The man who finds a truth lights a torch.
Robert G. Ingersoll

Truth is never alone; to know one will require the knowledge of many. They hang together in a chain of mutual dependence; you cannot draw one link without many others.
Joseph Glanvill

> I never can hide myself from me;
> I see what others may never see;
> I know what others may never know,
> I never can fool myself, and so
> Whatever happens, I want to be
> Self-respecting and conscience free.
> *Anonymous*

The grand character of truth is its capability of enduring

the test of universal experience, and coming unchanged out of every possible form of fair discussion.
Sir John Herschel

To thine own self be true,
And it must follow, as the night the day,
Thou canst not then be false to any man.
Shakespeare

Truth travels down from the heights of philosophy to the humblest walks of life, and up from the simplest perceptions of an awakened intellect to the discoveries which almost change the face of the world. At every stage of its progress it is genial, luminous, creative.
Edward Everett

Neither the clamor of the mob nor the voice of power will ever turn me by the breadth of a hair from the course I mark out for myself, guided by such knowledge as I can obtain, and controlled and directed by a solemn conviction of right and duty.
Robert M. LaFollette

To restore a common-place truth to its first uncommon lustre you need only translate it into action. But to do this you must have reflected on its truth.
Samuel Taylor Coleridge

Much of the glory and sublimity of truth is connected with its mystery. To understand everything we must be as God.
Tryon Edwards

Truth is such a fly-away, such a sly-boots, so untransportable and unbarrelable a commodity, that it is as bad to catch as light.   *Ralph Waldo Emerson*

When I look back upon the more than sixty years that I have spent on this entrancing earth and when I am asked which of all the changes that I have witnessed appears to me to be the most significant, I am inclined to answer that it is the loss of a sense of shame.
Harold Nicolson

Truth does not do as much good in the world, as its counterfeit does mischief.
François Duc de la Rochefoucauld

These are the things that ye shall do: Speak ye every man the truth to his neighbour; execute the judgment of truth and peace in your gates.
Zechariah 8:16

    When fiction rises pleasing to the eye,
    Men will believe, because they love the lie;
    But truth herself, if clouded with a frown,
    Must have some solemn proof to pass her down.
Charles Churchill

To keep clear of concealment, to keep clear of the need of concealment, to do nothing which he might not do out on the middle of Boston Common at noonday, I cannot say how more and more that seems to me to be the glory

of a young man's life. It is an awful hour when the first necessity of hiding anything comes. The whole life is different thenceforth. When there are questions to be feared and eyes to be avoided and subjects which must not be touched, then the bloom of life is gone. Put off that day as long as possible. Put it off forever if you can.
Phillips Brooks

Man with his burning soul has but an hour of breath to build a ship of truth in which his soul may sail—sail on the sea of death, for death takes toll of beauty, courage, youth, of all but truth. *John Masefield*

Truth without charity is often intolerant and even persecuting, as charity without truth is weak in concession and untrustworthy in judgment. But charity, loyal to truth and rejoicing in it, has the wisdom of the serpent with the harmlessness of the dove. *Josua Swartz*

"Your task . . . to build a better world," God said. I answered *"How?* . . . This world is such a large, vast place, so complicated now, and I so small and useless am, there's nothing I can do." But God in all his wisdom said, "Just build a better you."
Anonymous

To seek for the truth, for the sake of knowing the truth, is one of the noblest objects a man can live for.
William R. Inge

Truth is the disciple of the ascetic, the quest of the mystic, the faith of the simple, the ransom of the weak, the standard of the righteous, the doctrine of the meek, and the challenge of Nature. Together, all these constitute the Law of the Universe.
John H. Allison

Use what talents you possess: the woods would be very silent if no birds sang there except those that sang best.
Henry Van Dyke

What we have in us of the image of God is the love of truth and justice. *Demosthenes*

> We search the world for truth. We cull
> The good, the pure, the beautiful,
> From graven stone and written scroll,
> From all old flower-fields of the soul;
> And, weary seekers of the best,
> We come back laden from the quest,
> To find that all the sages said
> Is in the Book our mothers read.
> *John Greenleaf Whittier*

Prosperity, obtained through truth and righteousness, is built on a sure rock. Happiness derived from falsehood, injustice and lust, is built on sand.
Moses Maimonides

Still rule those minds on earth at whom sage Milton's wormwood words were hurled: *Truth like a bastard comes into the world never without ill-fame to him who gives her birth.*   *Thomas Hardy*

Truth! though the Heavens crush me for following her.
Thomas Carlyle

What a man is inwardly he will ultimately display outwardly. He may for a time, like the barren fig tree, make a great display of false profession, but the truth will come out, and he will be known for what he is.
Anonymous

Truths turn into dogmas the moment they are disputed.
G. K. Chesterton

Truth is incontrovertible. Panic may resent it; ignorance may deride it; malice may distort it; but there it is.
Winston Churchill

> That man is great, and he alone,
> Who serves a greatness not his own,
> For neither praise or pelf;
> Content to know and be unknown;
> Whole in himself.
> *Owen Meredith*

Of all duties, the love of truth, with faith and constancy in it, ranks first and highest. To love God and to love truth are one and the same.   *Silvio Pellico*

The greatest friend of truth is Time, her greatest enemy is Prejudice, and her constant companion is Humility.
Charles C. Colton

There is a time in every man's education when he arrives at the conviction that envy is ignorance, that imitation is suicide; that he must take himself for better or for worse, as his portion; that though the wide universe is full of good, no kernel of nourishing corn can come to him but through his toil bestowed on that plot of ground which is given to him to till. The power which resides in him is new in nature, and none but he knows what that is which he can do, nor does he know until he has tried.
Ralph Waldo Emerson

> Truth crushed to earth will rise again;
> The eternal years of God are hers;
> But error wounded writhes in pain
> And dies amid her worshippers.
> *William Cullen Bryant*

I have sworn eternal hostility to every form of tyranny over the mind of man. *Thomas Jefferson*